Cecil H. Russell

Euripides Hecuba

Part I

Cecil H. Russell

Euripides Hecuba

Part I

ISBN/EAN: 9783337168858

Printed in Europe, USA, Canada, Australia, Japan

Cover: Foto ©ninafisch / pixelio.de

More available books at **www.hansebooks.com**

Clarendon Press Series

EURIPIDES

HECUBA

EDITED

WITH INTRODUCTION AND NOTES

BY

CECIL H. RUSSELL, M.A.

Assistant Master at Clifton College
Late Scholar of Trinity College, Oxford

PART I.- INTRODUCTION AND TEXT

Oxford

AT THE CLARENDON PRESS

M DCCC LXXXIX

[*All rights reserved*]

PREFACE.

In preparing the Introduction and Notes, the following have been especially consulted—Hermann, Porson, Musgrave, Barnes, Dindorf, Kirchhoff, Nauck, Paley, Weil; with Dindorf's collection of the Scholia. Reference has been made to Jelf and Goodwin on grammatical points.

The text is based on that of Nauck; but W. Dindorf and Kirchhoff have been referred to throughout, and a list is added of the chief variations from the MSS. and the Oxford Text.

The Editor wishes to acknowledge gratefully the kindness of Mr. F. A. Haverfield, late Scholar of New College, who has looked over the manuscript of the Notes, and given valuable suggestions for these and the Introduction; of Mr. Evelyn Abbott, Fellow of Balliol College, who has revised the proof-sheets of the Introduction and Notes; of Mr. R. W. Raper, Fellow of Trinity College, who has corrected the Introduction; and of Mr. E. N. P. Moor, late Scholar of Balliol College, who has assisted in many of the Notes and looked through the proofs of the whole.

C. H. R.

INTRODUCTION.

1. Date of the Play.

THE date of the Hecuba is unknown; but internal evidence supplies some cue. The parody of line 172 in the Clouds of Aristophanes, which came out in 423 B.C., points to a period preceding this; while the apparent reference in line 458 to the purification of Delos by the Athenians, and, in line 649, to the capture of the Spartans in Sphacteria, is in favour of a time soon after 425 B.C., when those events took place. The date of the play has been fixed, therefore, for 424 B.C., the fourth year of the eighty-eighth Olympiad.

2. The Legend.

Hecuba, like Priam, is a type of misfortune in antiquity. Her story supplies one of the many plays based on the legend of Troy. The subject of Polyxena had been previously treated by Arctinus of Miletus (?), in the Taking of Troy; by Lesches of Mytilene (?), in the Lesser Iliad; by the lyric poet Ibycus; and by Sophocles, in the play which bears her name: of Polydorus only the Homeric legend remained. After Euripides, both episodes were largely embellished. According to Philostratus, Polyxena was the betrothed of Achilles: Achilles was slain by Paris in the temple of Thymbraean Apollo, where he had gone to receive his bride; and Polyxena fled to the Grecian camp and killed herself upon his tomb. Pacuvius, in the 'Iliona,' follows Euripides in committing Polydorus to the charge of Polymestor: but Iliona, wife of Polymestor and daughter of Priam, brings up Polydorus, her brother, as her own son Deiphilus, Deiphilus as Polydorus; and Polymestor, who is bribed by the Greeks to slay Polydorus, slays, by mistake, Deiphilus.

The antecedents of the 'Hecuba' are given in the opening speech. The plot of the play exhibits several variations from Homer and the received legend. Artistic reasons may account for some of these. The apparent position of Achilles' tomb at the scene of the play, the Thracian Chersonese (l. 37), may be more poetic than its acknowledged site in the Troad. In Homer, Polydorus is the son of Priam and Laothoe, and is killed in battle by Achilles: to make him the son of Hecuba (l. 3) and slay him by the hands of her friend Polymestor (l. 25), heightens the picture of her sorrows. The argument may require that Odysseus' entry into Troy should have been known to Hecuba (l. 243), not, as in Homer, to Helen only. But it is not clear why Hecuba, who in Homer is the daughter of Phrygian Dymas, becomes in Euripides (l. 3) the daughter of Cisseus. The object is perhaps to account for her friendship with Polymestor of Thrace: Cisseus being also a Thracian king. But all mention of this is omitted: while new details are added elsewhere, for which no sufficient reason can be given. Euripides is probably following some authority, perhaps the Lesser Iliad.

(*Note.* The story of Polyxena's betrothal to Achilles is apparently unknown to Euripides. Distinct reference must otherwise have been somewhere made to it (e.g. ll. 37, 135, 389): the first half of the play would have turned upon it. Yet, in ll. 97, 116, Achilles claims vaguely a sacrifice; and the more definite demand of ll. 40, 390, is evidently a reflection of the decision of the Greek council. (On νύμφην ἄνυμφον, l. 612, see note *ad loc.*). The legend, based perhaps on this play, belongs to later Greek and Latin romance,—Dictys of Crete, Dares the Phrygian, Philostratus, Hyginus.)

3. Analysis of the Play.

(The scene is laid throughout at the Greek encampment on the Thracian Chersonese.)

Prologus, 1-99.

The Shade of Polydorus appears above Agamemnon's tent. He tells of his own murder by Polymestor and of the coming sacrifice of Polyxena. He has haunted Hecuba in dreams: and to obtain burial, will be washed up by the sea at the feet of a Trojan woman. But hush! Hecuba herself is here, how fallen from her royal estate! (1-59.)

Hecuba approaches from the tent of Agamemnon, dressed as a slave and supported by Trojan women. She bewails her fortune, and tells how she has been distracted by visions of the night about the safety of Polydorus and Polyxena. The Shade of Achilles, also, has asked for the guerdon of a Trojan maid. (60-99.)

Parodus, 100-154.

The Chorus, composed of captive Trojan women, enter the orchestra, singing: 'Hecuba, we are come to bear thee ill-tidings. The Greeks have determined on the sacrifice of Polyxena. Pray Agamemnon and all the gods to save her.'

First Epeisodion, 155-443.

Hecuba, in anguish, calls forth Polyxena; who laments her fate for her mother's sake, but desires it for her own. (155-215.)

Odysseus enters. He informs Hecuba of the decree, and bids her obey it without resistance. She entreats him for the sake of past favour, of Polyxena's guiltlessness, and her own destitution, to dissuade the Greeks from their project. Odysseus answers: he will repay the favours by saving Hecuba who gave them; Polyxena he cannot save: on her sacrifice depends the honouring of heroes, which is the secret of Hellenic greatness. (216-331.)

Hecuba appeals to Polyxena to plead with Odysseus: he also has children and will pity her. But Polyxena is willing to die: she has fallen low in life: to live longer might only mean to fall yet lower. (332-378.)

Then Hecuba would die instead of her; or, at least, die with her. But Odysseus refuses. He leads away Polyxena ; and Hecuba is left, fainting with grief, upon the ground. (379-443.)

First Stasimon, 444-483.

The Chorus wonder to what land of captivity in Greece they will be taken. Alas! for their ruined country, which they have left for the tents of slavery.

Second Epeisodion, 484-625.

Talthybius enters. He pities the lot of Hecuba, and summons her to the burial of Polyxena ; whose noble death he describes. Hecuba, of all women, is the most blest in children, and the most unfortunate. (484-582.)

Hecuba laments the multitude of her sorrows. Yet Polyxena's nobleness lessens the grief at her loss: strange how strong is a noble nature. Commanding that no Greek shall touch the body, she sends a hand-maid to fetch sea-water for the laying out : she will bury her daughter as richly as she can. (583-625.)

Second Stasimon, 627-657.

Meanwhile the Chorus sing: It was an evil day when Paris sailed to Greece for Helen. His judgment of the goddesses on Ida has brought sorrow on Trojan women and on Greek alike.

Third Epeisodion, 658-904.

The hand-maid re-enters with the dead body of Polydorus, which she has found on the sea-shore. Hecuba bewails the fulfilment of her dream, and curses the treachery of Polymestor. (658-720.)

Agamemnon enters : Why has Hecuba delayed the burial of Polyxena ? At first she turns from him, immersed in thought ; but, seeing that, without his aid, she cannot avenge her son, raises his pity by showing him the body of Polydorus, and begs him, in the name of justice and his love for Cassandra, to help her to punish Polymestor. Agamemnon hesitates : Polymestor is a friend of the Greeks, Hecuba their enemy. Then let him, at least, connive at her vengeance : she can carry it out with the aid of her women. He consents; and an attendant is despatched for Polymestor. (721-904.)

Third Stasimon, 905-952.

The Chorus lament the fate of Troy, and describe how it fell at the dead of night, and they were led away captive to the sea, execrating the unholy marriage of Helen and Paris.

Exodus, 953-1295.

Polymestor enters with his children, and enquires of Hecuba why he has been summoned. She wishes to tell him of a place where gold has been buried in Troy. There is also with her a secret treasure, saved from Troy, of which she desires him to take charge. She takes him into the tent to receive the treasure. (953-1022.)

As the Chorus prophesy the fate of his crime, cries are heard from him within; and Hecuba enters saying that, with her women, she has put out Polymestor's eyes and slain his children. She retires as he bursts from the tent, groping wildly for the murderesses and bewailing his lost sight. (1023-1108.)

Agamemnon enters at the cries, and Polymestor sets forth his case to him. It was for the Greeks he killed Polydorus, and kept the gold. He then describes how, in the tent, the Trojan women clustered round his seat, holding him by force, while they murdered his children and put out his eyes. All this he has suffered for Agamemnon. (1109-1182.)

Then Hecuba speaks in turn. Her plea, she says, lies in facts. A barbarian, in the nature of things, could never be the friend of a Greek; if Polymestor had acted for the Greeks, why had he waited till the fall of Troy? He acted from greed of gold; and Agamemnon, if he supports him, will be a lover of evil. (1183-1251.)

Agamemnon decides in Hecuba's favour. Whereon Polymestor prophesies the metamorphosis of Hecuba into a dog, and Agamemnon's murder by Clytaemnestra. Agamemnon, in anger, orders him to be carried off to a desert island. (1251-1295.)

4. Remarks on the Play.

The play, on its artistic side, has been justly censured by Hermann and Schlegel. It violates the Aristotelean maxim, οὐ περὶ ἕνα ἀλλὰ περὶ μίαν πρᾶξιν,—wants unity of action, being (like the Andromache) divided into two distinct movements, the sacrifice of Polyxena, and the murder of Polydorus, with its punishment; movements not sufficiently combined in the proposed motive of 'the sorrows of Hecuba,'—especially as the last turns less on a sorrow than on its revenge. It exhibits the common faults of Euripides—the explanatory introduction, ll. 1-54 (condemned by Horace; partly, perhaps, due to a love for manipulating legend); the inappropriate choric odes, like the first stasimon, (l. 444); the forensic character of the dialogue, as in the scene between Hecuba and Polymestor (l. 1132: cf. on l. 299). The ferocity of Hecuba may be defensible in a barbarian; but there is a want of taste in Agamemnon going in person for Hecuba (l. 726), in his judgment and banishment of the Thracian king (l. 1285). The characters of Agamemnon and Polymestor are lifeless; and the force of the last episode is dissipated in a series of ingenious situations.

On the other hand, the episode of Polyxena is strong and human: the description of her death, like most of the poet's descriptions, possessing especial beauty. The inappropriateness of the choric odes is partly cancelled by their prettiness. And that the play as a whole must have appealed to at least some generations, is shown by the host of imitations, such as the Iliona of Pacuvius, which followed it, and of manuscripts, which have perpetuated it, surpassing in number those of any other play, except the Orestes and Phoenissae.

Other points in the play, the philosophic theory of religion, l. 799, and of morality, l. 592; the general sophistic tone, ll. 299, 1132; with the misogynism, l. 1178—all attacked by Aristophanes—have been referred to in the notes. They are well treated by Mr. Browning in his Aristophanes' Apology. It is sufficient here to say that in religion and morality, as in art,

Euripides reflected the free-thinking spirit of his age; that, if he helped to destroy the old, he did something to build the new; and that, if he took down tragedy from its divine basis of fate, he tried to reinstate it on the more appreciable basis of human nature. Later criticism may prefer the fateful grandeur of Aeschylus or the self-control of Sophocles; but the 'humanity' of Euripides possessed a wider and more general popularity with his immediate successors. It was by recitations from his plays, not from those of his two rivals, that the Athenian captives saved their lives at Syracuse; the Parthian king Orodes was attending an exhibition of the Bacchae when the news arrived of the defeat and death of Crassus in B.C. 55; the Byzantine drama, Χριστὸς Πάσχων, was little else than a cento of lines from Euripides.

5. Scenic arrangements of the Play.

('Right' and 'left' = the spectators' right and left.)

The Greek theatre, open to the sky, and generally built on the side of a hill, was divided into three parts: the seats of the spectators, the orchestra, and the stage.

Of these, the seats of the spectators, κοῖλον, or the hollow, formed the larger arc of a circle; the ends of which stretched towards either side of the stage.

The orchestra, ὀρχήστρα, or dancing-place, formed a segment of the circle. It was enclosed by the seats of the spectators and the stage, and lay at the ground-level, twelve feet below the lowest seats. The larger part of it, extending from the stage, was covered by a platform; called θυμέλη, from an altar of Bacchus (θυμέλη), which was in the centre of it. This platform is the part chiefly used by the chorus. It was six feet above the ground, and widened, as it approached the stage, into two passages, δρόμοι, which ran to right and left between the stage and the ends of the spectators' seats, and were entered from beneath the stage by two πάροδοι. The χορός were fifteen in number, and were under a leader, κορυφαῖος[1]. As they chanted the entrance-ode, (called, like the entrance itself, 'parodus'), they passed through one of the parodoi, (the right, if from the neighbourhood, as here, l. 100; the left, if from a distance), moved along the corresponding δρόμος, and so took up their station before the central altar; never leaving the orchestra till the end of the play. The other odes, called στάσιμα, or station-songs, they chanted from this station,—the στροφή, turning-song, moving to the left: the ἀντιστροφή, returning-song, to the right; the ἐπῳδός, after-song, remaining still. In these choric odes, the whole of the chorus took part, though often speaking of themselves in the singular, as in l. 476: in the dialogue, the coryphaeus alone spoke, taking the part of a fourth actor.

The stage, λογεῖον, or speaking place, was a straight narrow platform, stretching in front of the orchestral platform with its δρόμοι and six feet above it, i.e. on a level with the front seats of the spectators. The back-ground was formed by the palace of a king—here the tent of Agamemnon—and other buildings. In these there were three main entrances: a central one for the protagonist, by which Hecuba would always enter and leave (see on l. 54): one on the right for the deuteragonist, by which Polyxena probably enters (l. 178): one on the left for the tritagonist, perhaps not used in this play. There were also two other entrances, one at each end of the stage, the right for actors coming from the town or neighbourhood, the left for those from the country, as in the choric parodoi, which lay immediately below. By the first of these would enter Odysseus (l. 218), Talthybius (l. 484), Agamemnon (l. 726); by the last, the Attendant (l. 658), and Polymestor (l. 953). In front of these entrances (and apparently referring also to the underlying parodoi), were revolving doors in the form of a triangular prism, περίακτοι (sc. θύραι), which represented changes of scenery: that on the right here repre-

---

[1] To be distinguished from the χορηγός, who paid the chorus, and the χοροδιδάσκαλος, who taught them.

senting the camp; that on the left, first the sea-shore for the Attendant's entrance, then, by a revolution, the distant country, for the entrance of Polymestor. There were other stage contrivances, e.g. the crane, γέρανος, by which Polydorus is probably suspended above the tent of Agamemnon ; the moveable chamber, ἐκκύκλημα, which is rolled forward, disclosing the dead children of Polymestor in its interior, l. 1056. The actors, always men, were three only in number: the first actor, πρωταγωνιστής ; the second, δευτεραγωνιστής ; the third, τριταγωνιστής. Consequently one actor had often to take several parts, using for this purpose different masks. Thus, while the protagonist here takes the part of Hecuba throughout, the deuteragonist takes probably the parts of Polyxena, Talthybius, and Agamemnon ; the tritagonist, those of Polydorus, Odysseus, the Attendant, and Polymestor. But any number of mutes could be brought on the stage, as the attendants of Hecuba (l. 59); the children and guards of Polymestor (l. 953); the attendants of Agamemnon (l. 1109).

The play is divided into acts by the choric odes,—all that comes before the parodus being called the prologue, πρόλογος ; all that comes between two odes, an episode, ἐπεισόδιον ; all that comes after the last stasimon, the ἔξοδος.

6. MSS. and Scholia.

The text of Euripides was at the mercy of actors until the orator Lycurgus, circ. 330 B.C., procured an official text of the three great tragedians. Euripides became the most popular : but of his plays, the nineteen which have come down to us were preferred to the rest ; and, in Byzantine times, nine of these, one of which was the Hecuba, were selected as superior to the other ten ; the nine, again, being later narrowed down to three, the Orestes, Phoenissae, and Hecuba. The MSS. were written, some on parchment, some on paper. Their number and value correspond to the popularity of the text : few of Aeschylus and Sophocles remain, many of Euripides, especially of the favoured nine plays, and most especially, of the still more favoured three. The Hecuba, therefore, is one of the three best supported of Greek plays. The MSS. of Euripides date from the twelfth and thirteenth centuries. They have been arranged by Adolph Kirchhoff (Berlin, A.D. 1855), in an order of merit, designated by the letters of the alphabet. The best, containing the Hecuba, are 'A,' Marcianus, at Venice ('471'); 'B,' Vaticanus, at Rome, ('909'); 'E.' Parisinus, at Paris, ('2712'). The first printed edition of Euripides was from the press of Janus Lascaris, Florence, A.D. 1496, containing four plays, of which the Hecuba was not one; the second, from the Aldine Press in Venice, A.D. 1503, containing all but the Electra.

Commentaries were written on classical authors by ancient scholars, chiefly of Alexandria and Byzantium: of whom the Alexandrines, especially Dionysius Thrax, Aristarchus, Aristophanes of Byzantium, Didymus and Timachidas, contributed much that was useful; the Byzantines, though their work was voluminous, produced little that was of any value. These commentaries were of three kinds: (1) a few continuous commentaries; (2) 'glosses,' explanations of words written over the word explained; (3) 'scholia,' marginal notes written at the side of the text, often obscuring or corrupting the text, but occasionally suggesting correct readings from better MSS., since lost, which the Scholiast had at his command. The scholia of Euripides, which are very numerous, were mostly drawn from Didymus, and perhaps Dionysius Thrax: both of whom lived in the first century B.C. They were first printed by Bishop Arsenius in 1533; but his work was imperfect:—they have lately been published in a complete form by W. Dindorf, Oxford, 1863.

HECUBA.

DRAMATIS PERSONAE.

SHADE OF POLYDORUS, *son of Priam and Hecuba.*
HECUBA, *wife of Priam, and mother of Polydorus.*
POLYXENA, *daughter of Priam and Hecuba.*
ODYSSEUS, *king of Ithaca.*
TALTHYBIUS, *herald of Agamemnon.*
AGAMEMNON, *king of Mycenae.*
POLYMESTOR, *king of the Thracian Chersonese.*
ATTENDANT *of Hecuba.*
CHORUS *of captive Trojan women.*

PROLOGUE.

(*Scene:* Greek *encampment on coast of* THRACIAN CHERSONESE. *The Shade of* POLYDORUS *appears above the tent of* Agamemnon.)

Πολύδωρος.

Ἥκω νεκρῶν κευθμῶνα καὶ σκότου πύλας
λιπών, ἵν' Ἅιδης χωρὶς ᾤκισται θεῶν,
Πολύδωρος, Ἑκάβης παῖς γεγὼς τῆς Κισσέως,
Πριάμου τε πατρός, ὅς μ', ἐπεὶ Φρυγῶν πόλιν
5 κίνδυνος ἔσχε δορὶ πεσεῖν Ἑλληνικῷ,
δείσας ὑπεξέπεμψε Τρωικῆς χθονὸς
Πολυμήστορος πρὸς δῶμα, Θρηκίου ξένου,
ὃς τὴν ἀρίστην Χερσονησίαν πλάκα
σπείρει, φίλιππον λαὸν εὐθύνων δορί.
10 πολὺν δὲ σὺν ἐμοὶ χρυσὸν ἐκπέμπει λάθρᾳ
πατήρ, ἵν', εἴ ποτ' Ἰλίου τείχη πέσοι,
τοῖς ζῶσιν εἴη παισὶ μὴ σπάνις βίου.

νεώτατος δ' ἦν Πριαμιδῶν. ὃ καί με γῆς
ὑπεξέπεμψεν· οὔτε γὰρ φέρειν ὅπλα
15 οὔτ' ἔγχος οἷός τ' ἦν νέῳ βραχίονι.
ἕως μὲν οὖν γῆς ὄρθ' ἔκειθ' ὁρίσματα,
πύργοι τ' ἄθραυστοι Τρωικῆς ἦσαν χθονός,
Ἕκτωρ τ' ἀδελφὸς οὑμὸς ηὐτύχει δορί,
καλῶς παρ' ἀνδρὶ Θρῃκί, πατρῴῳ ξένῳ,
20 τροφαῖσιν, ὥς τις πτόρθος, ηὐξόμην τάλας.
ἐπεὶ δὲ Τροία θ' Ἕκτορός τ' ἀπόλλυται
ψυχή, πατρῷα θ' ἑστία κατεσκάφη,
αὐτὸς δὲ βωμῷ πρὸς θεοδμήτῳ πίτνει,
σφαγεὶς Ἀχιλλέως παιδὸς ἐκ μιαιφόνου,
25 κτείνει με χρυσοῦ τὸν ταλαίπωρον χάριν
ξένος πατρῷος, καὶ κτανὼν ἐς οἶδμ' ἁλὸς
μεθῆχ', ἵν' αὐτὸς χρυσὸν ἐν δόμοις ἔχῃ.
κεῖμαι δ' ἐπ' ἀκταῖς, ἄλλοτ' ἐν πόντου σάλῳ,
πολλοῖς διαύλοις κυμάτων φορούμενος,
30 ἄκλαυστος, ἄταφος· νῦν δ' ὑπὲρ μητρὸς φίλης
Ἑκάβης ἀΐσσω, σῶμ' ἐρημώσας ἐμόν,
τριταῖον ἤδη φέγγος αἰωρούμενος,
ὅσονπερ ἐν γῇ τῇδε Χερσονησίᾳ
μήτηρ ἐμὴ δύστηνος ἐκ Τροίας πάρα.
35 πάντες δ' Ἀχαιοὶ ναῦς ἔχοντες ἥσυχοι
θάσσουσ' ἐπ' ἀκταῖς τῆσδε Θρῃκίας χθονός·
ὁ Πηλέως γὰρ παῖς, ὑπὲρ τύμβου φανείς,
κατέσχ' Ἀχιλλεὺς πᾶν στράτευμ' Ἑλληνικόν,
πρὸς οἶκον εὐθύνοντας ἐναλίαν πλάτην·

40 αἰτεῖ δ' ἀδελφὴν τὴν ἐμὴν Πολυξένην
τύμβῳ φίλον πρόσφαγμα καὶ γέρας λαβεῖν.
καὶ τεύξεται τοῦδ', οὐδ' ἀδώρητος φίλων
ἔσται πρὸς ἀνδρῶν· ἡ πεπρωμένη δ' ἄγει
θανεῖν ἀδελφὴν τῷδ' ἐμὴν ἐν ἤματι.
45 δυοῖν δὲ παίδοιν δύο νεκρὼ κατόψεται
μήτηρ, ἐμοῦ τε τῆς τε δυστήνου κόρης.
φανήσομαι γάρ, ὡς τάφου τλήμων τύχω,
δούλης ποδῶν πάροιθεν ἐν κλυδωνίῳ.
τοὺς γὰρ κάτω σθένοντας ἐξῃτησάμην
50 τύμβου κυρῆσαι, κεἰς χέρας μητρὸς πεσεῖν.
τοὐμὸν μὲν οὖν, ὅσονπερ ἤθελον τυχεῖν,
ἔσται· γεραιᾷ δ' ἐκποδὼν χωρήσομαι
Ἑκάβῃ· περᾷ γὰρ ἥδ' ὑπὸ σκηνῆς πόδα
Ἀγαμέμνονος, φάντασμα δειμαίνουσ' ἐμόν.

(HECUBA *is seen coming out of the tent of Agamemnon, dressed as a slave and supported by Trojan women.*)

φεῦ·
55 ὦ μῆτερ, ἥτις ἐκ τυραννικῶν δόμων
δούλειον ἦμαρ εἶδες, ὡς πράσσεις κακῶς,
ὅσονπερ εὖ ποτ'· ἀντισηκώσας δέ σε
φθείρει θεῶν τις τῆς πάροιθ' εὐπραξίας.

(*The shade of* POLYDORUS *retires.* HECUBA *enters.*)

ἙΚΆΒΗ.
ἄγετ', ὦ παῖδες, τὴν γραῦν πρὸ δόμων.
60 ἄγετ', ὀρθοῦσαι τὴν ὁμόδουλον,
Τρῳάδες, ὑμῖν, πρόσθε δ' ἄνασσαν·

λάβετε, φέρετε, πέμπετ', ἀείρετέ μου
γεραιᾶς χειρὸς προσλαζύμεναι·
65 κἀγώ, σκολιῷ σκίπωνι χερὸς
διερειδομένα, σπεύσω βραδύπουν
ἤλυσιν ἄρθρων προτιθεῖσα.
ὦ στεροπὰ Διός, ὦ σκοτία νύξ,
τί ποτ' αἴρομαι ἔννυχος οὕτω
70 δείμασι, φάσμασιν; ὦ πότνια Χθών,
μελανοπτερύγων μᾶτερ ὀνείρων,
ἀποπέμπομαι ἔννυχον ὄψιν,
ἣν περὶ παιδὸς ἐμοῦ τοῦ σωζομένου κατὰ Θρῄκην
75 ἀμφὶ Πολυξείνης τε φίλης θυγατρὸς δι' ὀνείρων
φοβερὰν ὄψιν ἔμαθον, ἐδάην.
ὦ χθόνιοι θεοί, σώσατε παῖδ' ἐμόν,
80 ὃς μόνος οἴκων * ἄγκυρ' ἀμῶν
τὴν χιονώδη Θρῄκην κατέχει,
ξείνου πατρίου φυλακαῖσιν.
ἔσται τι νέον,
ἥξει τι μέλος γοερὸν γοεραῖς.
85 οὔποτ' ἐμὰ φρὴν ὧδ' ἀλίαστος
φρίσσει, ταρβεῖ.
ποῦ ποτε θείαν Ἑλένου ψυχὰν
ἢ Κασάνδραν ἐσίδω, Τρῳάδες,
ὥς μοι κρίνωσιν ὀνείρους;
90 εἶδον γὰρ βαλιὰν ἔλαφον λύκου αἵμονι χαλᾷ
σφαζομέναν, ἀπ' ἐμῶν γονάτων σπασθεῖσαν
ἀνάγκᾳ

οἰκτρῶς. καὶ τόδε δεῖμά μοι·
ἦλθ' ὑπὲρ ἄκρας τύμβου κορυφᾶς
95 φάντασμ' Ἀχιλέως· ᾔτει δὲ γέρας
τῶν πολυμόχθων τινὰ Τρωιάδων.
ἀπ' ἐμᾶς οὖν, ἀπ' ἐμᾶς τόδε παιδὸς
πέμψατε, δαίμονες, ἱκετεύω.

PARODUS.

Enter the CHORUS.

Χορός.

100 Ἑκάβη, σπουδῇ πρός σ' ἐλιάσθην,
τὰς δεσποσύνους σκηνὰς προλιποῦσ',
ἵν' ἐκληρώθην καὶ προσετάχθην
δούλη, πόλεως ἀπελαυνομένη
τῆς Ἰλιάδος, λόγχης αἰχμῇ
105 δοριθήρατος πρὸς Ἀχαιῶν,
οὐδὲν παθέων ἀποκουφίζουσ',
ἀλλ' ἀγγελίας βάρος ἀραμένη
μέγα, σοί τε, γύναι, κῆρυξ ἀχέων.
ἐν γὰρ Ἀχαιῶν πλήρει ξυνόδῳ
110 λέγεται δόξαι σὴν παῖδ' Ἀχιλεῖ
σφάγιον θέσθαι· τύμβου δ' ἐπιβὰς
οἶσθ' ὅτε χρυσέοις ἐφάνη σὺν ὅπλοις,
τὰς ποντοπόρους δ' ἔσχε σχεδίας,
λαίφη προτόνοις ἐπερειδομένας,

115 τάδε θωΰσσων·
ποῖ δή, Δαναοί, τὸν ἐμὸν τύμβον
στέλλεσθ' ἀγέραστον ἀφέντες;
πολλῆς δ' ἔριδος συνέπαισε κλύδων,
δόξα δ' ἐχώρει δίχ' ἂν Ἑλλήνων
120 στρατὸν αἰχμητήν, τοῖς μὲν διδόναι
τύμβῳ σφάγιον, τοῖς δ' οὐχὶ δοκοῦν.
ἦν δὲ τὸ μὲν σὸν σπεύδων ἀγαθὸν
τῆς μαντιπόλου Βάκχης ἀνέχων
λέκτρ' Ἀγαμέμνων·
125 τὼ Θησείδα δ', ὄζω Ἀθηνῶν,
δισσῶν μύθων ῥήτορες ἦσαν·
γνώμῃ δὲ μιᾷ συνεχωρείτην,
τὸν Ἀχίλλειον τύμβον στεφανοῦν
αἵματι χλωρῷ, τὰ δὲ Κασάνδρας
130 λέκτρ' οὐκ ἐφάτην τῆς Ἀχιλείας
πρόσθεν θήσειν ποτὲ λόγχης.
σπουδαὶ δὲ λόγων κατατεινομένων
ἦσαν ἴσαι πως, πρὶν ὁ ποικιλόφρων
κόπις, ἡδυλόγος, δημοχαριστής,
135 Λαερτιάδης πείθει στρατιὰν
μὴ τὸν ἄριστον Δαναῶν πάντων
δούλων σφαγίων οὕνεκ' ἀπωθεῖν,
μηδέ τιν' εἰπεῖν παρὰ Περσεφόνῃ
στάντα φθιμένων
140 ὡς ἀχάριστοι Δαναοὶ Δαναοῖς
τοῖς οἰχομένοις ὑπὲρ Ἑλλήνων

HECUBA

Τροίας πεδίων ἀπέβησαν.
ἥξει δ' Ὀδυσεὺς ὅσον οὐκ ἤδη,
πῶλον ἀφέλξων σῶν ἀπὸ μαστῶν,
145 ἔκ τε γεραιᾶς χερὸς ὁρμήσων.
ἀλλ' ἴθι ναούς, ἴθι πρὸς βωμούς,
ἵζ' Ἀγαμέμνονος ἱκέτις γονάτων,
κήρυσσε θεοὺς τούς τ' οὐρανίδας
τούς θ' ὑπὸ γαῖαν.
150 ἢ γάρ σε λιταὶ διακωλύσουσ'
ὀρφανὸν εἶναι παιδὸς μελέας,
ἢ δεῖ σ' ἐπιδεῖν τύμβου προπετῆ
φοινισσομένην αἵματι παρθένου
ἐκ χρυσοφόρου
δειρῆς νασμῷ μελαναυγεῖ.

FIRST EPEISODION.

Ἑκάβη.

155 οἲ 'γὼ μελέα, τί ποτ' ἀπύσω ;
ποίαν ἀχώ, ποῖον ὀδυρμόν ;
δειλαία δειλαίου γήρως,
δουλείας τᾶς οὐ τλατᾶς,
τᾶς οὐ φερτᾶς· ὤμοι μοι.
160 τίς ἀμύνει μοι ; ποία γέννα,
ποία δὲ πόλις ;
φροῦδος πρέσβυς, φροῦδοι παῖδες.
ποίαν, ἢ ταύταν ἢ κείναν,

στείχω; * ποῖ δ' ἥσω πόδα; τίς θεῶν
165 ἡ * δαίμων νῷν ἐπαρωγός;
ὦ κάκ' ἐνεγκοῦσαι Τρῳάδες, ὦ
κάκ' ἐνεγκοῦσαι
πήματ', ἀπωλέσατ', ὠλέσατ'· οὐκέτι μοι βίος
ἀγαστὸς ἐν φάει.
170 ὦ τλάμων ἄγησαί μοι
πούς, ἄγησαι τᾷ γραίᾳ
πρὸς τάνδ' αὐλάν· ὦ τέκνον, ὦ παῖ
δυστανοτάτας ματέρος, ἔξελθ',
ἔξελθ' οἴκων· ἄϊε ματέρος
175 αὐδάν, ὦ τέκνον, ὡς εἰδῇς
οἵαν οἵαν ἀΐω φάμαν
περὶ σᾶς ψυχᾶς.

(POLYXENA *enters from the tent.*

Πολυξένη.

ἰώ,
μᾶτερ μᾶτερ, τί βοᾷς; τί νέον
καρύξασ' οἴκων μ', ὥστ' ὄρνιν,
180 θάμβει τῷδ' ἐξέπταξας;

Ἑκάβη.
οἴμοι, τέκνον.

Πολυξένη.
τί με δυσφημεῖς; φροίμιά μοι κακά.

Ἑκάβη.
αἰαῖ, σᾶς ψυχᾶς..

Πολυξένη.
ἔξαυδα, μὴ κρύψῃς δαρόν.
185 δειμαίνω, δειμαίνω, μᾶτερ,
τί ποτ' ἀναστένεις.

Ἑκάβη.
τέκνον ὦ τέκνον μελέας ματρός.

Πολυξένη.
τί τόδ' ἀγγέλλεις;

Ἑκάβη.
σφάξαι σ' Ἀργείων κοινὰ
190 συντείνει πρὸς τύμβον γνώμα
*Πηλείᾳ γέννᾳ.

Πολυξένη.
οἴμοι, μᾶτερ, πῶς φθέγγει
ἀμέγαρτα κακῶν; μάνυσόν μοι.
μάνυσον, μᾶτερ.

Ἑκάβη.
195 αὐδῶ, παῖ, δυσφήμους φάμας·
ἀγγέλλουσ' Ἀργείων δόξαι
ψήφῳ τᾶς σᾶς περί μοι ψυχᾶς.

Πολυξένη.

ὦ δεινὰ παθοῦσ', ὦ παντλάμων,
ὦ δυστάνου μᾶτερ βιοτᾶς,
200 οἵαν οἵαν αὖ σοι λώβαν
ἐχθίσταν ἀρρήταν τ'
ὦρσέν τις δαίμων.
οὐκέτι σοι παῖς ἅδ' οὐκέτι δὴ
γήρᾳ δειλαίῳ δειλαία
συνδουλεύσω.
σκύμνον γάρ μ' ὥστ' οὐριθρέπταν
205 μόσχον δειλαία δειλαίαν
εἰσόψει χειρὸς ἀναρπαστὰν
σᾶς ἄπο, λαιμότομόν τ' Ἀίδᾳ
γᾶς ὑποπεμπομέναν σκότον, ἔνθα νεκρῶν μέτα
210 τάλαινα κείσομαι.
καὶ σὲ μέν, μᾶτερ δύστανε,
κλαίω πανδύρτοις θρήνοις·
τὸν ἐμὸν δὲ βίον, λώβαν λύμαν τ',
οὐ μετακλαίομαι, ἀλλὰ θανεῖν μοι
215 ξυντυχία κρείσσων ἐκύρησεν.

ODYSSEUS *is seen approaching from the camp.*

Χορός.

καὶ μὴν Ὀδυσσεὺς ἔρχεται σπουδῇ ποδός,
Ἑκάβη, νέον τι πρὸς σὲ σημανῶν ἔπος.

(*Enter* ODYSSEUS.

᾽Οδυσσεύς.

γύναι, δοκῶ μέν σ᾽ εἰδέναι γνώμην στρατοῦ
ψῆφόν τε τὴν κρανθεῖσαν· ἀλλ᾽ ὅμως φράσω.
220 ἔδοξ᾽ Ἀχαιοῖς παῖδα σὴν Πολυξένην
σφάξαι πρὸς ὀρθὸν χῶμ᾽ Ἀχιλλείου τάφου.
ἡμᾶς δὲ πομποὺς καὶ κομιστῆρας κόρης
τάσσουσιν εἶναι· θύματος δ᾽ ἐπιστάτης
ἱερεύς τ᾽ ἐπέσται τοῦδε παῖς Ἀχιλλέως.
225 οἶσθ᾽ οὖν ὃ δρᾶσον; μήτ᾽ ἀποσπασθῇς βίᾳ
μήτ᾽ εἰς χερῶν ἅμιλλαν ἐξέλθῃς ἐμοί·
γίγνωσκε δ᾽ ἀλκὴν καὶ παρουσίαν κακῶν
τῶν σῶν. σοφόν τοι κἂν κακοῖς ἃ δεῖ φρονεῖν.

Ἑκάβη.

αἰαῖ· παρέστηχ᾽, ὡς ἔοικ᾽, ἀγὼν μέγας,
230 πλήρης στεναγμῶν οὐδὲ δακρύων κενός.
*κἄγωγ᾽ ἄρ᾽ οὐκ ἔθνησκον οὗ μ᾽ ἐχρῆν θανεῖν,
οὐδ᾽ ὤλεσέν με Ζεύς, τρέφει δ᾽, ὅπως ὁρῶ
κακῶν κάκ᾽ ἄλλα μεῖζον᾽ ἡ τάλαιν᾽ ἐγώ.
εἰ δ᾽ ἔστι τοῖς δούλοισι τοὺς ἐλευθέρους
235 μὴ λυπρὰ μηδὲ καρδίας δηκτήρια
ἐξιστορῆσαι, σοὶ μὲν εἰρῆσθαι χρεών,
ἡμᾶς δ᾽ ἀκοῦσαι τοὺς ἐρωτῶντας τάδε.

Ὀδυσσεύς.

ἔξεστ᾽, ἐρώτα· τοῦ χρόνου γὰρ οὐ φθονῶ.

Ἑκάβη.
οἶσθ᾽ ἡνίκ᾽ ἦλθες Ἰλίου κατάσκοπος,
240 δυσχλαινίᾳ τ᾽ ἄμορφος, ὀμμάτων τ᾽ ἄπο
φόνου σταλαγμοὶ σὴν κατέσταζον γένυν;

Ὀδυσσεύς.
οἶδ᾽· οὐ γὰρ ἄκρας καρδίας ἔψαυσέ μου.

Ἑκάβη.
ἔγνω δέ σ᾽ Ἑλένη, καὶ μόνῃ κατεῖπ᾽ ἐμοί;

Ὀδυσσεύς.
μεμνήμεθ᾽ ἐς κίνδυνον ἐλθόντες μέγαν.

Ἑκάβη.
245 ἧψω δὲ γονάτων τῶν ἐμῶν ταπεινὸς ὤν;

Ὀδυσσεύς.
ὥστ᾽ ἐνθανεῖν γε σοῖς πέπλοισι χεῖρ᾽ ἐμήν.

Ἑκάβη.
τί δῆτ᾽ ἔλεξας, δοῦλος ὢν ἐμὸς τότε;

Ὀδυσσεύς.
πολλῶν λόγων εὑρήμαθ᾽, ὥστε μὴ θανεῖν.

Ἑκάβη.
ἔσωσα δῆτά σ᾽, ἐξέπεμψά τε χθονός;

Ὀδυσσεύς.
250 ὥστ᾽ εἰσορᾶν γε φέγγος ἡλίου τόδε.

Ἑκάβη.
οὔκουν κακύνει τοῖσδε τοῖς βουλεύμασιν,
ὃς ἐξ ἐμοῦ μὲν ἔπαθες οἷα φῂς παθεῖν,
δρᾷς δ' οὐδὲν ἡμᾶς εὖ, κακῶς δ' ὅσον δύνα ;
ἀχάριστον ὑμῶν σπέρμ', ὅσοι δημηγόρους
255 ζηλοῦτε τιμάς· μηδὲ γιγνώσκοισθέ μοι,
οἳ τοὺς φίλους βλάπτοντες οὐ φροντίζετε,
ἢν τοῖσι πολλοῖς πρὸς χάριν λέγητέ τι.
ἀτὰρ τί δὴ σόφισμα τοῦθ' ἡγούμενοι
εἰς τήνδε παῖδα ψῆφον ὥρισαν φόνου ;
260 πότερα τὸ χρῆν σφ' ἐπήγαγ' ἀνθρωποσφαγεῖν
πρὸς τύμβον, ἔνθα βουθυτεῖν μᾶλλον πρέπει;
ἢ τοὺς κτανόντας ἀνταποκτεῖναι θέλων
εἰς τήνδ' Ἀχιλλεὺς ἐνδίκως τείνει φόνον ;
ἀλλ' οὐδὲν αὐτὸν ἥδε γ' εἴργασται κακόν.
265 Ἑλένην νιν αἰτεῖν χρῆν τάφῳ προσφάγματα·
κείνη γὰρ ὤλεσέν νιν εἰς Τροίαν τ' ἄγει.
εἰ δ' αἰχμαλώτων χρή τιν' ἔκκριτον θανεῖν
κάλλει θ' ὑπερφέρουσαν, οὐχ ἡμῶν τόδε·
ἡ Τυνδαρὶς γὰρ εἶδος ἐκπρεπεστάτη,
270 ἀδικοῦσά θ' ἡμῶν οὐδὲν ἧσσον ηὑρέθη.
τῷ μὲν δικαίῳ τόνδ' ἁμιλλῶμαι λόγον·
ἃ δ' ἀντιδοῦναι δεῖ σ', ἀπαιτούσης ἐμοῦ,
ἄκουσον. ἥψω τῆς ἐμῆς, ὡς φῄς, χερὸς
καὶ τῆσδε γραίας προσπίτνων παρηίδος·
275 ἀνθάπτομαί σου τῶνδε τῶν αὐτῶν ἐγὼ
χάριν τ' ἀπαιτῶ τὴν τόθ', ἱκετεύω τέ σε,

μή μου τὸ τέκνον ἐκ χερῶν ἀποσπάσῃς,
μηδὲ κτάνητε· τῶν τεθνηκότων ἅλις.
[ταύτῃ γέγηθα κἀπιλήθομαι κακῶν·]
280 ἥδ' ἀντὶ πολλῶν ἐστί μοι παραψυχή,
πόλις, τιθήνη, βάκτρον, ἡγεμὼν ὁδοῦ.
οὐ τοὺς κρατοῦντας χρὴ κρατεῖν ἃ μὴ χρεών,
οὐδ' εὐτυχοῦντας εὖ δοκεῖν πράξειν ἀεί·.
κἀγὼ γὰρ ἦν ποτ', ἀλλὰ νῦν οὐκ εἴμ' ἔτι,
285 τὸν πάντα δ' ὄλβον ἦμαρ ἕν μ' ἀφείλετο.
ἀλλ' ὦ φίλον γένειον, αἰδέσθητί με,
οἴκτειρον· ἐλθὼν δ' εἰς Ἀχαϊκὸν στρατὸν
παρηγόρησον, ὡς ἀποκτείνειν φθόνος
γυναῖκας, ἃς τὸ πρῶτον οὐκ ἐκτείνατε
290 βωμῶν ἀποσπάσαντες, ἀλλ' ᾠκτείρατε.
νόμος δ' ἐν ὑμῖν τοῖς τ' ἐλευθέροις ἴσος
καὶ τοῖσι δούλοις αἵματος κεῖται πέρι.
τὸ δ' ἀξίωμα, κἂν κακῶς * λέγῃς, τὸ σὸν
πείσει· λόγος γὰρ ἔκ τ' ἀδοξούντων ἰὼν
295 κἀκ τῶν δοκούντων αὑτὸς οὐ ταὐτὸν σθένει.

Χορός.
οὐκ ἔστιν οὕτω στερρὸς ἀνθρώπου φύσις,
ἥτις γόων σῶν καὶ μακρῶν ὀδυρμάτων
κλύουσα θρήνους οὐκ ἂν ἐκβάλοι δάκρυ.

Ὀδυσσεύς.
Ἑκάβη, διδάσκου, μηδὲ τῷ θυμουμένῳ
300 τὸν εὖ λέγοντα δυσμενῆ ποιοῦ φρενί.

ἐγὼ τὸ μὲν σὸν σῶμ', ὑφ' οὗπερ ηὐτύχουν,
σώζειν ἕτοιμός εἰμι, κοὐκ ἄλλως λέγω·
ἃ δ' εἶπον εἰς ἅπαντας, οὐκ ἀρνήσομαι,
Τροίας ἁλούσης ἀνδρὶ τῷ πρώτῳ στρατοῦ
305 σὴν παῖδα δοῦναι σφάγιον ἐξαιτουμένῳ.
ἐν τῷδε γὰρ κάμνουσιν αἱ πολλαὶ πόλεις,
ὅταν τις ἐσθλὸς καὶ πρόθυμος ὢν ἀνὴρ
μηδὲν φέρηται τῶν κακιόνων πλέον.
ἡμῖν δ' Ἀχιλλεὺς ἄξιος τιμῆς, γύναι,
310 θανὼν ὑπὲρ γῆς Ἑλλάδος κάλλιστ' ἀνήρ.
οὔκουν τόδ' αἰσχρόν, εἰ βλέποντι μὲν φίλῳ
χρώμεσθ', ἐπεὶ δ' ὄλωλε, μὴ χρώμεσθ' ἔτι;
εἶεν· τί δῆτ' ἐρεῖ τις, ἤν τις αὖ φανῇ
στρατοῦ τ' ἄθροισις πολεμίων τ' ἀγωνία;
315 πότερα μαχούμεθ', ἢ φιλοψυχήσομεν,
τὸν κατθανόνθ' ὁρῶντες οὐ τιμώμενον;
καὶ μὴν ἔμοιγε ζῶντι μέν, καθ' ἡμέραν,
κεἰ σμίκρ' ἔχοιμι, πάντ' ἂν ἀρκούντως ἔχοι·
τύμβον δὲ βουλοίμην ἂν ἀξιούμενον
τὸν ἐμὸν ὁρᾶσθαι· διὰ μακροῦ γὰρ ἡ χάρις..
εἰ δ' οἰκτρὰ πάσχειν φῄς, τάδ' ἀντάκουέ μου.
εἰσὶν παρ' ἡμῖν οὐδὲν ἧσσον ἄθλιαι
γραῖαι γυναῖκες ἠδὲ πρεσβῦται σέθεν,
νύμφαι τ' ἀρίστων νυμφίων τητώμεναι,
325 ὧν ἥδε κεύθει σώματ' Ἰδαία κόνις.
τόλμα τάδ'· ἡμεῖς δ', εἰ κακῶς νομίζομεν
τιμᾶν τὸν ἐσθλόν, ἀμαθίαν ὀφλήσομεν·

οἱ βάρβαροι δὲ μήτε τοὺς φίλους φίλους
ἡγεῖσθε μήτε τοὺς καλῶς τεθνηκότας
330 θαυμάζεθ', ὡς ἂν ἡ μὲν Ἑλλὰς εὐτυχῇ,
ὑμεῖς δ' ἔχηθ' ὅμοια τοῖς βουλεύμασιν.

Χορός.
αἰαῖ· τὸ δοῦλον ὡς κακὸν *πέφυκ' ἀεί,
τολμᾷ θ' ἃ μὴ χρή, τῇ βίᾳ νικώμενον.

Ἑκάβη.
ὦ θύγατερ, οὑμοὶ μὲν λόγοι πρὸς αἰθέρα
335 φροῦδοι μάτην ῥιφθέντες ἀμφὶ σοῦ φόνου·
σὺ δ' εἴ τι μείζω δύναμιν ἢ μήτηρ ἔχεις,
σπούδαζε, πάσας ὥστ' ἀηδόνος στόμα
φθογγὰς ἱεῖσα, μὴ στερηθῆναι βίου.
πρόσπιπτε δ' οἰκτρῶς τοῦδ' Ὀδυσσέως γόνυ,
340 καὶ πεῖθ'· ἔχεις δὲ πρόφασιν· ἔστι γὰρ τέκνα
καὶ τῷδε, τὴν σὴν ὥστ' ἐποικτεῖραι τύχην.

Πολυξένη.
ὁρῶ σ', Ὀδυσσεῦ, δεξιὰν ὑφ' εἵματος
κρύπτοντα χεῖρα, καὶ πρόσωπον ἔμπαλιν
στρέφοντα, μή σου προσθίγω γενειάδος.
345 θάρσει· πέφευγας τὸν ἐμὸν ἱκέσιον Δία·
ὡς ἕψομαί γε, τοῦ τ' ἀναγκαίου χάριν
θανεῖν τε χρῄζουσ'· εἰ δὲ μὴ βουλήσομαι,
κακὴ φανοῦμαι καὶ φιλόψυχος γυνή.

τί γάρ με δεῖ ζῆν; ἦ πατὴρ μὲν ἦν ἄναξ
350 Φρυγῶν ἁπάντων· τοῦτό μοι πρῶτον βίου·
ἔπειτ' ἐθρέφθην ἐλπίδων καλῶν ὕπο
βασιλεῦσι νύμφη, ζῆλον οὐ σμικρὸν γάμων
ἔχουσ', ὅτου δῶμ' ἑστίαν τ' ἀφίξομαι·
δέσποινα δ' ἡ δύστηνος Ἰδαίαισιν ἦν
355 γυναιξὶ παρθένοις τ' ἀπόβλεπτος μέτα,
ἴση θεοῖσι, πλὴν τὸ κατθανεῖν μόνον·
νῦν δ' εἰμὶ δούλη. πρῶτα μέν με τοὔνομα
θανεῖν ἐρᾶν τίθησιν, οὐκ εἰωθὸς ὄν·
ἔπειτ' ἴσως ἂν δεσποτῶν ὠμῶν φρένας
360 τύχοιμ' ἄν, ὅστις ἀργύρου μ' ὠνήσεται,
τὴν Ἕκτορός τε χἀτέρων πολλῶν κάσιν,
προσθεὶς δ' ἀνάγκην σιτοποιὸν ἐν δόμοις,
σαίρειν τε δῶμα κερκίσιν τ' ἐφεστάναι
λυπρὰν ἄγουσαν ἡμέραν μ' ἀναγκάσει·
365 λέχη δὲ τἀμὰ δοῦλος ὠνητός ποθεν
χρανεῖ, τυράννων πρόσθεν ἠξιωμένα.
οὐ δῆτ'· ἀφίημ' ὀμμάτων ἐλεύθερον
φέγγος τόδ', Ἅιδῃ προστιθεῖσ' ἐμὸν δέμας.
ἄγ' οὖν μ', Ὀδυσσεῦ, καὶ διέργασαί μ' ἄγων·
370 οὔτ' ἐλπίδος γὰρ οὔτε του δόξης ὁρῶ
θάρσος παρ' ἡμῖν ὥς ποτ' εὖ πρᾶξαί με χρή.
μῆτερ, σὺ δ' ἡμῖν μηδὲν ἐμποδὼν γένῃ,
λέγουσα * μήτε δρῶσα· συμβούλου δέ μοι
θανεῖν πρὶν αἰσχρῶν μὴ κατ' ἀξίαν τυχεῖν.
375 ὅστις γὰρ οὐκ εἴωθε γεύεσθαι κακῶν,

φέρει μέν, ἀλγεῖ δ᾽ αὐχέν᾽ ἐντιθεὶς ζυγῷ·
θανὼν δ᾽ ἂν εἴη μᾶλλον εὐτυχέστερος
ἢ ζῶν· τὸ γὰρ ζῆν μὴ καλῶς μέγας πόνος.

Χορός.
δεινὸς χαρακτὴρ κἀπίσημος ἐν βροτοῖς
380 ἐσθλῶν γενέσθαι, κἀπὶ μεῖζον ἔρχεται
τῆς εὐγενείας ὄνομα τοῖσιν ἀξίοις.

Ἑκάβη.
καλῶς μὲν εἶπας, θύγατερ· ἀλλὰ τῷ καλῷ
λύπη πρόσεστιν. εἰ δὲ δεῖ τῷ Πηλέως
χάριν γενέσθαι παιδὶ καὶ ψόγον φυγεῖν
385 ὑμᾶς, Ὀδυσσεῦ, τήνδε μὲν μὴ κτείνετε,
ἡμᾶς δ᾽ ἄγοντες πρὸς πυρὰν Ἀχιλλέως
κεντεῖτε, μὴ φείδεσθ᾽· ἐγὼ ᾽τεκον Πάριν,
ὃς παῖδα Θέτιδος ὤλεσεν τόξοις βαλών.

Ὀδυσσεύς.
οὐ σ᾽, ὦ γεραιά, κατθανεῖν Ἀχιλλέως
390 φάντασμ᾽ Ἀχαιούς, ἀλλὰ τήνδ᾽, ᾐτήσατο.

Ἑκάβη.
ὑμεῖς δέ μ᾽ ἀλλὰ θυγατρὶ συμφονεύσατε,
καὶ δὶς τόσον * πῶμ᾽ αἵματος γενήσεται
γαίᾳ νεκρῷ τε τῷ τάδ᾽ ἐξαιτουμένῳ.

Ὀδυσσεύς.
ἅλις κόρης εἷς θάνατος, οὐ προσοιστέος
395 ἄλλος πρὸς ἄλλῳ· μηδὲ τόνδ᾽ ὠφείλομεν.

Ἑκάβη.
πολλή γ' ἀνάγκη θυγατρὶ συνθανεῖν ἐμέ.

Ὀδυσσεύς.
πῶς; οὐ γὰρ οἶδα δεσπότας κεκτημένος.

Ἑκάβη.
ὁποῖα κισσὸς δρυὸς ὅπως τῆσδ' ἕξομαι.

Ὀδυσσεύς.
οὔκ, ἤν γε πείθῃ τοῖσι σοῦ σοφωτέροις.

Ἑκάβη.
400 ὡς τῆσδ' ἑκοῦσα παιδὸς οὐ μεθήσομαι.

Ὀδυσσεύς.
ἀλλ' οὐδ' ἐγὼ μὴν τήνδ' ἄπειμ' αὐτοῦ λιπών.

Πολυξένη.
μῆτερ, πιθοῦ μοι· καὶ σύ, παῖ Λαερτίου,
χάλα τοκεῦσιν εἰκότως θυμουμένοις,
σύ τ', ὦ τάλαινα, τοῖς κρατοῦσι μὴ μάχου.
405 βούλει πεσεῖν πρὸς οὖδας ἑλκῶσαί τε σὸν
γέροντα χρῶτα πρὸς βίαν ὠθουμένη,
ἀσχημονῆσαί τ' ἐκ νέου βραχίονος
σπασθεῖσ'; ἃ πείσει· μὴ σύ γ'· οὐ γὰρ ἄξιον.
ἀλλ' ὦ φίλη μοι μῆτερ, ἡδίστην χέρα
410 δὸς καὶ παρειὰν προσβαλεῖν παρηίδι·
ὡς οὔποτ' αὖθις, ἀλλὰ νῦν πανύστατον,
ἀκτῖνα κύκλον θ' ἡλίου προσόψομαι.

τέλος δέχει δὴ τῶν ἐμῶν προσφθεγμάτων.
ὦ μῆτερ, ὦ τεκοῦσ'· ἄπειμι δὴ κάτω.

Ἑκάβη.
415 ὦ θύγατερ, ἡμεῖς δ' ἐν φάει δουλεύσομεν.

Πολυξένη.
ἄνυμφος ἀνυμέναιος, ὧν μ' ἐχρῆν τυχεῖν.

Ἑκάβη.
οἰκτρὰ σύ, τέκνον, ἀθλία δ' ἐγὼ γυνή.

Πολυξένη.
ἐκεῖ δ' ἐν Ἅιδου κείσομαι χωρὶς σέθεν.

Ἑκάβη.
οἴμοι· τί δράσω; ποῖ τελευτήσω βίον;

Πολυξένη.
420 δούλη θανοῦμαι, πατρὸς οὖσ' ἐλευθέρου.

Ἑκάβη.
ἡμεῖς δὲ πεντήκοντά γ' ἄμμοροι τέκνων.

Πολυξένη.
τί σοι πρὸς Ἕκτορ' ἢ γέροντ' εἴπω πόσιν;

Ἑκάβη.
ἄγγελλε πασῶν ἀθλιωτάτην ἐμέ.

Πολυξένη.
ὦ στέρνα, μαστοί θ', οἵ μ' ἐθρέψαθ' ἡδέως.

Ἑκάβη.
ὦ τῆς ἀώρου θύγατερ ἀθλίας τύχης.

Πολυξένη.
χαῖρ', ὦ τεκοῦσα, χαῖρε Κασάνδρα τ' ἐμοί.

Ἑκάβη.
χαίρουσιν ἄλλοι, μητρὶ δ' οὐκ ἔστιν τόδε.

Πολυξένη.
ὅ τ' ἐν φιλίπποις Θρῃξὶ Πολύδωρος κάσις.

Ἑκάβη.
εἰ ζῇ γ'· ἀπιστῶ δ'· ὧδε πάντα δυστυχῶ.

Πολυξένη.
ζῇ, καὶ θανούσης ὄμμα συγκλῄσει τὸ σόν.

Ἑκάβη.
τέθνηκ' ἔγωγε, πρὶν θανεῖν, κακῶν ὕπο.

Πολυξένη.
κόμιζ', Ὀδυσσεῦ, μ' ἀμφιθεὶς κάρα πέπλοις·
ὡς πρὶν σφαγῆναί γ' ἐκτέτηκα καρδίαν
θρήνοισι μητρός, τήνδε τ' ἐκτήκω γόοις.
ὦ φῶς· προσειπεῖν γὰρ σὸν ὄνομ' ἔξεστί μοι,
μέτεστι δ' οὐδὲν πλὴν ὅσον χρόνον ξίφους
βαίνω μεταξὺ καὶ πυρᾶς Ἀχιλλέως.

Ἑκάβη.
οἲ 'γώ, προλείπω· λύεται δέ μου μέλη.
ὦ θύγατερ, ἅψαι μητρός, ἔκτεινον χέρα,

440 δός· μὴ λίπῃς μ' ἄπαιδ'. ἀπωλόμην, φίλαι.
[ὡς τὴν Λάκαιναν σύγγονον Διοσκόροιν
Ἑλένην ἴδοιμι· διὰ καλῶν γὰρ ὀμμάτων
αἴσχιστα Τροίαν εἷλε τὴν εὐδαίμονα.]

(POLYXENA *is led away by* ODYSSEUS, *and* HECUBA *sinks fainting upon the ground.*)

FIRST STASIMON.

Χορός.

Strophe I.

αὔρα, ποντιὰς αὔρα,
445 ἅτε ποντοπόρους κομίζεις
θοὰς ἀκάτους ἐπ' οἶδμα λίμνας.
ποῖ με τὰν μελέαν πορεύσεις ;
τῷ δουλόσυνος πρὸς οἶκον
κτηθεῖσ' ἀφίξομαι ;
450 ἦ Δωρίδος ὅρμον αἴας,
ἦ Φθιάδος, ἔνθα καλλί-
στων ὑδάτων πατέρα
φασὶν Ἀπιδανὸν * γύας λιπαίνειν ;

Antistrophe I

455 ἦ νάσων, ἁλιήρει
κώπᾳ πεμπομέναν τάλαιναν,
οἰκτρὰν βιοτὰν ἔχουσαν οἴκοις.
ἔνθα πρωτόγονός τε φοῖνιξ
δάφνα θ' ἱεροὺς ἀνέσχε

460 πτόρθους Λατοῖ φίλᾳ,
ὠδῖνος ἄγαλμα Δίας;
σὺν Δηλιάσιν τε κούραις
Ἀρτέμιδός τε θεᾶς
465 χρυσέαν ἄμπυκα τόξα τ' εὐλογήσω;

Strophe II.

ἢ Παλλάδος ἐν πόλει
τᾶς καλλιδίφρου * θεᾶς
* ναίουσ', ἐν κροκέῳ πέπλῳ
ζεύξομαι * ἆρα πώλους, ἐν
470 δαιδαλέαισι ποικίλλουσ'
ἀνθοκρόκοισι πήναις,
ἢ Τιτάνων γενεάν,
τὰν Ζεὺς ἀμφιπύρῳ
κοιμίζει φλογμῷ Κρονίδας;

Antistrophe II.

475 ὤμοι τεκέων ἐμῶν,
ὤμοι πατέρων χθονός θ',
ἃ καπνῷ κατερείπεται
τυφομένα, * δορίκτητος
Ἀργείων· ἐγὼ δ' ἐν ξεί-
480 νᾳ χθονὶ δὴ κέκλημαι
δούλα, λιποῦσ' Ἀσίαν,
Εὐρώπας θεράπναν,
ἀλλάξασ' Ἅιδα θαλάμους.

SECOND EPEISODION.

(*Enter* Talthybius *from the camp.* Hecuba *is lying upon the ground.*)

Ταλθύβιος.

ὗ τὴν ἄνασσαν δή ποτ' οὖσαν Ἰλίου
485 Ἑκάβην ἂν ἐξεύροιμι, Τρῳάδες κόραι;

Χορός.

αὕτη πέλας σοῦ, νῶτ' ἔχουσ' ἐπὶ χθονί,
Ταλθύβιε, κεῖται, συγκεκλῃμένη πέπλοις.

Ταλθύβιος.

ὦ Ζεῦ, τί λέξω; πότερά σ' ἀνθρώπους ὁρᾶν;
ἢ δόξαν ἄλλως τήνδε κεκτῆσθαι μάτην
490 ψευδῆ, δοκοῦντας δαιμόνων εἶναι γένος,
τύχην δὲ πάντα τἀν βροτοῖς ἐπισκοπεῖν;
οὐχ ἥδ' ἄνασσα τῶν πολυχρύσων Φρυγῶν,
οὐχ ἥδε Πριάμου τοῦ μέγ' ὀλβίου δάμαρ;
καὶ νῦν πόλις μὲν πᾶσ' ἀνέστηκεν δορί,
495 αὐτὴ δὲ δούλη, γραῦς, ἄπαις, ἐπὶ χθονὶ
κεῖται, κόνει φύρουσα δύστηνον κάρα.
φεῦ φεῦ· γέρων μέν εἰμ', ὅμως δέ μοι θανεῖν
εἴη, πρὶν αἰσχρᾷ περιπεσεῖν τύχῃ τινί.
ἀνίστασ', ὦ δύστηνε, καὶ μετάρσιον
500 πλευρὰν ἔπαιρε καὶ τὸ πάλλευκον κάρα.

Ἑκάβη.

ἔα· τίς οὗτος σῶμα τοὐμὸν οὐκ ἐᾷς
κεῖσθαι; τί κινεῖς μ', ὅστις εἶ, λυπουμένην;

Ταλθύβιος.

Ταλθύβιος ἥκω, Δαναϊδῶν ὑπηρέτης,
Ἀγαμέμνονος πέμψαντος, ὦ γύναι, μέτα.

Ἑκάβη.

505 ὦ φίλτατ', ἆρα κἄμ' ἐπισφάξαι τάφῳ
δοκοῦν Ἀχαιοῖς ἦλθες; ὡς φίλ' ἂν λέγοις.
σπεύδωμεν, ἐγκονῶμεν· ἡγοῦ μοι, γέρον.

(*Raising herself.*)

Ταλθύβιος.

σὴν παῖδα κατθανοῦσαν ὡς θάψῃς, γύναι,
ἥκω μεταστείχων σε· πέμπουσιν δέ με
510 δισσοί τ' Ἀτρεῖδαι καὶ λεὼς Ἀχαϊκός.

Ἑκάβη.

οἴμοι, τί λέξεις; οὐκ ἄρ' ὡς θανουμένους
μετῆλθες ἡμᾶς, ἀλλὰ σημανῶν κακά;
ὄλωλας, ὦ παῖ, μητρὸς ἁρπασθεῖσ' ἄπο·
ἡμεῖς δ' ἄτεκνοι τοὐπὶ σ'· ὦ τάλαιν' ἐγώ.
515 πῶς καί νιν ἐξεπράξατ'; ἆρ' αἰδούμενοι;
ἢ πρὸς τὸ δεινὸν ἤλθεθ', ὡς ἐχθράν, γέρον,
κτείνοντες; εἰπέ, καίπερ οὐ λέξων φίλα.

Ταλθύβιος.

διπλᾶ με χρῄζεις δάκρυα κερδᾶναι, γύναι,
σῆς παιδὸς οἴκτῳ· νῦν τε γὰρ λέγων κακὰ
520 τέγξω τόδ' ὄμμα, πρὸς τάφῳ θ', ὅτ' ὤλλυτο.
παρῆν μὲν ὄχλος πᾶς Ἀχαιοῦ στρατοῦ
πλήρης πρὸ τύμβου σῆς κόρης ἐπὶ σφαγάς·

λαβὼν δ' Ἀχιλλέως παῖς Πολυξένην χερὸς
ἔστησ' ἐπ' ἄκρου χώματος, πέλας δ' ἐγώ·
525 λεκτοί τ' Ἀχαιῶν ἔκκριτοι νεανίαι,
σκίρτημα μόσχου σῆς καθέξοντες χεροῖν,
ἕσποντο. πλῆρες δ' ἐν χεροῖν λαβὼν δέπας
πάγχρυσον αἴρει χειρὶ παῖς Ἀχιλλέως,
χοὰς θανόντι πατρί· σημαίνει δέ μοι
530 σιγὴν Ἀχαιῶν παντὶ κηρῦξαι στρατῷ.
κἀγὼ παραστὰς εἶπον ἐν μέσοις τάδε·
σιγᾶτ', Ἀχαιοί, σῖγα πᾶς ἔστω λεώς,
σίγα, σιώπα· νήνεμον δ' ἔστησ' ὄχλον.
ὁ δ' εἶπεν· ὦ παῖ Πηλέως, πατὴρ δ' ἐμός,
535 δέξαι χοάς μοι τάσδε κηλητηρίους,
νεκρῶν ἀγωγούς· ἐλθὲ δ' ὡς πίῃς μέλαν
κόρης ἀκραιφνὲς αἷμ', ὅ σοι δωρούμεθα
στρατός τε κἀγώ· πρευμενὴς δ' ἡμῖν γενοῦ,
λῦσαί τε πρύμνας καὶ χαλινωτήρια
540 νεῶν δὸς ἡμῖν, πρευμενοῦς τ' ἀπ' Ἰλίου
νόστου τυχόντας πάντας εἰς πάτραν μολεῖν.
τοσαῦτ' ἔλεξε, πᾶς δ' ἐπηύξατο στρατός.
εἶτ' ἀμφίχρυσον φάσγανον κώπης λαβὼν
ἐξεῖλκε κολεοῦ, λογάσι δ' Ἀργείων στρατοῦ
545 νεανίαις ἔνευσε παρθένον λαβεῖν.
ἡ δ', ὡς ἐφράσθη, τόνδ' ἐσήμηνεν λόγον·
ὦ τὴν ἐμὴν πέρσαντες Ἀργεῖοι πόλιν,
ἑκοῦσα θνῄσκω· μή τις ἅψηται χροὸς
τοὐμοῦ· παρέξω γὰρ δέρην εὐκαρδίως.

HECUBA 41

550 ἐλευθέραν δέ μ', ὡς ἐλευθέρα θάνω,
πρὸς θεῶν μεθέντες κτείνατ'· ἐν νεκροῖσι γὰρ
δούλη κεκλῆσθαι βασιλὶς οὖσ' αἰσχύνομαι.
λαοὶ δ' ἐπερρόθησαν, Ἀγαμέμνων τ' ἄναξ
εἶπεν μεθεῖναι παρθένον νεανίαις.
555 [οἱ δ', ὡς τάχιστ' ἤκουσαν ὑστάτην ὄπα,
μεθῆκαν, οὗπερ καὶ μέγιστον ἦν κράτος.]
κἀπεὶ τόδ' εἰσήκουσε δεσποτῶν ἔπος,
λαβοῦσα πέπλους ἐξ ἄκρας ἐπωμίδος
ἔρρηξε λαγόνος ἐς μέσον παρ' ὀμφαλόν,
560 μαστούς τ' ἔδειξε στέρνα θ', ὡς ἀγάλματος,
κάλλιστα, καὶ καθεῖσα πρὸς γαῖαν γόνυ
ἔλεξε πάντων τλημονέστατον λόγον·
ἰδοὺ τόδ', εἰ μὲν στέρνον, ὦ νεανία,
παίειν προθυμεῖ, παῖσον, εἰ δ' ὑπ' αὐχένα
565 χρῄζεις, πάρεστι λαιμὸς εὐτρεπὴς ὅδε.
ὁ δ', οὐ θέλων τε καὶ θέλων οἴκτῳ κόρης,
τέμνει σιδήρῳ πνεύματος διαρροάς·
κρουνοὶ δ' ἐχώρουν. ἡ δὲ καὶ θνῄσκουσ' ὅμως
πολλὴν πρόνοιαν εἶχεν εὐσχήμως πεσεῖν,
570 κρύπτουσ' ἃ κρύπτειν ὄμματ' ἀρσένων χρεών.
ἐπεὶ δ' ἀφῆκε πνεῦμα θανασίμῳ σφαγῇ,
οὐδεὶς τὸν αὐτὸν εἶχεν Ἀργείων πόνον·
ἀλλ' οἱ μὲν αὐτῶν τὴν θανοῦσαν ἐκ χερῶν
φύλλοις ἔβαλλον, οἱ δὲ πληροῦσιν πυράν,
575 κορμοὺς φέροντες πευκίνους, ὁ δ' οὐ φέρων
πρὸς τοῦ φέροντος τοιάδ' ἤκουεν κακά·

ἕστηκας, ὦ κάκιστε, τῇ νεάνιδι
οὐ πέπλον οὐδὲ κόσμον ἐν χεροῖν ἔχων;
οὐκ εἶ τι δώσων τῇ περίσσ' εὐκαρδίῳ
580 ψυχήν τ' ἀρίστῃ; τοιάδ' ἀμφὶ σῆς λέγω
παιδὸς θανούσης· εὐτεκνωτάτην δὲ σὲ
πασῶν γυναικῶν δυστυχεστάτην θ' ὁρῶ.

Χορός.

δεινόν τι πῆμα Πριαμίδαις ἐπέζεσε
πόλει τε τῇμῇ· θεῶν ἀναγκαῖον τόδε.

Ἑκάβη.

585 ὦ θύγατερ, οὐκ οἶδ' εἰς ὅ τι βλέψω κακῶν,
πολλῶν παρόντων· ἢν γὰρ ἅψωμαί τινος,
τόδ' οὐκ ἐᾷ με, παρακαλεῖ δ' ἐκεῖθεν αὖ
λύπη τις ἄλλη, διάδοχος κακῶν κακοῖς.
καὶ νῦν τὸ μὲν σὸν ὥστε μὴ στένειν πάθος
590 οὐκ ἂν δυναίμην ἐξαλείψασθαι φρενός·
τὸ δ' αὖ λίαν παρεῖλες, ἀγγελθεῖσά μοι
γενναῖος. οὔκουν δεινόν, εἰ γῆ μὲν κακή,
τυχοῦσα καιροῦ θεόθεν, εὖ στάχυν φέρει,
χρηστὴ δ', ἁμαρτοῦσ' ὧν χρεὼν αὐτὴν τυχεῖν,
595 κακὸν δίδωσι καρπόν; ἄνθρωποι δ' ἀεί,
ὁ μὲν πονηρὸς οὐδὲν ἄλλο πλὴν κακός,
ὁ δ' ἐσθλὸς ἐσθλός, οὐδὲ συμφορᾶς ὕπο
φύσιν διέφθειρ', ἀλλὰ χρηστός ἐστ' ἀεί;
ἆρ' οἱ τεκόντες διαφέρουσιν, ἢ τροφαί;

600 ἔχει γέ τοί τι καὶ τὸ θρεφθῆναι καλῶς
δίδαξιν ἐσθλοῦ· τοῦτο δ' ἤν τις εὖ μάθῃ,
οἶδεν τό γ' αἰσχρόν, κανόνι τοῦ καλοῦ μαθών.
καὶ ταῦτα μὲν δὴ νοῦς ἐτόξευσεν μάτην·
σὺ δ' ἐλθὲ καὶ σήμηνον Ἀργείοις τάδε,
605 μὴ θιγγάνειν μοι μηδέν, ἀλλ' εἴργειν ὄχλον
τῆς παιδός. ἔν τοι μυρίῳ στρατεύματι
ἀκόλαστος ὄχλος ναυτική τ' ἀναρχία
κρείσσων πυρός, κακὸς δ' ὁ μή τι δρῶν κακόν.

Exit TALTHYBIUS.

σὺ δ' αὖ λαβοῦσα τεῦχος, ἀρχαία λάτρι,
610 βάψασ' ἔνεγκε δεῦρο ποντίας ἁλός,
ὡς παῖδα λουτροῖς τοῖς πανυστάτοις ἐμήν,
νύμφην τ' ἄνυμφον παρθένον τ' ἀπάρθενον,
λούσω προθῶμαί θ'· ὡς μὲν ἀξία, πόθεν;
οὐκ ἂν δυναίμην· ὡς δ' ἔχω· τί γὰρ πάθω;
615 κόσμον τ' ἀγείρασ' αἰχμαλωτίδων πάρα,
αἵ μοι πάρεδροι τῶνδ' ἔσω σκηνωμάτων
ναίουσιν, εἴ τις τοὺς νεωστὶ δεσπότας
λαθοῦσ' ἔχει τι κλέμμα τῶν αὑτῆς δόμων.

Exit ATTENDANT.

ὦ σχήματ' οἴκων, ὦ ποτ' εὐτυχεῖς δόμοι,
620 ὦ πλεῖστ' ἔχων κάλλιστά τ', εὐτεκνώτατε
Πρίαμε, γεραιά θ' ἥδ' ἐγὼ μήτηρ τέκνων,
ὡς ἐς τὸ μηδὲν ἥκομεν, φρονήματος
τοῦ πρὶν στερέντες. εἶτα δῆτ' ὀγκούμεθα,

ὁ μέν τις ἡμῶν πλουσίοις ἐν δώμασιν,
625 ὁ δ' ἐν πολίταις τίμιος κεκλημένος.
τὰ δ' οὐδέν· ἄλλως φροντίδων βουλεύματα,
γλώσσης τε κόμποι. κεῖνος ὀλβιώτατος,
ὅτῳ κατ' ἦμαρ τυγχάνει μηδὲν κακόν.

(HECUBA *enters the tent.*)

SECOND STASIMON.

Χορός.

Strophe.

ἐμοὶ χρῆν συμφοράν,
630 ἐμοὶ χρῆν πημονὰν γενέσθαι,
Ἰδαίαν ὅτε πρῶτον ὕλαν
Ἀλέξανδρος εἰλατίναν
ἐτάμεθ', ἅλιον ἐπ' οἶδμα ναυστολήσων
635 Ἑλένας ἐπὶ λέκτρα, τὰν
καλλίσταν ὁ χρυσοφαὴς
Ἅλιος αὐγάζει.

Antistrophe.

πόνοι γὰρ καὶ πόνων
ἀνάγκαι κρείσσονες κυκλοῦνται.
640 κοινὸν δ' ἐξ ἰδίας ἀνοίας
κακὸν τᾷ Σιμουντίδι γᾷ
ὀλέθριον ἔμολε, συμφορά τ' ἀπ' ἄλλων.
ἐκρίθη δ' ἔρις, ἃν ἐν Ἴ-
645 δᾳ κρίνει τρισσὰς μακάρων
παῖδας ἀνὴρ βούτας,

HECUBA

Epodus.

ἐπὶ δορὶ καὶ φόνῳ καὶ ἐμῶν μελάθρων λώβᾳ·
650 στένει δὲ καί τις ἀμφὶ τὸν εὔροον Εὐρώταν
Λάκαινα πολυδάκρυτος ἐν δόμοις κόρα,
πολιόν τ' ἐπὶ κρᾶτα μάτηρ
τέκνων θανόντων
655 τίθεται χέρα δρύπτεταί τε παρειάν,
δίαιμον ὄνυχα τιθεμένα σπαραγμοῖς.

THIRD EPEISODION.

(*Re-enter* ATTENDANT *from the sea-shore, with the body of* POLYDORUS, *veiled.*)

Θεράπαινα.

γυναῖκες, Ἑκάβη ποῦ ποθ' ἡ παναθλία,
ἡ πάντα νικῶσ' ἄνδρα καὶ θῆλυν σπορὰν
660 κακοῖσιν; οὐδεὶς στέφανον ἀνθαιρήσεται.

Χορός.

τί δ', ὦ τάλαινα σῆς κακογλώσσου βοῆς;
ὡς οὔποθ' εὕδει λυπρά σου κηρύγματα.

Θεράπαινα.

Ἑκάβῃ φέρω τόδ' ἄλγος· ἐν κακοῖσι δὲ
οὐ ῥᾴδιον βροτοῖσιν εὐφημεῖν στόμα.

Χορός.

665 καὶ μὴν περῶσα τυγχάνει δόμων ὕπο
ἥδ', ἐς δὲ καιρὸν σοῖσι φαίνεται λόγοις.

(*Re-enter* HECUBA.)

Θεράπαινα.
ὦ παντάλαινα, κἄτι μᾶλλον ἢ λέγω,
δέσποιν᾽, ὄλωλας, οὐκέτ᾽ εἶ βλέπουσα φῶς,
ἄπαις, ἄνανδρος, ἄπολις, ἐξεφθαρμένη.

Ἑκάβη.
670 οὐ καινὸν εἶπας, εἰδόσιν δ᾽ ὠνείδισας.
ἀτὰρ τί νεκρὸν τόνδε μοι Πολυξένης
ἥκεις κομίζουσ᾽, ἧς ἀπηγγέλθη τάφος
πάντων Ἀχαιῶν διὰ χερὸς σπουδὴν ἔχειν;

Θεράπαινα.
ἥδ᾽ οὐδὲν οἶδεν, ἀλλά μοι Πολυξένην
675 θρηνεῖ, νέων δὲ πημάτων οὐχ ἅπτεται.

Ἑκάβη.
οἲ ᾽γὼ τάλαινα· μῶν τὸ βακχεῖον κάρα
τῆς θεσπιῳδοῦ δεῦρο Κασάνδρας φέρεις;

Θεράπαινα.
ζῶσαν λέλακας, τὸν θανόντα δ᾽ οὐ στένεις
τόνδ᾽· ἀλλ᾽ ἄθρησον σῶμα γυμνωθὲν νεκροῦ.
680 εἴ σοι φανεῖται θαῦμα καὶ παρ᾽ ἐλπίδας.

(Unveils the body.)

Ἑκάβη.
οἴμοι, βλέπω δὴ παῖδ᾽ ἐμὸν τεθνηκότα,
Πολύδωρον, ὅν μοι Θρὴξ ἔσῳζ᾽ οἴκοις ἀνήρ.
ἀπωλόμην δύστηνος, οὐκέτ᾽ εἰμὶ δή.

ὦ τέκνον τέκνον,
685 αἰαῖ, κατάρχομαι νόμον
βακχεῖον, ἐξ ἀλάστορος
ἀρτιμαθὴς κακῶν.

Θεράπαινα.
ἔγνως γὰρ ἄτην παιδός, ὦ δύστηνε σύ;

Ἑκάβη.
ἄπιστ' ἄπιστα, καινὰ καινὰ δέρκομαι.
690 ἕτερα δ' ἀφ' ἑτέρων κακὰ κακῶν κυρεῖ·
οὐδέποτ' ἀστένακτος ἀδάκρυτος ἁ-
μέρα ἐπισχήσει.

Χορός.
δείν', ὦ τάλαινα, δεινὰ πάσχομεν κακά.

Ἑκάβη.
ὦ τέκνον τέκνον ταλαίνας ματρός,
695 τίνι μόρῳ θνήσκεις,
τίνι πότμῳ κεῖσαι;
πρὸς τίνος ἀνθρώπων;

Θεράπαινα.
οὐκ οἶδ'· ἐπ' ἀκταῖς νιν κυρῶ θαλασσίαις.

Ἑκάβη.
ἔκβλητον, ἢ πέσημα φονίου δορός,
700 ἐν ψαμάθῳ λευρᾷ;

Θεράπαινα.
πόντου νιν ἐξήνεγκε πελάγιος κλύδων.

Ἑκάβη.
ὤμοι, αἰαῖ, ἔμαθον ἐνύπνιον ὀμμάτων
ἐμῶν ὄψιν, οὔ με παρέβα φάσμα μελανόπτερον,
ἂν ἐσεῖδον ἀμφὶ σ᾽,
ὦ τέκνον, οὐκέτ᾽ ὄντα Διὸς ἐν φάει.

Χορός.
τίς γάρ νιν ἔκτειν᾽; οἶσθ᾽ ὀνειρόφρων φράσαι;

Ἑκάβη.
ἐμὸς ἐμὸς ξένος, Θρήκιος ἱππότας,
ἵν᾽ ὁ γέρων πατὴρ ἔθετό νιν κρύψας.

Χορός.
ὤμοι, τί λέξεις; χρυσὸν ὡς ἔχοι κτανών;

Ἑκάβη.
ἄρρητ᾽, ἀνωνόμαστα, θαυμάτων πέρα,
οὐχ ὅσι᾽, οὐδ᾽ ἀνεκτά. ποῦ δίκα ξένων; ?
ὦ κατάρατ᾽ ἀνδρῶν, ὡς διεμοιράσω
χρόα, σιδαρέῳ τεμὼν φασγάνῳ
μέλεα τοῦδε παιδός, οὐδ᾽ ᾠκτίσω.

Χορός.
ὦ τλῆμον, ὥς σε πολυπονωτάτην βροτῶν
δαίμων ἔθηκεν, ὅστις ἐστί σοι βαρύς.

ἀλλ', εἰσορῶ γὰρ τοῦδε δεσπότου δέμας
725 Ἀγαμέμνονος, τοὐνθένδε σιγῶμεν, φίλαι.

Enter AGAMEMNON *from the camp.*)

Ἀγαμέμνων.

Ἑκάβη, τί μέλλεις παῖδα σὴν κρύπτειν τάφῳ
ἐλθοῦσ', ἐφ' οἷσπερ Ταλθύβιος ἤγγειλέ μοι
μὴ θιγγάνειν σῆς μηδέν' Ἀργείων κόρης;
ἡμεῖς μὲν οὖν ἐῶμεν, οὐδὲ ψαύομεν·
730 σὺ δὲ σχολάζεις, ὥστε θαυμάζειν ἐμέ.
ἥκω δ' ἀποστελῶν σε· τἀκεῖθεν γὰρ εὖ
πεπραγμέν' ἐστίν, εἴ τι τῶνδ' ἐστὶν καλῶς.

(*Sees the dead body.*

ἔα· τίν' ἄνδρα τόνδ' ἐπὶ σκηναῖς ὁρῶ
θανόντα Τρώων; οὐ γὰρ Ἀργεῖον πέπλοι
735 δέμας περιπτύσσοντες ἀγγέλλουσί μοι.

Ἑκάβη. (*Aside.*

δύστην', ἐμαυτὴν γὰρ λέγω λέγουσα σέ,
Ἑκάβη, τί δράσω; πότερα προσπέσω γόνυ
Ἀγαμέμνονος τοῦδ', ἢ φέρω σιγῇ κακά;

Ἀγαμέμνων.

τί μοι προσώπῳ νῶτον ἐγκλίνασα σὸν
740 δύρει, τὸ πραχθὲν δ' οὐ λέγεις; τίς ἔσθ' ὅδε;

Ἑκάβη. (*Aside.*

ἀλλ' εἴ με δούλην πολεμίαν θ' ἡγούμενος
γονάτων ἀπώσαιτ', ἄλγος ἂν προσθείμεθ' ἄν.

D

Ἀγαμέμνων.

οὔτοι πέφυκα μάντις, ὥστε μὴ κλύων
ἐξιστορῆσαι σῶν ὁδὸν βουλευμάτων.

Ἑκάβη.   (Aside.

745 ἆρ' ἐκλογίζομαί γε πρὸς τὸ δυσμενὲς
μᾶλλον φρένας τοῦδ', ὄντος οὐχὶ δυσμενοῦς;

Ἀγαμέμνων.

εἴ τοί με βούλει τῶνδε μηδὲν εἰδέναι,
ἐς ταὐτὸν ἥκεις· καὶ γὰρ οὐδ' ἐγὼ κλύειν.

Ἑκάβη.   (Aside.)

οὐκ ἂν δυναίμην τοῦδε τιμωρεῖν ἄτερ
750 τέκνοισι τοῖς ἐμοῖσι. τί στρέφω τάδε;
τολμᾶν ἀνάγκη, κἂν τύχω κἂν μὴ τύχω.

(To Agamemnon.)

Ἀγάμεμνον, ἱκετεύω σε τῶνδε γουνάτων
καὶ σοῦ γενείου δεξιᾶς τ' εὐδαίμονος.

Ἀγαμέμνων.

τί χρῆμα μαστεύουσα; μῶν ἐλεύθερον
755 αἰῶνα θέσθαι; ῥᾴδιον γάρ ἐστί σοι.

Ἑκάβη.

[οὐ δῆτα· τοὺς κακοὺς δὲ τιμωρουμένη,
αἰῶνα τὸν ξύμπαντα δουλεῦσαι θέλω.

Ἀγαμέμνων.

καὶ δὴ τίν' ἡμᾶς εἰς ἐπάρκειαν καλεῖς;]

Ἑκάβη.
οὐδέν τι τούτων ὧν σὺ δοξάζεις, ἄναξ.
760 ὁρᾷς νεκρὸν τόνδ', οὗ καταστάζω δάκρυ·

Ἀγαμέμνων.
ὁρῶ· τὸ μέντοι μέλλον οὐκ ἔχω μαθεῖν.

Ἑκάβη.
τοῦτόν ποτ' ἔτεκον κἄφερον ζώνης ὕπο.

Ἀγαμέμνων.
ἔστιν δὲ τίς σῶν οὗτος, ὦ τλῆμον, τέκνων;

Ἑκάβη.
οὐ τῶν θανόντων Πριαμιδῶν ὑπ' Ἰλίῳ.

Ἀγαμέμνων.
765 ἦ γάρ τιν' ἄλλον ἔτεκες ἢ κείνους, γύναι;

Ἑκάβη.
ἀνόνητά γ', ὡς ἔοικε, τόνδ' ὃν εἰσορᾷς.

Ἀγαμέμνων.
ποῦ δ' ὢν ἐτύγχαν', ἡνίκ' ὤλλυτο πτόλις;

Ἑκάβη.
πατήρ νιν ἐξέπεμψεν, ὀρρωδῶν θανεῖν.

Ἀγαμέμνων.
ποῖ τῶν τότ' ὄντων χωρίσας τέκνων μόνον;

Ἑκάβη.
770 εἰς τήνδε χώραν, οὗπερ ηὑρέθη θανών.

Ἀγαμέμνων.
πρὸς ἄνδρ᾽ ὃς ἄρχει τῆσδε Πολυμήστωρ χθονός;

Ἑκάβη.
ἐνταῦθ᾽ ἐπέμφθη, πικροτάτου χρυσοῦ φύλαξ.

Ἀγαμέμνων.
θνήσκει δὲ πρὸς τοῦ, καὶ τίνος πότμου τυχών;

Ἑκάβη.
- τίνος δ᾽ ὑπ᾽ ἄλλου; Θρῇξ νιν ὤλεσε ξένος.

Ἀγαμέμνων.
775 ὦ τλῆμον· ἦ που χρυσὸν ἠράσθη λαβεῖν;

Ἑκάβη.
τοιαῦτ᾽, ἐπειδὴ συμφορὰν ἔγνω Φρυγῶν.

Ἀγαμέμνων.
εὗρες δὲ ποῦ νιν, ἢ τίς ἤνεγκεν νεκρόν;

Ἑκάβη.
ἥδ᾽, ἐντυχοῦσα ποντίας ἀκτῆς ἔπι.

Ἀγαμέμνων.
τοῦτον ματεύουσ᾽, ἢ πονοῦσ᾽ ἄλλον πόνον;

Ἑκάβη.
780 λουτρ᾽ ᾤχετ᾽ οἴσουσ᾽ ἐξ ἁλὸς Πολυξένῃ.

Ἀγαμέμνων.
κτανών νιν, ὡς ἔοικεν, ἐκβάλλει ξένος.

Ἑκάβη.
θαλασσόπλαγκτόν γ', ὧδε διατεμὼν χρόα.

Ἀγαμέμνων.
ὦ σχετλία σὺ τῶν ἀμετρήτων πόνων.

Ἑκάβη.
ὄλωλα, κοὐδὲν λοιπόν, Ἀγάμεμνον, κακῶν.

Ἀγαμέμνων.
785 φεῦ φεῦ· τίς οὕτω δυστυχὴς ἔφυ γυνή;

Ἑκάβη.
οὐκ ἔστιν, εἰ μὴ τὴν τύχην αὐτὴν λέγοις.
ἀλλ' ὧνπερ οὕνεκ' ἀμφὶ σὸν πίπτω γόνυ,
ἄκουσον. εἰ μὲν ὅσιά σοι παθεῖν δοκῶ,
στέργοιμ' ἄν· εἰ δὲ τοὔμπαλιν, σύ μοι γενοῦ
790 τιμωρὸς ἀνδρὸς ἀνοσιωτάτου ξένου,
ὃς οὔτε τοὺς γῆς νέρθεν οὔτε τοὺς ἄνω
δείσας δέδρακεν ἔργον ἀνοσιώτατον,
[κοινῆς τραπέζης πολλάκις τυχὼν ἐμοὶ
ξενίας τ', ἀριθμῷ πρῶτα τῶν ἐμῶν φίλων·
795 τυχὼν δ' ὅσων δεῖ καὶ λαβὼν προμηθίαν
ἔκτεινε, τύμβου δ', εἰ κτανεῖν ἐβούλετο,
οὐκ ἠξίωσεν, ἀλλ' ἀφῆκε πόντιον.]
ἡμεῖς μὲν οὖν δοῦλοί τε κἀσθενεῖς ἴσως·

ἀλλ᾽ οἱ θεοὶ σθένουσι χὠ κείνων κρατῶν
800 νόμος· νόμῳ γὰρ τοὺς θεοὺς ἡγούμεθα,
καὶ ζῶμεν ἄδικα καὶ δίκαι᾽ ὡρισμένοι·
ὃς εἰς σ᾽ ἀνελθὼν εἰ διαφθαρήσεται,
καὶ μὴ δίκην δώσουσιν οἵτινες ξένους
κτείνουσιν ἢ θεῶν ἱερὰ τολμῶσιν φέρειν,
805 οὐκ ἔστιν οὐδὲν τῶν ἐν ἀνθρώποις ἴσον.
ταῦτ᾽ οὖν ἐν αἰσχρῷ θέμενος αἰδέσθητί με·
οἴκτειρον ἡμᾶς, ὡς γραφεύς τ᾽ ἀποσταθεὶς
ἰδοῦ με κἀνάθρησον οἷ᾽ ἔχω κακά.
τύραννος ἦν ποτ᾽, ἀλλὰ νῦν δούλη σέθεν,
810 εὔπαις ποτ᾽ οὖσα, νῦν δὲ γραῦς ἄπαις θ᾽ ἅμα,
ἄπολις, ἔρημος, ἀθλιωτάτη βροτῶν.

(AGAMEMNON *turns away*.

οἴμοι τάλαινα, ποῖ μ᾽ ὑπεξάγεις πόδα;
ἔοικα πράξειν οὐδέν· ὦ τάλαιν᾽ ἐγώ.
τί δῆτα θνητοὶ τἆλλα μὲν μαθήματα
815 μοχθοῦμεν ὡς χρὴ πάντα καὶ μαστεύομεν,
πειθὼ δὲ τὴν τύραννον ἀνθρώποις μόνην
οὐδέν τι μᾶλλον ἐς τέλος σπουδάζομεν,
μισθοὺς διδόντες, μανθάνειν, ἵν᾽ *ἦν ποτε
πείθειν ἅ τις βούλοιτο τυγχάνειν θ᾽ ἅμα;
820 πῶς οὖν ἔτ᾽ ἄν τις ἐλπίσαι πράξειν καλῶς;
οἱ μὲν γὰρ ὄντες παῖδες οὐκέτ᾽ εἰσί μοι,
αὐτὴ δ᾽ ἐπ᾽ αἰσχροῖς αἰχμάλωτος οἴχομαι·
καπνὸν δὲ πόλεως τόνδ᾽ ὑπερθρῴσκονθ᾽ ὁρῶ.
καὶ μὴν—ἴσως μὲν τοῦ λόγου κενὸν τόδε,

825 Κύπριν προβάλλειν· ἀλλ' ὅμως εἰρήσεται·—
πρὸς σοῖσι πλευροῖς παῖς ἐμὴ κοιμίζεται,
ἡ φοιβάς, ἣν καλοῦσι Κασάνδραν Φρύγες.
ποῦ τὰς φίλας δῆτ' εὐφρόνας δείξεις, ἄναξ,
ἢ τῶν ἐν εὐνῇ φιλτάτων ἀσπασμάτων
830 χάριν τίν' ἕξει παῖς ἐμή, κείνης δ' ἐγώ;
[ἐκ τοῦ σκότου γὰρ τῶν τε νυκτέρων βροτοῖς
φίλτρων μεγίστη γίγνεται βροτοῖς χάρις.]
ἄκουε δή νυν· τὸν θανόντα τόνδ' ὁρᾷς;
τοῦτον καλῶς δρῶν, ὄντα κηδεστὴν σέθεν
835 δράσεις. ἑνός μοι μῦθος ἐνδεὴς ἔτι·
εἴ μοι γένοιτο φθόγγος ἐν βραχίοσι
καὶ χερσὶ καὶ κόμαισι καὶ ποδῶν βάσει,
ἢ Δαιδάλου τέχναισιν ἢ θεῶν τινος,
ὡς πάνθ' ὁμαρτῇ σῶν ἔχοιντο γουνάτων
840 κλαίοντ', ἐπισκήπτοντα παντοίους λόγους.
ὦ δέσποτ', ὦ μέγιστον Ἕλλησιν φάος,
πιθοῦ, παράσχες χεῖρα τῇ πρεσβύτιδι
τιμωρόν, εἰ καὶ μηδέν ἐστιν, ἀλλ' ὅμως.
ἐσθλοῦ γὰρ ἀνδρὸς τῇ δίκῃ θ' ὑπηρετεῖν
845 καὶ τοὺς κακοὺς δρᾶν πανταχοῦ κακῶς ἀεί.

Χορός.

δεινόν γε, θνητοῖς ὡς ἅπαντα συμπίτνει,
καὶ τὰς ἀνάγκας οἱ νόμοι διώρισαν,
φίλους τιθέντες τούς τε πολεμιωτάτους,
ἐχθρούς τε τοὺς πρὶν εὐμενεῖς ποιούμενοι.

Ἀγαμέμνων.

850 ἐγὼ σὲ καὶ σὸν παῖδα καὶ τύχας σέθεν,
Ἑκάβη, δι' οἴκτου χεῖρά θ' ἱκεσίαν ἔχω,
καὶ βούλομαι θεῶν θ' οὕνεκ' ἀνόσιον ξένον
καὶ τοῦ δικαίου τήνδε σοι δοῦναι δίκην,
εἴ πως φανείη γ' ὥστε σοί τ' ἔχειν καλῶς,
855 στρατῷ τε μὴ δόξαιμι Κασάνδρας χάριν
Θρῄκης ἄνακτι τόνδε βουλεῦσαι φόνον.
ἔστιν γὰρ ᾗ ταραγμὸς ἐμπέπτωκέ μοι·
τὸν ἄνδρα τοῦτον φίλιον ἡγεῖται στρατός,
τὸν κατθανόντα δ' ἐχθρόν· εἰ δὲ σοὶ φίλος
860 ὅδ' ἐστί, χωρὶς τοῦτο κοὐ κοινὸν στρατῷ.
πρὸς ταῦτα φρόντιζ'· ὡς θέλοντα μέν μ' ἔχεις
σοὶ ξυμπονῆσαι καὶ ταχὺν προσαρκέσαι,
βραδὺν δ', Ἀχαιοῖς εἰ διαβληθήσομαι.

Ἑκάβη.

φεῦ·
οὐκ ἔστι θνητῶν ὅστις ἔστ' ἐλεύθερος·
865 ἢ χρημάτων γὰρ δοῦλός ἐστιν ἢ τύχης,
ἢ πλῆθος αὐτὸν πόλεος ἢ νόμων γραφαὶ
εἴργουσι χρῆσθαι μὴ κατὰ γνώμην τρόποις.
ἐπεὶ δὲ ταρβεῖς τῷ τ' ὄχλῳ πλέον νέμεις,
ἐγώ σε θήσω τοῦδ' ἐλεύθερον φόβου.
870 ξύνισθι μὲν γάρ, ἤν τι βουλεύσω κακὸν
τῷ τόνδ' ἀποκτείναντι, συνδράσῃς δὲ μή.
ἢν δ' ἐξ Ἀχαιῶν θόρυβος ἢ 'πικουρία,

HECUBA

πάσχοντος ἀνδρὸς Θρῃκὸς οἷα πείσεται,
φανῇ τις, εἶργε, μὴ δοκῶν ἐμὴν χάριν.
875 τὰ δ' ἄλλα θάρσει· πάντ' ἐγὼ θήσω καλῶς,

Ἀγαμέμνων.

πῶς οὖν; τί δράσεις; πότερα φάσγανον χερὶ
λαβοῦσα γραίᾳ φῶτα βάρβαρον κτενεῖς,
ἢ φαρμάκοισιν ἢ 'πικουρίᾳ τίνι;
τίς σοι ξυνέσται χείρ; πόθεν κτήσει φίλους;

Ἑκάβη.
880 στέγαι κεκεύθασ' αἵδε Τρῳάδων ὄχλον.

Ἀγαμέμνων.
τὰς αἰχμαλώτους εἶπας, Ἑλλήνων ἄγραν;

Ἑκάβη.
σὺν ταῖσδε τὸν ἐμὸν φονέα τιμωρήσομαι.

Ἀγαμέμνων.
καὶ πῶς γυναιξὶν ἀρσένων ἔσται κράτος;

Ἑκάβη.
δεινὸν τὸ πλῆθος, σὺν δόλῳ τε δύσμαχον.

Ἀγαμέμνων.
885 δεινόν· τὸ μέντοι θῆλυ μέμφομαι γένος.

Ἑκάβη.
τί δ'; οὐ γυναῖκες εἷλον Αἰγύπτου τέκνα,
καὶ Λῆμνον ἄρδην ἀρσένων ἐξῴκισαν;

ἀλλ' ὡς γενέσθω· τόνδε μὲν μέθες λόγον,
πέμψον δέ μοι τήνδ' ἀσφαλῶς διὰ στρατοῦ
890 γυναῖκα. (*To Attendant*
καὶ σὺ Θρῃκὶ πλαθεῖσα ξένῳ
λέξον· καλεῖ σ' ἄνασσα δή ποτ' Ἰλίου
Ἑκάβη, σὸν οὐκ ἔλασσον ἢ κείνης χρέος.
καὶ παῖδας· ὡς δεῖ καὶ τέκν' εἰδέναι λόγους
τοὺς ἐξ ἐκείνης. (*Exit Attendant.*)
τὸν δὲ τῆς νεοσφαγοῦς
895 Πολυξένης ἐπίσχες, Ἀγάμεμνον, τάφον,
ὡς τώδ' ἀδελφὼ πλησίον μιᾷ φλογί,
δισσὴ μέριμνα μητρί, κρυφθῆτον χθονί.

Ἀγαμέμνων.

ἔσται τάδ' οὕτω· καὶ γὰρ εἰ μὲν ἦν στρατῷ
πλοῦς, οὐκ ἂν εἶχον τήνδε σοι δοῦναι χάριν·
900 νῦν δ', οὐ γὰρ ἵησ' οὐρίας πνοὰς θεός,
μένειν ἀνάγκη πλοῦν ὁρῶντας ἥσυχον.
γένοιτο δ' εὖ πως· πᾶσι γὰρ κοινὸν τόδε
ἰδίᾳ θ' ἑκάστῳ καὶ πόλει, τὸν μὲν κακὸν
κακόν τι πάσχειν, τὸν δὲ χρηστὸν εὐτυχεῖν.

(*Exit* AGAMEMNON. HECUBA *goes into the tent.*

THIRD STASIMON.

Χορός.

Strophe I.

905 σὺ μέν, ὦ πατρὶς Ἰλιάς,
τῶν ἀπορθήτων πόλις οὐκέτι λέξει·

τοῖοι Ἑλλάνων νέφος ἀμφί σε κρύπτει
δορὶ δὴ δορὶ πέρσαν.
910 ἀπὸ δὲ στεφάναν κέκαρσαι
πύργων, κατὰ δ' αἰθάλου
κηλῖδ' οἰκτροτάταν κέχρωσαι·
τάλαιν', οὐκέτι σ' ἐμβατεύσω.

Antistrophe I.

μεσονύκτιος ὠλλύμαν,
915 ἦμος ἐκ δείπνων ὕπνος ἡδὺς ἐπ' ὄσσοις
κίδναται, μολπᾶν δ' ἄπο καὶ χαροποιῶν
θυσιᾶν καταπαύσας
πόσις ἐν θαλάμοις ἔκειτο,
920 ξυστὸν δ' ἐπὶ πασσάλῳ,
ναύταν οὐκέθ' ὁρῶν ὅμιλον
Τροίαν Ἰλιάδ' ἐμβεβῶτα.

Strophe II.

ἐγὼ δὲ πλόκαμον ἀναδέτοις
μίτραισιν ἐρρυθμιζόμαν
925 χρυσέων ἐνόπτρων
λεύσσουσ' ἀτέρμονας εἰς αὐγάς,
ἐπιδέμνιος ὡς πέσοιμ' ἐς εὐνάν.
ἀνὰ δὲ κέλαδος ἔμολε πόλιν·
κέλευσμα δ' ἦν κατ' ἄστυ Τροίας τόδ'· ὦ
930 παῖδες Ἑλλάνων, πότε δὴ πότε τὰν
Ἰλιάδα σκοπιὰν
πέρσαντες ἥξετ' οἴκους;

Antistrophe II.

λέχη δὲ φίλια μονόπεπλος
λιποῦσα, Δωρὶς ὡς κόρα,
935 σεμνὰν προσίζουσ᾽
οὐκ ἤνυσ᾽ Ἄρτεμιν ἁ τλάμων·
ἄγομαι δὲ θανόντ᾽ ἰδοῦσ᾽ ἀκοίταν
τὸν ἐμὸν ἅλιον ἐπὶ πέλαγος,
πόλιν τ᾽ ἀποσκοποῦσ᾽, ἐπεὶ νόστιμον
940 ναῦς ἐκίνησεν πόδα καί μ᾽ ἀπὸ γᾶς
ὥρισεν Ἰλιάδος,
τάλαιν᾽, ἀπεῖπον ἄλγει,

Epodus.

τὰν τοῖν Διοσκόροιν Ἑλέναν κάσιν
Ἰδαῖόν τε βούταν
945 αἰνόπαριν κατάρᾳ
διδοῦσ᾽, ἐπεί με γᾶς
ἐκ πατρῴας ἀπώλεσεν
ἐξῴκισέν τ᾽ οἴκων γάμος, οὐ γάμος,
ἀλλ᾽ ἀλάστορός τις οἰζύς·
950 ἃν μήτε πέλαγος ἅλιον ἀπαγάγοι πάλιν,
μήτε πατρῷον ἵκοιτ᾽ ἐς οἶκον.

EXODUS.

HECUBA *comes out of the tent. Enter* POLYMESTOR, *with his children, from the country, attended by Thracian guards.*)

Πολυμήστωρ.

ὦ φίλτατ᾽ ἀνδρῶν Πρίαμε, φιλτάτη δὲ σύ,
Ἑκάβη, δακρύω σ᾽ εἰσορῶν πόλιν τε σήν,

955 τήν τ' ἀρτίως θανοῦσαν ἔκγονον σέθεν.
φεῦ·
οὐκ ἔστιν οὐδὲν πιστόν, οὔτ' εὐδοξία
οὔτ' αὖ καλῶς πράσσοντα μὴ πράξειν κακῶς.
φύρουσι δ' αὐτὰ θεοὶ πάλιν τε καὶ πρόσω,
ταραγμὸν ἐντιθέντες, ὡς ἀγνωσίᾳ
960 σέβωμεν αὐτούς. ἀλλὰ ταῦτα μὲν τί δεῖ
θρηνεῖν, προκόπτοντ' οὐδὲν εἰς πρόσθεν κακῶν;
σὺ δ', εἴ τι μέμφει τῆς ἐμῆς ἀπουσίας,
σχές· τυγχάνω γὰρ ἐν μέσοις Θρῄκης ὅροις
ἀπών, ὅτ' ἦλθες δεῦρ'· ἐπεὶ δ' ἀφικόμην,
965 ἤδη πόδ' ἔξω δωμάτων αἴροντί μοι
ἐς ταὐτὸν ἥδε συμπίτνει δμωῒς σέθεν,
λέγουσα μύθους ὧν κλύων ἀφικόμην.

Ἑκάβη.
αἰσχύνομαί σε προσβλέπειν ἐναντίον,
Πολυμῆστορ, ἐν τοιοῖσδε κειμένη κακοῖς.
970 ὅτῳ γὰρ ὤφθην εὐτυχοῦσ', αἰδώς μ' ἔχει
ἐν τῷδε πότμῳ τυγχάνουσ' ἵν' εἰμὶ νῦν,
κοὐκ ἂν δυναίμην προσβλέπειν ὀρθαῖς κόραις.
ἀλλ' αὐτὸ μὴ δύσνοιαν ἡγήσῃ σέθεν,
Πολυμῆστορ· ἄλλως δ' αἴτιόν τι καὶ νόμος,
975 γυναῖκας ἀνδρῶν μὴ βλέπειν ἐναντίον.

Πολυμήστωρ.
καὶ θαυμά γ' οὐδέν. ἀλλὰ τίς χρεία σ' ἐμοῦ;
τί χρῆμ' ἐπέμψω τὸν ἐμὸν ἐκ δόμων πόδα;

Ἑκάβη.
ἴδιον ἐμαυτῆς δή τι πρὸς σὲ βούλομαι ,
καὶ παῖδας εἰπεῖν σούς· ὀπάονας δέ μοι
980 χωρὶς κέλευσον τῶνδ' ἀποστῆναι δόμων.

Πολυμήστωρ. *(To the Guards.)*
χωρεῖτ'· ἐν ἀσφαλεῖ γὰρ ἥδ' ἐρημία.
The Guards retire.
φίλη μὲν εἶ σύ, προσφιλὲς δέ μοι τόδε
στράτευμ' Ἀχαιῶν. ἀλλὰ σημαίνειν σε χρή,
τί χρὴ τὸν εὖ πράσσοντα μὴ πράσσουσιν εὖ
985 φίλοις ἐπαρκεῖν· ὡς ἕτοιμός εἰμ' ἐγώ.

Ἑκάβη.
πρῶτον μὲν εἰπὲ παῖδ' ὃν ἐξ ἐμῆς χερὸς
Πολύδωρον ἔκ τε πατρὸς ἐν δόμοις ἔχεις,
εἰ ζῇ· τὰ δ' ἄλλα δεύτερόν σ' ἐρήσομαι.

Πολυμήστωρ.
μάλιστα· τοὐκείνου μὲν εὐτυχεῖς μέρος.

Ἑκάβη.
990 ὦ φίλταθ', ὡς εὖ κἀξίως σέθεν λέγεις.

Πολυμήστωρ.
τί δῆτα βούλει δεύτερον μαθεῖν ἐμοῦ;

Ἑκάβη.
εἰ τῆς τεκούσης τῆσδε μέμνηταί τί μου.

Πολυμήστωρ.
καὶ δεῦρό γ' ὡς σὲ κρύφιος ἐζήτει μολεῖν.

Ἑκάβη.
χρυσὸς δὲ σῶς, ὃν ἦλθεν ἐκ Τροίας ἔχων;

Πολυμήστωρ.
995 σῶς, ἐν δόμοις γε τοῖς ἐμοῖς φρουρούμενος.

Ἑκάβη.
σῶσόν νυν αὐτόν, μηδ' ἔρα τῶν πλησίον.

Πολυμήστωρ.
ἥκιστ'· ὀναίμην τοῦ παρόντος, ὦ γύναι.

Ἑκάβη.
οἶσθ' οὖν ἃ λέξαι σοί τε καὶ παισὶν θέλω;

Πολυμήστωρ.
οὐκ οἶδα· τῷ σῷ τοῦτο σημανεῖς λόγῳ.

Ἑκάβη.
1000 *ἔστ', ὦ φιληθεὶς ὡς σὺ νῦν ἐμοὶ φιλεῖ,

Πολυμήστωρ.
τί χρῆμ', ὃ κἀμὲ καὶ τέκν' εἰδέναι χρεών;

Ἑκάβη.
χρυσοῦ παλαιαὶ Πριαμιδῶν κατώρυχες.

Πολυμήστωρ.
ταῦτ' ἔσθ' ἃ βούλει παιδὶ σημῆναι σέθεν;

Ἑκάβη.
μάλιστα, διὰ σοῦ γ'· εἰ γὰρ εὐσεβὴς ἀνήρ.

Πολυμήστωρ.
1005 τί δῆτα τέκνων τῶνδε δεῖ παρουσίας;

Ἑκάβη.
ἄμεινον, ἢν σὺ κατθάνῃς, τούσδ' εἰδέναι.

Πολυμήστωρ.
καλῶς ἔλεξας· τῇδε καὶ σοφώτερον.

Ἑκάβη.
οἶσθ' οὖν Ἀθάνας Ἰλίας ἵνα στέγαι;

Πολυμήστωρ.
ἐνταῦθ' ὁ χρυσός ἐστι; σημεῖον δὲ τί;

Ἑκάβη.
1010 μέλαινα πέτρα γῆς ὑπερτέλλουσ' ἄνω.

Πολυμήστωρ.
ἔτ' οὖν τι βούλει τῶν ἐκεῖ φράζειν ἐμοί;

Ἑκάβη.
σῶσαί σε χρήμαθ' οἷς συνεξῆλθον θέλω.

Πολυμήστωρ.
ποῦ δῆτα; πέπλων ἐντὸς ἢ κρύψασ' ἔχεις;

Ἑκάβη.
σκύλων ἐν ὄχλῳ ταῖσδε σώζεται στέγαις.

Πολυμήστωρ.
ποῦ δ'; αἵδ' Ἀχαιῶν ναύλοχοι περιπτυχαί.

Ἑκάβη.
ἴδιαι γυναικῶν αἰχμαλωτίδων στέγαι.

Πολυμήστωρ.
τἄνδον δὲ πιστά, κἀρσένων ἐρημία;

Ἑκάβη.
οὐδεὶς Ἀχαιῶν ἔνδον, ἀλλ' ἡμεῖς μόναι.
ἀλλ' ἕρπ' ἐς οἴκους· καὶ γὰρ Ἀργεῖοι νεῶν
λῦσαι ποθοῦσιν οἴκαδ' ἐκ Τροίας πόδα·
ὡς πάντα πράξας ὧν σε δεῖ στείχῃς πάλιν
ξὺν παισὶν οὗπερ τὸν ἐμὸν ᾤκισας γόνον.

(HECUBA *conducts* POLYMESTOR *into the tent*.

Χορός.
οὔπω δέδωκας, ἀλλ' ἴσως δώσεις δίκην·
ἀλίμενόν τις ὡς εἰς ἄντλον πεσὼν
λέχριος, * ἐκπεσεῖ φίλας καρδίας,
ἀμέρσας βίον. τὸ γὰρ ὑπέγγυον
δίκᾳ καὶ θεοῖσιν *οὗ ξυμπίτνει,
ὀλέθριον ὀλέθριον κακόν.
ψεύσει σ' ὁδοῦ τῆσδ' ἐλπίς, ἥ σ' ἐπήγαγεν
θανάσιμον πρὸς Ἀίδαν, ὦ τάλας·
ἀπολέμῳ δὲ χειρὶ λείψεις βίον.

Πολυμήστωρ.   *Within.*
1035 ὤμοι. τυφλοῦμαι φέγγος ὀμμάτων τάλας.

Χορός.
ἠκούσατ' ἀνδρὸς Θρῃκὸς οἰμωγήν, φίλαι·

Πολυμήστωρ.   *Within.*
ὤμοι μάλ' αὖθις, τέκνα, δυστήνου σφαγῆς.

Χορός.
φίλαι, πέπρακται καίν' ἔσω δόμων κακά.

Πολυμήστωρ.   *Within.*
ἀλλ' οὔτι μὴ φύγητε λαιψηρῷ ποδί·
1040 βάλλων γὰρ οἴκων τῶνδ' ἀναρρήξω μυχούς.

Χορός.
ἰδού, βαρείας χειρὸς ὁρμᾶται βέλος.
βούλεσθ' ἐπεισπέσωμεν; ὡς ἀκμὴ καλεῖ
Ἑκάβῃ παρεῖναι Τρῳάσιν τε συμμάχους.

(Re-enter HECUBA.*)*

Ἑκάβη.
ἄρασσε, φείδου μηδέν, ἐκβάλλων πύλας·
1045 οὐ γάρ ποτ' ὄμμα λαμπρὸν ἐνθήσεις κόραις,
οὐ παῖδας ὄψει ζῶντας, οὓς ἔκτειν' ἐγώ.

Χορός.
ἦ γὰρ καθεῖλες Θρῇκα καὶ κρατεῖς ξένου,
δέσποινα, καὶ δέδρακας οἷάπερ λέγεις;

Ἑκάβη.

ὄψει νιν αὐτίκ' ὄντα δωμάτων πάρος,
1050 τυφλὸν τυφλῷ στείχοντα παραφόρῳ ποδί,
παίδων τε δισσῶν σώμαθ', οὓς ἔκτειν' ἐγὼ
σὺν ταῖς ἀρίσταις Τρῳάσιν· δίκην δέ μοι
δέδωκε· χωρεῖ δ', ὡς ὁρᾷς, ὅδ' ἐκ δόμων.
ἀλλ' ἐκποδὼν ἄπειμι κἀποστήσομαι
1055 θυμῷ ῥέοντι Θρῃκὶ δυσμαχωτάτῳ.

[HECUBA *retires to the side, as* POLYMESTOR *staggers upon the stage, his eyes streaming with blood.*]

Πολυμήστωρ.

ὤμοι ἐγώ, πᾷ βῶ,
πᾷ στῶ, πᾷ κέλσω;
τετράποδος βάσιν θηρὸς ὀρεστέρου
τιθέμενος ἐπὶ χεῖρα κατ' ἴχνος; ποίαν,
1060 ἢ ταύταν ἢ τάνδ',
ἐξαλλάξω, τὰς
ἀνδροφόνους μάρψαι
χρῄζων Ἰλιάδας, αἵ με διώλεσαν;
τάλαιναι κόραι τάλαιναι Φρυγῶν,
ὦ κατάρατοι,
1065 ποῖ καί με φυγᾷ πτώσσουσι μυχῶν;
εἴθε μοι ὀμμάτων αἱματόεν βλέφαρον
ἀκέσσαι' ἀκέσσαι', Ἅλιε, τυφλὸν
φέγγος ἀπαλλάξας.
ἀᾶ.

σίγα· κρυπτὰν βάσιν αἰσθάνομαι
1070 τάνδε γυναικῶν. πᾷ πόδ' ἐπᾴξας
σαρκῶν ὀστέων τ' ἐμπλησθῶ,
θοίναν ἀγρίων τιθέμενος θηρῶν,
ἀρνύμενος λώβαν,
λύμας ἀντίποιν' ἐμᾶς; ὦ τάλας. .

(*Turning towards the tent.*)

1075 ποῖ πᾷ φέρομαι τέκν' ἔρημα λιπὼν
Βάκχαις "Αιδου διαμοιρᾶσαι,
σφακτὰν κυσί τε φονίαν δαῖτ' ἀνήμερον
οὐρείαν τ' ἐκβολάν;
πᾷ στῶ, πᾷ κάμψω, [πᾷ βῶ,]
1080 ναῦς ὅπως ποντίοις πείσμασι λινόκροκον
φᾶρος στέλλων, ἐπὶ τάνδε συθεὶς
τέκνων ἐμῶν φύλαξ
ὀλέθριον κοίταν;

Χορός.

1085 ὦ τλῆμον, ὥς σοι δύσφορ' εἴργασται κακά·
δράσαντι δ' αἰσχρὰ δεινὰ τἀπιτίμια
[δαίμων ἔδωκεν, ὅστις ἐστί σοι βαρύς].

Πολυμήστωρ.

αἰαῖ, ἰὼ Θρῄκης
λογχοφόρον, ἔνοπλον, εὔιππον, Ἄ-
1090 ρει κάτοχον γένος.
ἰὼ Ἀχαιοί, ἰὼ Ἀτρεῖδαι.
βοὰν βοὰν ἀϋτῶ, βοάν·

HECUBA

ἴτε, μόλετε πρὸς θεῶν.
κλύει τις, ἢ οὐδεὶς ἀρκέσει; τί μέλλετε;
1095 γυναῖκες ὤλεσάν με,
γυναῖκες αἰχμαλώτιδες·
δεινὰ δεινὰ πεπόνθαμεν.
ὤμοι ἐμᾶς λώβας.
ποῖ τράπωμαι, ποῖ πορευθῶ;
1100 [αἰθέρ'] ἀμπτάμενος οὐράνιον
ὑψιπετὲς ἐς μέλαθρον, Ὠρίων
ἢ Σείριος ἔνθα πυρὸς φλογέας ἀφίησιν ὄσσων αὐγάς, ἢ τὸν * Ἅιδα
1105 μελανόχρωτα πορθμὸν ἄξω τάλας;

Χορός.
συγγνώσθ', ὅταν τις κρεῖσσον' ἢ φέρειν κακὰ
πάθῃ, ταλαίνης ἐξαπαλλάξαι * ζόης.

(Enter AGAMEMNON, with Attendants.

Ἀγαμέμνων.
κραυγῆς ἀκούσας ἦλθον· οὐ γὰρ ἥσυχος
1110 πέτρας ὀρείας παῖς λέλακ' ἀνὰ στρατὸν
Ἠχώ, διδοῦσα θόρυβον· εἰ δὲ μὴ Φρυγῶν
πύργους πεσόντας * ᾖσμεν Ἑλλήνων δορί,
φόβον παρέσχεν οὐ μέσως ὅδε κτύπος.

Πολυμήστωρ.
ὦ φίλτατ', ᾐσθόμην γάρ, Ἀγάμεμνον, σέθεν
1115 φωνῆς ἀκούσας, εἰσορᾷς ἃ πάσχομεν;

Ἀγαμέμνων.

ἔα·

Πολυμῆστορ ὦ δύστηνε, τίς σ' ἀπώλεσε;
τίς ὄμμ' ἔθηκε τυφλόν, αἱμάξας κόρας,
παῖδάς τε τούσδ' ἔκτεινεν; ἢ μέγαν χόλον
σοὶ καὶ τέκνοισιν εἶχεν, ὅστις ἦν ἄρα.

Πολυμήστωρ.

1120 Ἑκάβη με σὺν γυναιξὶν αἰχμαλώτισιν
ἀπώλεσ'. οὐκ ἀπώλεσ', ἀλλὰ μειζόνως.

Ἀγαμέμνων. (*Turning to* HECUBA.)
τί φῄς; σὺ τοὔργον εἴργασαι τόδ', ὡς λέγει;
σὺ τόλμαν, Ἑκάβη, τήνδ' ἔτλης ἀμήχανον;

Πολυμήστωρ.

ὤμοι, τί λέξεις; ἦ γὰρ ἐγγύς ἐστί που;
1125 σήμηνον, εἰπὲ ποῦ 'σθ', ἵν' ἁρπάσας χεροῖν
διασπάσωμαι καὶ καθαιμάξω χρόα.

Ἀγαμέμνων.

οὗτος, τί πάσχεις;

Πολυμήστωρ.

πρὸς θεῶν σε λίσσομαι,
μέθες μ' ἐφεῖναι τῇδε μαργῶσαν χέρα.

Ἀγαμέμνων.

ἴσχ'· ἐκβαλὼν δὲ καρδίας τὸ βάρβαρον
1130 λέγ', ὡς ἀκούσας σοῦ τε τῆσδέ τ' ἐν μέρει
κρίνω δικαίως, ἀνθ' ὅτου πάσχεις τάδε.

Πολυμήστωρ.
λέγοιμ' ἄν. ἦν τις Πριαμιδῶν νεώτατος
Πολύδωρος, Ἑκάβης παῖς, ὃν ἐκ Τροίας ἐμοὶ
πατὴρ δίδωσι Πρίαμος ἐν δόμοις τρέφειν,
1135 ὕποπτος ὢν δὴ Τρωικῆς ἁλώσεως.
τοῦτον κατέκτειν'· ἀνθ' ὅτου δ' ἔκτεινά νιν,
ἄκουσον, ὡς εὖ καὶ σοφῇ προμηθίᾳ. *precaution*
ἔδεισα μὴ σοὶ πολέμιος λειφθεὶς ὁ παῖς
Τροίαν ἀθροίσῃ καὶ ξυνοικίσῃ πάλιν,
1140 γνόντες δ' Ἀχαιοὶ ζῶντα Πριαμιδῶν τινα
Φρυγῶν ἐς αἶαν αὖθις ἄρειαν στόλον,
κἄπειτα Θρῄκης πεδία τρίβοιεν τάδε
ληλατοῦντες, γείτοσιν δ' εἴη κακὸν
Τρώων, ἐν ᾧπερ νῦν, ἄναξ, ἐκάμνομεν.
1145 Ἑκάβη δὲ παιδὸς γνοῦσα θανάσιμον μόρον,
λόγῳ με τοιῷδ' ἤγαγ', ὡς κεκρυμμένας
θήκας φράσουσα Πριαμιδῶν ἐν Ἰλίῳ
χρυσοῦ· μόνον δὲ σὺν τέκνοισί μ' εἰσάγει
δόμους, ἵν' ἄλλος μή τις εἰδείη τάδε.
1150 ἵζω δὲ κλίνης ἐν μέσῳ κάμψας γόνυ·
πολλαὶ δὲ * χειρὸς αἱ μὲν ἐξ ἀριστερᾶς,
αἱ δ' ἔνθεν, ὡς δὴ παρὰ φίλῳ, Τρώων κόραι
*θάκους ἔχουσαι, κερκίδ' Ἠδωνῆς χερὸς
ᾔνουν, * ὑπ' αὐγὰς τούσδε λεύσσουσαι πέ-
πλους·
1155 ἄλλαι δὲ κάμακα Θρῃκίαν θεώμεναι
γυμνόν μ' ἔθηκαν διπτύχου στολίσματος.

ὅσαι δὲ τοκάδες ἦσαν, ἐκπαγλούμεναι
τέκν' ἐν χεροῖν ἔπαλλον, ὡς πρόσω πατρὸς
γένοιντο, διαδοχαῖς ἀμείβουσαι χεροῖν.
1160 κᾆτ' ἐκ γαληνῶν—πῶς δοκεῖς;—προσφθεγμάτων
εὐθὺς λαβοῦσαι φάσγαν' ἐκ πέπλων ποθὲν
κεντοῦσι παῖδας, αἱ δὲ πολεμίων δίκην
ξυναρπάσασαι τὰς ἐμὰς εἶχον χέρας
καὶ κῶλα· παισὶ δ' ἀρκέσαι χρῄζων ἐμοῖς,
1165 εἰ μὲν πρόσωπον ἐξανισταίην ἐμόν,
κόμης κατεῖχον, εἰ δὲ κινοίην χέρας,
πλήθει γυναικῶν οὐδὲν ἤνυον τάλας.
τὸ λοίσθιον δέ, πῆμα πήματος πλέον,
ἐξειργάσαντο δείν'· ἐμῶν γὰρ ὀμμάτων,
1170 πόρπας λαβοῦσαι, τὰς ταλαιπώρους κόρας
κεντοῦσιν, αἱμάσσουσιν· εἶτ' ἀνὰ στέγας
φυγάδες ἔβησαν· ἐκ δὲ πηδήσας ἐγώ,
θὴρ ὥς, διώκω τὰς μιαιφόνους κύνας,
ἅπαντ' ἐρευνῶν τοῖχον, ὡς κυνηγέτης,
1175 βάλλων, ἀράσσων. τοιάδε σπεύδων χάριν
πέπονθα τὴν σήν, πολέμιόν τε σὸν κτανών,
Ἀγάμεμνον. ὡς δὲ μὴ μακροὺς τείνω λόγους,
εἴ τις γυναῖκας τῶν πρὶν εἴρηκεν κακῶς,
ἢ νῦν λέγων τίς ἐστιν, ἢ μέλλει λέγειν,
1180 ἅπαντα ταῦτα συντεμὼν ἐγὼ φράσω·
γένος γὰρ οὔτε πόντος οὔτε γῆ τρέφει
τοιόνδ'· ὁ δ' ἀεὶ ξυντυχὼν ἐπίσταται.

Χορός.

μηδὲν θρασύνου, μηδὲ τοῖς σαυτοῦ κακοῖς
τὸ θῆλυ συνθεὶς ὧδε πᾶν μέμψῃ γένος·
1185 [πολλαὶ γὰρ ἡμῶν, αἱ μὲν εἰσ᾿ ἐπίφθονοι,
αἱ δ᾿ εἰς ἀριθμὸν τῶν κακῶν πεφύκαμεν.]

Ἑκάβη.

Ἀγάμεμνον, ἀνθρώποισιν οὐκ ἐχρῆν ποτε
τῶν πραγμάτων τὴν γλῶσσαν ἰσχύειν πλέον·
ἀλλ᾿ εἴτε χρήστ᾿ ἔδρασε, χρήστ᾿ ἔδει λέγειν,
1190 εἴτ᾿ αὖ πονηρά, τοὺς λόγους εἶναι σαθρούς,
καὶ μὴ δύνασθαι τἄδικ᾿ εὖ λέγειν ποτέ.
σοφοὶ μὲν οὖν εἰσ᾿ οἱ τάδ᾿ ἠκριβωκότες,
ἀλλ᾿ οὐ δύνανται διὰ τέλους εἶναι σοφοί,
κακῶς δ᾿ ἀπώλοντ᾿· οὔτις ἐξήλυξέ πω.
1195 καί μοι τὸ μὲν σὸν ὧδε φροιμίοις ἔχει·
πρὸς τόνδε δ᾿ εἶμι καὶ λόγοις ἀμείψομαι,
ὃς φήσ᾿ Ἀχαιῶν πόνον ἀπαλλάσσων διπλοῦν
Ἀγαμέμνονός θ᾿ ἕκατι παῖδ᾿ ἐμὸν κτανεῖν.
ἀλλ᾿, ὦ κάκιστε, πρῶτον οὔποτ᾿ ἂν φίλον
1200 τὸ βάρβαρον γένοιτ᾿ ἂν Ἕλλησιν γένος,
οὐδ᾿ ἂν δύναιτο. τίνα δὲ καὶ σπεύδων χάριν
πρόθυμος ἦσθα; πότερα κηδεύσων τινά,
ἢ ξυγγενὴς ὤν, ἢ τίν᾿ αἰτίαν ἔχων;
ἢ σῆς ἔμελλον γῆς τεμεῖν βλαστήματα,
1205 πλεύσαντες αὖθις; τίνα δοκεῖς πείσειν τάδε;
ὁ χρυσός, εἰ βούλοιο τἀληθῆ λέγειν,

ἔκτεινε τὸν ἐμὸν παῖδα, καὶ κέρδη τὰ σά.
ἐπεὶ δίδαξον τοῦτο· πῶς, ὅτ' ηὐτύχει
Τροία, πέριξ δὲ πύργος εἶχ' ἔτι πτόλιν,
1210 ἔζη τε Πρίαμος, Ἕκτορός τ' ἤνθει δόρυ,
τί δ' οὐ τότ', εἴπερ τῷδ' ἐβουλήθης χάριν
θέσθαι, τρέφων τὸν παῖδα κἀν δόμοις ἔχων
ἔκτεινας, ἢ ζῶντ' ἦλθες Ἀργείοις ἄγων;
ἀλλ' ἡνίχ' ἡμεῖς οὐκέτ' ἦμεν ἐν φάει,
1215 καπνῷ δ' ἐσήμην' ἄστυ πολεμίων ὕπο,
ξένον κατέκτας σὴν μολόντ' ἐφ' ἑστίαν.
πρὸς τοῖσδε νῦν ἄκουσον, ὡς φανῇς κακός.
χρῆν σ', εἴπερ ἦσθα τοῖς Ἀχαιοῖσιν φίλος,
τὸν χρυσὸν ὃν φῂς οὐ σόν, ἀλλὰ τοῦδ', ἔχειν,
1220 δοῦναι φέροντα πενομένοις τε καὶ χρόνον
πολὺν πατρῴας γῆς ἀπεξενωμένοις·
σὺ δ' οὐδὲ νῦν πω σῆς ἀπαλλάξαι χερὸς
τολμᾷς, ἔχων δὲ καρτερεῖς ἔτ' ἐν δόμοις.
καὶ μὴν τρέφων μὲν ὥς σε παῖδ' ἐχρῆν τρέφειν
1225 σώσας τε τὸν ἐμόν, εἶχες ἂν καλὸν κλέος·
ἐν τοῖς κακοῖς γὰρ ἀγαθοὶ σαφέστατοι
φίλοι· τὰ χρηστὰ δ' αὔθ' ἕκαστ' ἔχει φίλους.
εἰ δ' ἐσπάνιζες χρημάτων, ὁ δ' ηὐτύχει,
θησαυρὸς ἄν σοι παῖς ὑπῆρχ' οὑμὸς μέγας·
1230 νῦν δ' οὔτ' ἐκεῖνον ἄνδρ' ἔχεις σαυτῷ φίλον,
χρυσοῦ τ' ὄνησις οἴχεται παῖδές τε σοι,
αὐτός τε πράσσεις ὧδε. σοὶ δ' ἐγὼ λέγω,
Ἀγάμεμνον, εἰ τῷδ' ἀρκέσεις, κακὸς φανεῖ·

οὔτ' εὐσεβῆ γὰρ οὔτε πιστὸν οἷς ἐχρῆν,
1235 οὐχ ὅσιον, οὐ δίκαιον εὖ δράσεις ξένον·
αὐτὸν δὲ χαίρειν τοῖς κακοῖς σὲ φήσομεν
τοιοῦτον ὄντα· δεσπότας δ' οὐ λοιδορῶ.

Χορός.
φεῦ φεῦ· βροτοῖσιν ὡς τὰ χρηστὰ πράγματα
χρηστῶν ἀφορμὰς ἐνδίδωσ' ἀεὶ λόγων.

Ἀγαμέμνων.
1240 ἀχθεινὰ μέν μοι τἀλλότρια κρίνειν κακά,
ὅμως δ' ἀνάγκη· καὶ γὰρ αἰσχύνην φέρει,
πρᾶγμ' ἐς χέρας λαβόντ' ἀπώσασθαι τόδε.
ἐμοὶ δ', ἵν' εἰδῇς, οὔτ' ἐμὴν δοκεῖς χάριν
οὔτ' οὖν Ἀχαιῶν ἄνδρ' ἀποκτεῖναι ξένον,
1245 ἀλλ' ὡς ἔχῃς τὸν χρυσὸν ἐν δόμοισι σοῖς.
λέγεις δὲ σαυτῷ πρόσφορ' ἐν κακοῖσιν ὤν.
τάχ' οὖν παρ' ὑμῖν ῥᾴδιον ξενοκτονεῖν·
ἡμῖν δέ γ' αἰσχρὸν τοῖσιν Ἕλλησιν τόδε.
πῶς οὖν σε κρίνας μὴ ἀδικεῖν φύγω ψόγον;
1250 οὐκ ἂν δυναίμην. ἀλλ' ἐπεὶ τὰ μὴ καλὰ
πράσσειν ἐτόλμας, τλῆθι καὶ τὰ μὴ φίλα.

Πολυμήστωρ.
οἴμοι, γυναικός, ὡς ἔοιχ', ἡσσώμενος
δούλης, ὑφέξω τοῖς κακίοσιν δίκην.

Ἑκάβη.
οὐκοῦν δικαίως, εἴπερ εἰργάσω κακά;

Πολυμήστωρ.
οἴμοι τέκνων τῶνδ' ὀμμάτων τ' ἐμῶν, τάλας.

Ἑκάβη.
ἀλγεῖς· τί δαὶ 'μέ; παιδὸς οὐκ ἀλγεῖν δοκεῖς;

Πολυμήστωρ.
χαίρεις ὑβρίζουσ' εἰς ἔμ', ὦ πανοῦργε σύ;

Ἑκάβη.
οὐ γάρ με χαίρειν χρή σε τιμωρουμένην;

Πολυμήστωρ.
ἀλλ' οὐ τάχ', ἡνίκ' ἄν σε ποντία νοτὶς

Ἑκάβη.
μῶν ναυστολήσῃ γῆς ὅρους Ἑλληνίδος;

Πολυμήστωρ.
κρύψῃ μὲν οὖν πεσοῦσαν ἐκ καρχησίων.

Ἑκάβη.
πρὸς τοῦ βιαίων τυγχάνουσαν ἁλμάτων;

Πολυμήστωρ.
αὐτὴ πρὸς ἱστὸν ναὸς ἀμβήσει ποδί.

Ἑκάβη.
ὑποπτέροις νώτοισιν; ἢ ποίῳ τρόπῳ;

Πολυμήστωρ.
κύων γενήσει πύρσ' ἔχουσα δέργματα.

Ἑκάβη.
πῶς δ' οἶσθα μορφῆς τῆς ἐμῆς μετάστασιν ;

Πολυμήστωρ.
ὁ Θρῃξὶ μάντις εἶπε Διόνυσος τάδε.

Ἑκάβη.
σοὶ δ' οὐκ ἔχρησεν οὐδὲν ὧν ἔχεις κακῶν ;

Πολυμήστωρ.
οὐ γάρ ποτ' ἂν σύ μ' εἷλες ὧδε σὺν δόλῳ.

Ἑκάβη.
1270 θανοῦσα δ' ἢ ζῶσ' ἐνθάδ' ἐκπλήσω βίον ;

Πολυμήστωρ.
θανοῦσα· τύμβῳ δ' ὄνομα σῷ κεκλήσεται

Ἑκάβη.
μορφῆς ἐπῳδόν, ἢ τί, τῆς ἐμῆς ἐρεῖς ;

Πολυμήστωρ.
κυνὸς ταλαίνης σῆμα, ναυτίλοις τέκμαρ.

Ἑκάβη.
οὐδὲν μέλει μοι σοῦ γέ μοι δόντος δίκην.

Πολυμήστωρ.
1275 καὶ σὴν γ' ἀνάγκη παῖδα Κασάνδραν θανεῖν.

Ἑκάβη.
ἀπέπτυσ'· αὐτῷ ταῦτα σοὶ δίδωμ' ἔχειν.

Πολυμήστωρ.
κτενεῖ νιν ἡ τοῦδ' ἄλοχος, οἰκουρὸς πικρά.

Ἑκάβη.
μήπω μανείη Τυνδαρὶς τοσόνδε παῖς.

Πολυμήστωρ.
καὐτόν γε τοῦτον, πέλεκυν ἐξάρασ' ἄνω.

Ἀγαμέμνων.
1280 οὗτος σύ, μαίνει, καὶ κακῶν ἐρᾷς τυχεῖν;

Πολυμήστωρ.
κτεῖν', ὡς ἐν Ἄργει φόνια λουτρά σ' ἀμμένει.

Ἀγαμέμνων. (*To Attendants.*
οὐχ ἕλξετ' αὐτόν, δμῶες, ἐκποδὼν βίᾳ;

Πολυμήστωρ.
ἀλγεῖς ἀκούων;

Ἀγαμέμνων.
οὐκ ἐφέξετε στόμα;

Πολυμήστωρ.
ἐγκλῄετ'· εἴρηται γάρ.

Ἀγαμέμνων.
οὐχ ὅσον τάχος
1285 νήσων ἐρήμων αὐτὸν ἐκβαλεῖτέ που,
ἐπείπερ οὕτω καὶ λίαν θρασυστομεῖ;

Ἑκάβη, σὺ δ', ὦ τάλαινα, διπτύχους νεκροὺς
στείχουσα θάπτε· δεσποτῶν δ' ὑμᾶς χρεὼν
σκηναῖς πελάζειν. Τρῳάδες· καὶ γὰρ πνοὰς
πρὸς οἶκον ἤδη τάσδε πομπίμους ὁρῶ.
εὖ δ' ἐς πάτραν πλεύσαιμεν, εὖ δὲ τἀν δόμοις
ἔχοντ' ἴδοιμεν, τῶνδ' ἀφειμένοι πόνων.

Χορός.
ἴτε πρὸς λιμένας σκηνάς τε, φίλαι,
τῶν δεσποσύνων πειρασόμεναι
μόχθων· στερρὰ γὰρ ἀνάγκη.

Clarendon Press Series

EURIPIDES
HECUBA

EDITED

WITH INTRODUCTION AND NOTES

BY

CECIL H. RUSSELL, M.A.

*Assistant Master at Clifton College
Late Scholar of Trinity College, Oxford*

PART II.—NOTES

Oxford
AT THE CLARENDON PRESS
M DCCC LXXXIX

[*All rights reserved*]

London
HENRY FROWDE

OXFORD UNIVERSITY PRESS WAREHOUSE
AMEN CORNER, E.C.

NOTES.

☞ *The less elementary notes are enclosed in square brackets.*

(For the parts taken by the actors, see Introduction, p. 13.)

PROLOGUS, 1-99. The shade of Polydorus tells of his murder by Polymestor and of the coming sacrifice of Polyxena. Hecuba tells of her dreams and the fears they have caused for Polydorus and Polyxena.

(The tent of Agamemnon is in the centre of the stage. On the method of Polydorus's appearance, see Introd. p. 13.)

Compare the shade of Darius in the 'Persae' and of Clytaemnestra in the 'Eumenides.'

l. 1. σκότος, in the drama, generally masculine. Elsewhere, also neuter (genitive -εος).

l. 2. ᾤκισται, 'dwells'; lit. 'has made his dwelling'; in middle sense. [Others, passive: 'has been set to dwell,' at the division of the world with his brothers, Zeus and Poseidon. χωρὶς θεῶν. Cf. Hom. Il. xx. 65 οἰκία—σμερδαλέ' εὐρώεντα τά τε στυγέουσι θεοί περ.]

l. 3. Ἑκάβης παῖς γεγώς. According to Homer (Il. xxi. 88), Polydorus was son of Laothoe. Κισσέως. Cf. Verg. Aen. x. 705, Cisseis. Cisseus was a Thracian king. According to Homer, Hecuba was daughter of the Phrygian Dymas. [Euripides perhaps makes the change to account for Priam's friendship with Polymestor; but see for this and for 'Εκ π., Introd. p. 6, on the legend.]

l. 5. πεσεῖν, construc. ad sens. as if πόλις ἐκινδύνευσε had preceded. [πεσεῖν: on the question whether such infinitives should be regarded as datives or as accusatives (here cog. acc.), see Appendix, p. 64.]

l. 6. ὑπεξέπεμψε. ὑπο-, 'secretly.' Τρωικῆς χθονός, genitive after the ἐξ- in ὑπεξέπεμψε.

l. 7. ξένου, 'friend,' or 'friend of his house,' 'a Thracian.' A ξένος was one with whom the rights of hospitality were interchanged. The relation was hereditary. ['Guest-friend' and 'host-friend' have been suggested as translations, but are not satisfactory. There is no exact equivalent in English.]

l. 8. τήν: almost 'this'; as Polym. was king of the whole Chersonese: cf. 1052, inf. ταῖς. (The subject, with the article, generally

HECUBA.

implies a comparison, 'most,' not 'very.') πλάκα, 'steppe'; lit. 'flat,' with which it is perhaps philologically connected. The word does not apply well to the Chersonese. [τήν, MS.; Herm. emend. τήνδ'.]

l. 9. δορί, not merely 'sceptro' (Musgrave), but of a warlike sway.

l. 10. ἐκπέμπει, Historic Present.

ll. 11-12. ἵν'.. εἴη.. μή, met. grat. for ἵνα μὴ εἴη (Dind.). εἴη, not ᾖ, after the Historic Present, because 'the Historic Present is a secondary tense, as it refers to the past.' Goodw. M. & T. § 32. 2.

l. 13. ὅ, not nominative to ὑπεξέπεμψεν (Porson), but in the sense of δι' ὅ, 'wherefore;' an adverbial acc. [Orig. an accusative of respect ('with reference to which'), whose antecedent is the preceding sentence: cf. Eur. Phoen. 155 and 262 ὃ καὶ δέδοικα μὴ κ.τ.λ., and perhaps Hom. Od. xviii. 392 ὃ καὶ μεταμώνια βάζεις; also the Latin 'quod,' e.g. Terent. Hec. 3. 2. 3 Quod te, Aesculapi, et te, Salus, ne quid sit hujus, oro, and often in Plautus. The conjunctions in Greek and Latin were originally cases of nouns or pronouns; and ὅ would thus illustrate the transition from one to the other.]

l. 15. οἷός τε, 'able': orig. 'such as to' (hence with infin.): τοιοῦτος being understood and τε being indefinite, like que in quandoque (cf. Homeric τε); [or τε, the copula,—the relative οἷος orig. demonstrative. Jelf, 823. Obs. 4.]

l. 16. ἔκειθ', 'stood': κεῖμαι being used as the passive of τίθημι. ὁρίσματα, 'the walls which bounded it.' [2, the boundaries or land-marks: columnae, termini: Musgrave.]

l. 18. ηὐτύχει. An unaugmented form, εὐτύχει, also exists: cf. on ηὑρέθη, inf. 270. [MSS. and Editors waver between the augmented and the unaugmented form in most of the historic tenses of εὐτυχέω, εὑρίσκω, εὔχομαι, and several other verbs beginning in εὐ-. See Veitch's Greek Verbs.]

l. 20. τροφαῖσιν ηὐξόμην τάλας, 'I grew and was nurtured up to my sorrow.' ηὐξ-, imperf. midd. of αὔξω, more common in Eur. than the parallel form αὐξάνω.

ll. 21-2. Ἕκτορος ψυχή, 'the great Hector.' Such periphrases are not pleonastic. They express awe, affection, or reverence; being adjectival in character. [See on inf. 87 Ἑλένου ψυχάν; 1210 Ἕκτορος δόρυ; and cf. the Homeric βία, μένος, ἴς, e.g. βίη Διομήδεος, ἱερὸν μένος Ἀλκινόοιο, ἱερὴ ἲς Τηλεμάχοιο. Cf. on 619 inf. σχῆμάτ' οἴκων.]

l. 23. αὐτός, sc. πατήρ (Πρίαμος), contained in πατρῴα. βωμῷ, of Ζεὺς Ἑρκεῖος. Θεοδμήτῳ, 'holy altar of the god'·lit. built for a god: generally, built by a god.

NOTES. LINES 8—40.

l. 24. Ἀχιλλέως παιδός, Pyrrhus or Neoptolemus: -εως, as one syllable, ͜ͅͅͅͅͅͅͅͅͅͅͅͅͅͅͅͅͅͅͅͅ͏jως, by synizesis. [Priam's death is described in Verg. Aen. ii. 550 sqq.]

l. 25. κτείνει με. According to Homer (Il. xx. 407), Polydorus was killed by Achilles. [See Introd., p. 6.]

l. 26. ξένος πατρῷος, 'he, my father's friend': emphatically placed late in the sentence and at the beginning of a line.

l. 27. ἔχῃ, more strictly ἔχοι: the subj. is a return to present narration, as in 1139 inf., ἔδεισα μὴ ἀθροίσῃ: [or (2) shows present possession of the money (Hermann; Jelf, G. G. 806. 1, after aor. with perf. force).]

l. 28. ἐπ' ἀκταῖς, sc. ἄλλοτε: cf. Soph. Trach. 11 φοιτῶν ἐναργὴς ταῦρος, ἄλλοτ' αἰόλος δράκων ἑλικτός.

l. 29. διαύλοις: 'borne about by many a running and returning wave.' The δίαυλος was the double 'channel,' going and returning, of a racecourse.

l. 30. ὑπέρ, 'above,' sc. her head (Schol.); i. e. in dreams (see inf. 75, etc.). [Cf. the Homeric visions, e. g. Il. ii. 20 στῆ δ' ἄρ' ὑπὲρ κεφαλῆς (ὄνειρος).]

l. 31. ἀΐσσω, 'glance,' or 'move.' The α is long in Homer.

l. 32. τριταῖον κ.τ.λ., 'it being now the third light of day that I hover in the air,—the third light of day that my mother' etc.; accusatives of duration of time. τριτ. = not merely τρίτον, but 'of the third day.' ὅσονπερ, 'even so long as.' [τρ., cf. Hdt. ii. 89 τριταῖος γενόμενος, 'on the third day after death.']

l. 34. πάρα, i. e. πάρεστι. N.B. the accent.

l. 35. ναῦς ἔχοντες, 'with their ships.' [Others, improbably, 'landing,' navem appellentes (as in Od. x. 91, etc.), which would be σχόντες.]

l. 37. ὑπὲρ τύμβου. The tomb of Achilles was at Sigeum, in the Troad: Euripides here places it, by poetic license, in the Chersonese. [See Introd., p. 6. Others imagine a cenotaph at the Chersonese; or refer the line to a previous event, and make the Greek army return to the Troad for the sacrifice of Polyxena, (Paley).]

l. 39. εὐθύνοντας, agreeing, κατὰ σύνεσιν, with Ἕλληνας, contained in πᾶν στράτευμ' Ἑλληνικόν: cf. Aesch. Ag. 577 Τροίαν ἑλόντες δή ποτ' Ἀργείων στόλος.

l. 40. Πολυξένην. Cf. inf. 390. On the other hand, in 97 inf., only τινὰ Τρωιάδων. The lines may be reconciled by considering that Achilles demanded Polyxena, but indirectly only, as the fairest of the captives. There is no reference in the play to a previous betrothal of Achilles and Polyxena: see Introd., p. 6. [For the sacrifice of

5

HECUBA.

Polyxena to appease the winds on the homeward voyage, compare that of Iphigenia, with the same purpose, on the outward voyage.]

l. 41. λαβεῖν, probably epexegetic (lit. 'so as to receive it'); not after αἰτεῖ.

l. 42. φίλων, emphatic.

l. 43. ἡ πεπρωμένη, sc. μοῖρα.

l. 44. ἐν ἤματι. ἐν, with the dative, of time, strictly = 'within.'

l. 45. δυοῖν δύο. For these 'vain repetitions,' in which the tragedians ' rejoice,' cf. Med. 513 σὺν τέκνοις μόνη μόνοις.

l. 48. δούλης κ.τ.λ. See inf. 778 sqq.

l. 49. ἐξῃτησάμην, I prayed them, and won my prayer,—ἐξ-; cf. ex in Lat. exoro. [Cf. the disquiet of the unburied Elpenor in Hom. Od. xi. 51 sqq.]

l. 51. τοὐμόν, not adverb.acc., 'as to me,' (Weil), but nominative,'my desire' (ἔσται, 'shall be accomplished'). ὅσονπερ. For the accusative after τυγχάνω, cf. Med. 259 τοσοῦτον οὖν σου τυγχάνειν βουλήσομαι.

l. 53. Ἑκάβῃ, ethic dative. περᾷ γὰρ κ.τ.λ., 'see, here she bends her steps from beneath the tent.' ὑπὸ σκηνῆς : ὑπό, with the genitive, in this sense, frequent in Homer, but rare in Attic Greek. πόδα, direct accusative after περᾷ, poetically used as transitive. [Or (2) ' cognate, Jelf, 558. 2; or (3) of respect. Cf. inf. 1070 πύδ' ἐπᾴξας, and Eur. Elect. 94 βαίνω πόδα, and perhaps inf. 528 MS. ἔρρει χοάς. ὑπό, see on inf. 665 δόμων ὕπο; and cf. Androm. 441 νεοσσὸν τόνδ' ὑπὸ πτερῶν σπάσας (Paley): Musgrave and Porson, ὑπὲρ σκηνήν, ' past the tent.']

l. 54. Ἀγαμέμνονος: prob. only because the entrance of the protagonist was through the central doorway: see Notes ad init., and Introd., p. 12. [Put thoughtlessly, Weil. Others: Hecuba was in Agamemnon's tent (1) because she had fallen to his lot at the division of the spoil (though. in the Troades, to that of Odysseus); or (2) because she was waiting there for the division of the spoil, which had not yet taken place; or (3) because she had gone there to consult Cassandra about the dream (Schol.: supported perhaps by 87-8 inf.). See on sup. 53 ὑπὲρ σκηνήν.]

l. 55. ἥτις. quippe quae: 'seeing that thou,' etc. ἐκ, 'after,' as in ἐκ δείπνων, inf. 915, [and ἐκ γαληνῶν προσφθεγμάτων 1160: (2) local. ἥτ., ὅστις is used of a particular object only when a general notion (i. e. a cause) is implied.]

l. 56. ὡς, 'how': exclamatory.

l. 57. ὅσονπερ, as if τοσοῦτον, not ὡς, had preceded,—'how ill thou farest now—as ill as well of old.'

6

NOTES. LINES 40—75.

ll. 57-9. ἀντισηκώσας δέ κ.τ.λ. 'Some god doth ruin thee, to countervail thy former happiness.' ἀντισ., 'compensating for'; a metaphor from the scales: here, as in Aesch. Pers. 437 (ὡς τοῦδε καὶ δὶς ἀντισηκῶσαι ῥοπῇ), probably intransitive, σε being after φθείρει. τῆς εὐπραξίας, genitive after the ἀντι- in ἀντισηκώσας.

(Hecuba, as protagonist, enters by the central doorway: cf. sup. 54, and see Introd., p. 12. The Trojan women on the stage here (cf. perhaps inf. 1069) must be distinguished from the chorus, who enter only at l. 100, and then never leave the orchestra. See Introd., p. 12.)

l. 60. ὀρθοῦσαι, 'supporting.'

l. 61. ὑμῖν: dative of resemblance after the ὁμο- in ὁμόδουλον.

l. 62. πέμπετ', 'guide me.' μου—χειρός: both partitive genitives after προσλαζύμεναι by the σχῆμα καθ' ὅλον καὶ μέρος, 'whole and part figure': cf. inf. 275 ἀνθάπτομαί σου τῶνδε. [So, when the main verb takes dat., inf. 202 συνδουλεύσω σοι γήρᾳ; when acc., inf. 432 μ' ἀμφιθεὶς κάρα.]

l. 65. σκολιῷ σκίπωνι χερός, 'on the bent staff of my hand': viz. on the bent staff which is in my hand; the genitive being possessive: [Schol., Weil; or (2) metaphorically, on the hand of my maidens, as on a bent staff; the genitive being one of material. Blaydes emend. δέμας for χερός.]

ll. 66-7. σπεύσω κ.τ.λ., lit. 'I will put forward in haste the slow-footed going of my limbs'; σπ. being prob. intrans. ⌐[Others separate σπ. and πρ.: I will hasten the slow-footed going of my limbs, setting one before the other. Weil understands σκίπωνα after προτιθεῖσα.]

l. 68. στεροπὰ Διός, viz. light of day. [Cf. Soph. Trach. 99 ὦ (ἥλιε) λαμπρᾷ στεροπᾷ φλεγέθων. Schol., wrongly, ὦ ὄνειρον.]

l. 69. αἴρομαι, 'I am moved,' 'excited.'

ll. 70-1. Χθών . . μᾶτερ ὀνείρων: Hades, their home, being in the recesses of the earth. μελανοπτερύγων: as the children of Hades, and also as dark-omened. Cf. inf. 704 φάσμα μελανόπτερον. [χθ. μ. ο.: cf. Hom. Od. xix. 562, xxiv. 12; Verg. Aen. vi. 283 and 893. Also Eur. Iph. Taur. 1262 νυχία χθὼν ἐτεκνώσατο φάσματ' ὀνείρων. The night, however, is the accredited mother of dreams: so Hermann and Wakefield, on a v. l. of the Schol., transpose ὦ σκοτία νύξ (l. 68) and ὦ ποτνία χθών (l. 70).]

l. 72. ἀποπέμπομαι, 'I would drive from me'; lit. I am driving or trying to drive. Present, of attempted action: Middle, from myself. Lat. abominor, to deprecate as ill-omened.

l. 73. τοῦ σωζομένου, 'who is in safety.'

l. 75. δι' ὀνείρων, 'in dreams': lit. through, by means of.

7

HECUBA.

l. 76. **φοβεράν ὄψιν**: picking up in the relative clause the previous ὄψιν which is antecedent to that clause, 'the nightly vision, the dread vision which I have learnt.' etc.

l. 77. **χθόνιοι**: of Hades: [Schol.; less probably, (2\), of this land. Dind., Herm. ἐγχώριοι: cp. Soph. Oed. Col. 948 "Ἀρεος πάγον χθόνιον.]

l. 80. **ἄγκυρ' ἁμῶν**: ἁμός poet. for ἐμός. [Nauck.—Vulg. ἄγκυρά τ' ἐμῶν (viz. coupled to μόνος). Reiske, followed by Porson, emends to ἄγκυρ' ἅτ' ἐμῶν.]

l. 81. **κατέχει**, 'dwells in.'

l. 82. **φυλακαῖσιν**: local dat.; plur. for sing.

l. 85. **ἀλίαστος**, 'and will not be comforted': lit. continuously, unswervingly.

l. 86. **φρίσσει, ταρβεῖ**: the present may be shown in transl., ' never, as now, has my soul so shuddered, so trembled.'

l. 87. **θείαν**, 'divine'; viz. divinely-inspired, prophetic. **Ἑλένου ψυχάν**: 'the inspired Helenus.' On the periphr., see sup. 21. **Ἕκτορος ψυχή**. Helenus was son of Priam and Hecuba. He afterwards received from the Greeks part of Epirus and married Andromache. [See Verg. Aen. iii. 295, 333, etc. Paley, however, with others, translates, ' the shade of Helenus,' and emphasises the difference of case in Ἑλένου and Κασάνδραν (though the vulg. is Κασάνδρας) as implying a distinction between the dead and the living.]

l. 88. **Κασάνδραν**. Cassandra was daughter of Priam and Hecuba. Apollo gave her prophetic power, but afterwards cancelled his gift by making men disbelieve her prophecies. **ἐσίδω**, deliberate conjunctive. [Goodw. (M. & T. § 88 remark) explains the delib. subj. by an ellipse of βούλει or some such word: this word being sometimes expressed, (see inf. 1042 βούλεσθ' ἐπισπέσωμεν). Monro II. G. § 277, more probably makes it direct, with future force; (N.B. the doubt between aor. subj. and fut. indic., 155 inf. ἀπύσω, 419 δράσω.]

l. 89. **κρίνωσιν**, 'that they may read me my dreams.'

l. 90. **χαλᾷ**. χηλή is more often used of the hoof of a horse or the claw of a bird. The hind, in Hecuba's dream, is Polyxena; the wolf, Odysseus.

l. 93. **τόδε**, i.e. the following.

l. 96. **γέρας**, acc. in apposition to τινά.

l. 97. **τινὰ Τρωιάδων**. See on sup. 40.

(The chorus (see sup. on 59) enter the orchestra by the right-hand parodus, singing: see Introd., p. 12.)

PARODUS, 100-154. **The Chorus tell Hecuba that the Greek Council has decided on the sacrifice of Polyxena.**

NOTES. LINES 76—114.

'*Hecuba, we have come from the tents of captivity, to bring thee tidings of sorrow. The shade of Achilles has demanded a victim : and the Greeks in conclave have determined on the sacrifice of thy daughter. Agamemnon, for Cassandra's sake, defended thy cause, but the sons of Theseus spoke for the honour of Achilles ; and Odysseus, urging that the Greeks should not stand guilty of ingratitude to the dead, hath turned the scale against thee. He is even now on his way to fetch Polyxena. Pray, therefore, to the gods of heaven and earth, that so thou mayst save thy child from death.*'

l. 100. ἐλιάσθην, ' I have bent my steps.'

l. 101. δεσποσύνους, 'of my master': attributive adj.: cf. inf. 1294 δεσποσύνων μόχθων.

l. 102. ἵν' ἐκληρώθην καὶ προσετάχθην, ' to which I was assigned by lot.' The best of the spoils and captives were reserved for the chief and called ἐξαίρετα. For the rest, every warrior put a marked lot into a helmet: the helmet was shaken; and each portion of the spoil in turn fell to the man whose lot first sprang out.

ll. 104–5. λόγχης αἰχμῇ δοριθήρατος, ' spear-taken at the lance's point.' [For the pleonasm, cf. Med. 434 ἀνάνδρου κοίτας λέκτρον.]

l. 106. παθέων, viz. ' thy woes:' gen. after οὐδέν. ἀποκουφίζουσα, i.e. by the news to bring. [παθ. (2), after ἀπο-; οὐδέν being adverbial, and σε understood, object of ἀποκ.: supported by Or. 1341.]

l. 107. ἀραμένη, ' having taken on me' (Middle); i.e. to bear to thee.

l. 110. δόξαι, 'that it has seemed good.'

l. 111. σφάγιον θέσθαι, ' make sacrifice of thy daughter;' i.e. σφάζειν. Such periphrases are more common with the active of τίθημι.

l. 112. οἶσθ' ὅτε, to be taken before τύμβον. N.B. ὅτε is a relative; so, sc. τὸν χρόνον ὅτε: otherwise ὁπότε, the interrog., would seem necessary. [The phrase has become virtually parenthetic, like εὖ οἶδ' ὅτι, etc., Jelf, 798. 2. οἶσθ' ὅτι, indeed, has been conjectured here, but unnecessarily: cf. inf. 239 οἶσθ' ἡνίκ'. See on 225 inf. οἶσθ' οὖν ὃ δρᾶσον.]

l. 113. ἔσχε, ' stayed '; like κατέσχε.

l. 114. λαίφη . . ἐπερειδομέναις, ' with their sails braced up by the stays:' lit. ' being stayed, as to their sails, by the ropes ': ἐπ., pass.; λαίφη, acc. of respect ; προτ. dat. instrum. The πρότονοι were properly the two ropes from the mast-head to the bows, which raised the mast from the stern and held it in its place, as in Homer, e. g. Il. i. 434 ἱστὸν προτόνοισιν ὑφέντες; here, perhaps, the haulyards which raised

HECUBA.

the sails themselves, as in Iph. Taur. 1134 ἰστία πρότονοι ἐκπετάσουσι. [L. and S. make ἐπ. trans. middle.]

l. 118. συνέπαισε, intransitive: 'dashed together.' [MSS. συνέπεσε.]

l. 119. ἐχώρει δίχ', 'ran two ways.' [Cf. Hom. Il. xviii. 510 δίχα δέ σφισιν ἥνδανε βουλή.]

l. 121. τύμβῳ, locative; 'at the tomb': prose would require ἐν, except with proper names. δοκοῦν, explanatory of δόξα; an accusative absolute like ἐξόν, etc. [Weil, a nominative, in apposition to δόξα.]

l. 122. τὸ μὲν σὸν σπεύδων ἀγαθόν, 'urging thy interest': σπ. trans., more often intrans. ἣν σπεύδων: for participle used as adjective, cf. inf. 358 εἰωθὸς ὄν and see on inf. 579.

l. 123. τῆς μαντιπόλου Βάκχης, Cassandra: see on 88 sup. She was now the concubine of Agamemnon. ἀνέχων, 'upholding,' i.e. honouring. [Cf. ? Soph. Ajax 211 ἐπεί σε λέχος δουριάλωτον στέρξας ἀνέχει θούριος Αἴας.]

l. 125. τὼ Θησείδα. Demophon and Acamas, sons of Theseus and Phaedra.

l. 126. δισσῶν, i.e. δυοῖν, 'two.' [Schol., ἐπεὶ δύο οἱ λέγοντες. Cf. Soph. Aj. 57 δισσοὺς Ἀτρείδας; also διπτύχους νεκρούς inf. 1287; and duplices palmas Verg. Aen. i. 93. Hermann, however, and Paley translate 'opposed,' i.e. while the two sons of Theseus agreed that someone should be sacrificed, one of them said this should be Polyxena, the other, someone else. (Cf. Aesch. Ag. 122 λήμασι δισσούς.) But l. 130 inf. seems against this interpretation.]

l. 128. στεφανοῦν, 'crown,' as with a wreath of flowers. [Cf. Soph. Antig. 431 χοαῖσι τρισπόνδοισι τὸν νέκυν στέφει.]

l. 129. αἵματι χλωρῷ, 'fresh young blood'; cf. Soph. Tr. 1055; χλ. lit. 'green,' of young leaves, etc.

ll. 129-131. τὰ δὲ Κασάνδρας κ.τ.λ. The relationship of Polyxena to Agamemnon through Cassandra must not prevail against the services of Achilles to the Greek army. Ἀχιλλείας, 'of Achilles': attrib. adj.: cf. sup. 101 δεσποσύνους.

l. 132. σπουδαὶ λόγων κατατεινομένων, 'the keen contending arguments.'

l. 133. ἴσαι πως, 'nearly balanced.'

l. 134. κόπις, lit. 'chopper;' used here in metaphorical sense of one who 'splits words,' 'a quibbler.' [One scholiast, λάλος ὅθεν καὶ κόβαλος καὶ κομψός. Another schol. συντόμως καὶ ὀξύς; Paley, 'incisive.' 'of cutting speech.' The dictionaries distinguish κόπις, 'a wrangler,' m., from κοπίς, f., 'an axe'; but the first is

10

NOTES. LINES 114—164.

only found here and twice in Lycophron; and it is doubtful if it exists, except as a metaph. use of the last.]

l. 137. δούλων σφαγίων οὕνεκ', ' for the sake of a slave-sacrifice '; δούλων being used adjectivally: cf. 921 inf. ναύταν ὅμιλον.

l. 138. μηδέ τιν' εἰπεῖν, i.e. μηδὲ ἐᾶν τιν' εἰπεῖν: Dind.

l. 140. Δαναοῖς, dat. incomm. after ἀχ.

l. 143. ὅσον οὐκ ἤδη, 'all but now'; like μόνον οὐ. Literally, 'so far (sc. τοσοῦτον, understood) as just not at once.'

l. 144. πῶλον, cf. μόσχος inf. 205, 526.

l. 146. ναούς, probably not accusative of motion to, but accusative after πρός. [Cp. Eur. Hel. 863 Τροίας τε σωθεὶς κἀπὸ βαρβάρου χθονός, and Hor. Od. iii. 25. 2 Quae nemora aut quos agor in specus. (Cf. ἄλλοτε sup. 28.) Still, N.B. a preposition only further defines the idea primarily contained in the case.]

l. 147. 'Αγαμέμνονος, γονάτων: both objective genitives after ἱκέτις by σχῆμα καθ' ὅλον καὶ μέρος; [rather than γον. obj. gen., 'Αγ. partit.—Or (2) γον. genitive of cause (cf. inf. 746 ἱκετεύω σε τῶνδε γονάτων;—more often expressed by πρός), 'in supplication of Agamemnon, by his knees' Cf. Thuc. iii. 59. 2 ἱκέται ὑμῶν τῶν πατρῴων τάφων; where Shepherd and Evans support the latter view.]

l. 148. κήρυσσε, 'call upon'; like a κῆρυξ.

l. 149. γαῖαν, the acc., with idea of previous motion to (as in πρὸς τύμβον 190 inf.), 'those that have passed beneath the earth.'

l. 151. ὀρφανός, more commonly of three terminations. παιδός, priv. gen. after ὀρφ.

l. 152. τύμβου, genitive of relation after the προ- in προπετῆ.

l. 153. χρυσοφόρου: as a mark of youth.

l. 154. νασμῷ, in apposition to αἵματι.

FIRST EPEISODION, 155–443. **Polyxena is led away by Odysseus to sacrifice.**

l. 155. ἀπύσω: ῡ: either 1st aor. subj. or fut. indic.; prob. the first. [See on 88 sup.]

l. 157. γήρως, genitive of cause: cf. inf. 783 σχετλία πόνων: [or respect; Weil, ' au sujet de'; cf. Med. 997 τάλαινα παίδων.]

l. 160. μοι, dat. com. ποία γέννα: ' what race of man?' [Or, perhaps, ' what child of mine:' Schol.]

l. 162. φροῦδος πρέσβυς, 'my lord is dead.' The copula, εἰμί, is generally omitted with φροῦδος.

l. 163. ποίαν, sc. ὁδόν: cognate accusative; expressing motion along: cf. inf. 1060.

l. 164. ποῖ δ' ἥσω πόδα; τίς; [Reiske and Musgr., for MSS.

HECUBA.

ποῖ δ' ἥσω; ποῦ τις (supplying πύδα with ἥσω Kirch. and Nauck.); Weil, ποῖ πύδα δ' ἥσω:]

ll. 166-8. κἄκ' ἐνεγκοῦσαι πήματ', ' that have brought me tidings of evil woes.' ἀπωλέσατ', sc. με.

l. 172. ὦ τέκνον κ.τ.λ. [Parodied by Aristoph. Clouds 1165 ὦ τέκνον, ὦ παῖ, ἐξέλθ' οἴκων, ἄϊε τοῦ πατρός. See Introd., p. 5, on date of play.]

Polyxena, as deuteragonist, enters by the right-hand door: see Introd., p. 12.)

l. 180. ἐξέπταξας; ' hast thou startled me forth in this amaze?' πτήσσω is commonly intransitive: cf. περᾷ, sup. 53. θάμβει, dat. of manner.

l. 182. τί με κ.τ.λ.: ' why dost thou thus ominously speak of me? an evil prelude, I fear.'   μοι, ethic dative.

l. 183. σᾶς ψυχᾶς: genitive of cause: cf. inf. 661 τάλαινα βοῆς.

l. 186. τί ποτ', interrogative after the idea of wonder contained in δειμαίνω. [Or τί ποτ' may begin a fresh sentence.]

l. 188. τί τόδ', ' what is this that,' etc.

ll. 189-91. σφάξαι κ.τ.λ.: ' the general voice of the Argives is eager to sacrifice thee at the tomb to the offspring of Peleus.' i. e. to Achilles. πρὸς τύμβον, 'at the tomb,' with the idea of previous motion to: cf. inf. πρὸς χῶμα 221 and Latin ' ad'; and see on sup. 149 ὑπὸ γαῖαν. [Πηλείᾳ γέννᾳ: Weil: cf. Eur. Iph. Taur. 1290 'Αγαμεμνονείας παιδός. Other readings are: (1) Πηλείδᾳ γέννᾳ Kirch. and Nauck.: cf. ? 1277 inf. Τυνδαρὶς παῖς,; (2) Πηλείδα γέννᾳ (Brunck, Dind.: i. e. Neoptolemus`; (3) Πηλείδα, γέννα vocative, Porson`: (4 Πηλείδα γέννα (nom., with κοίνᾳ γνώμῃ (when the Schol. joins γέννα Ἀργείων). An objection to the last two readings is that, in the nom. and voc., the α of γέννα is short: Paley.]

l. 192. πῶς; ' how is it that?' Weil.

l. 193. ἀμέγαρτα˙ κακῶν, ' most unenviable ills;' not quite ἀμέγαρτα κακά, but almost superlative in force. ἀμέγ. as contrasted with other κακά. [Cf. inf. 717 ὦ κατάρατ' ἀνδρῶν; Hipp. 848 φίλα γυναικῶν; and the Lat. per opaca viarum, etc.]

ll. 196-7. Ἀργείων κ.τ.λ.: ' that thy life, O my daughter (μοι: ethic dative), hath by vote of the Argives been resolved upon.' Lit. ' a vote has been passed about thy life.'

l. 199. δυστάνου βιοτᾶς, descriptive genitive = ' mother of hapless life.' [Or, perhaps, causal genitive of exclamation (' mother, O for thy hapless life!'); see on 661 inf. βοῆς. Cf. 425 inf. θύγατερ ἀθλίας τύχης.]

l. 202. παῖς ἅδ' like ἀνὴρ ὅδε)=' I ': so, συνδουλεύσω.   σοι, γήρᾳ: both after συνδουλεύσω, by the σχῆμα καθ' ὅλον καὶ μέρος, Weil: 'for τῷ σου γήρᾳ.' [Cf. Med. 992 παισὶν ὄλεθρον βιοτῷ προσάγεις, and see on 62 sup. Or (2) σοι, eth. dat.; γηρ., dat. after συνδουλ.]

l. 203. δειλαίῳ δειλαία, 'mingling my grief with thine': cf. inf. 205 δειλαία δειλαίαν.

l. 205. μόσχον: cf. πῶλον sup. 144. Yet σκύμνον, sup.: perhaps there is an intentional contrast between the two (Hav.),—'thy gentle heifer, like a wild whelp of the mountains.' δειλαία δειλαίαν, 'alas for thee, alas for me': cf. sup. 203 δειλαίῳ δειλαία.

ll. 207–8. λαιμότομόν τ' κ.τ.λ.: 'sent throat-severed to Hades, to the gloom beneath the earth.' Ἀίδᾳ: perhaps dative of motion to: cf. Hom. Il. i. 3 "Ἄιδι προΐαψεν, and Verg. Aen. ii. 398 multos demittimus Orco. But, as both Hades and Orcus are primarily persons (cf. sup. l. 2), the dative in each case may contain some idea of recipience. γᾶς: after σκότον. σκότον, after ὑπο-: 'beneath,' i. e. ' to beneath:' cf. Verg. Aen. iv. 243 sub Tartara mittit, 'to the shades below.' [Others take Ἀίδᾳ after λαιμότομον.]

l. 213. τὸν ἐμὸν κ.τ.λ.: 'but for my life, the outrage and shame of it, I weep not.' μετακλ., 'regret:' cf. the Engl. 'mourn after.' [Paley further emphasises μετα-: 'weep, when it is too late.' It is also, improbably, taken as 'again,' or 'with thee.' For the compound, cf. μετακλαύσεσθαι Hom. Il. xi. 763; μεταστένομαι Eur. Med. 996; μεταλγεῖς Aesch. Supp. 405.]

l. 214. θανεῖν, sc. τὸ θανεῖν: the nominative. (Goodw. M. & T. § 91.) See Appendix, p. 64.

l. 216. καὶ μήν often introduces a new person on to the stage.

l. 217. πρὸς σέ: 'to thee': cf. 422 inf. πρὸς Ἕκτορ' εἴπω. πρός and acc., of the words directed to a person: [Jelf, 638. 3; distinguish inf. 303 εἶπον εἰς ἅπαντας. Less probably, 'with reference to thee.']

(Odysseus enters by the right-hand side-door: see Introd., p. 12.)

l. 221. πρὸς χῶμ', 'at the tomb': with idea of previous motion to: cf. on 190 πρὸς τύμβον.

l. 224. ἐπέστη, 'is set.' [Nauck, followed by Kirch., considers this weak after ἐπιστάτης, and emends to ἐπέσται. It is perhaps only an oversight.]

l. 225. μήτ' ἀποσπασθῇς: N.B. tense: in prohibitions of the second or third person, with μή, the present imperative or aorist subjunctive are used. οἶσθ' οὖν ὃ δρᾶσον, lit. 'do, dost thou know what?' Bentley: οἶσθ' ὅ having almost become one expression, like Lat. nescio quid. The phrase is common in Greek drama. [E. g. Eur. Hel. 315, 1233; and occurs even with the third person,

13

HECUBA

as Iph. Taur. 1203 οἶσθά νυν ἅ μοι γενέσθω: cf. οἶσθ ὡς with the imperat., e. g. Soph. O. T. 543 οἶσθ' ὡς ποίησον. οἶσθ' ὅ, virtually = τόδε; and may orig. have been οἶσθα τοῦτο ὅ (cf. on οἶσθ' ὅτε 112, οἶσθ' ἡνίκ' 239); otherwise ὅ,τι would seem necessary (cf. England on Iph. T. 759 οἶσθ' ὃ δράσω): but the relative appears sometimes to be used interrogatively in indirect questions, e. g. Hdt. ii. 2 ἀνευρεῖν οἳ γενοίατο πρῶτοι ἀνθρώπων (cf. ? Soph. O. T. 1068; Aj. 1259). Others tr. δρᾶσον, 'you ought to do' (Thompson, Syntax, § 134); which is open to the same difficulty: (Hav).]

l. 227. γίγνωσκε, 'learn,' 'recognise;' not, 'know.' ἀλκήν, probably '*thy* strength,' viz. its smallness: [Weil. It is also taken. '*my* strength,' viz. its greatness.]

l. 231. ἆρ', 'it seems.'

l. 235. καρδίας, objective genitive after an adjective with active sense: cf. inf. 687 ἀρτιμαθὴς κακῶν; 1135 ὕποπτος ἁλώσεως.

l. 236-7. ἐξιστορῆσαι. For the double accusative with such verbs, implying two notions, the act and the patient, cf. Lat. rogo, and 264 inf. οὐδὲν αὐτὸν εἴργασται κακόν. σοὶ μὲν κ.τ.λ. 'to thee should my speech first (perf.) be addressed; then I that ask these things should hear thy answer.' Paley: σοί being dative of the person spoken to; εἰρῆσθαι, the 'formula of peroration.' τοὺς ἐρωτῶντας. For the plur., and the masc., which in such cases (according to Dawes's Canon: cf. Jelf, 390 c., always goes with it, cf. 511 inf. θανουμένους ἡμᾶς. [This form is only a variant for the fem. sing.; and differs from τοκεῦσι θυμουμένοις, inf. 403, where the plur. generalises. εἰρῆσθ., Herm.; see e. g. 1284 inf. εἴρηται γάρ; and Or. 1203, Phoen. 1012, etc. εἴρηται λόγος: or εἰρῆσθ. simply poet. for present.—Others, e. g. Weil, regard σοί as dative of agent; and some take ἡμᾶς as object of ἀκοῦσαι; but the acc. of the person after ἀκούω seems unsupported.]

l. 238. χρόνου, gen. of cause; σοι being understood after φθονῶ: Jelf. 499: 'I bear you no ill-will for the delay.'

l. 239. οἶσθ' ἡνίκ', sc. τὸν χρόνον ἡνίκ': see sup. on 112 οἶσθ' ὅτε. Odysseus mutilated himself, and entered Troy as a deserter who had been ill-treated by the Greeks. [On οἶσθ' ἡνίκ', see 225 οἶσθ' ὅ.]

l. 241. φόνου σταλαγμοί, 'drops of carnage,' i.e. of blood: abstract for concrete: cf. Tennyson, Morte d'Arthur, 'drops of onset': genitive of material. κατέσταξον, intrans.; γένυν being after κατά: see on 760 inf. καταστάξω δάκρυ. [φόν.: cf. Soph. Ant. 114 χιόνος πτέρυγι. φόβου and δόλου (Musgr.) have been conjectured: when σταλαγμοί might mean 'tears.']

14

NOTES. LINES 225—264.

l. 242. **ἄκρας καρδίας**, 'the surface only of my heart': partit. gen. after ψαύω, a verb of touching. ἄκρ., like ὦμον ἄκρον, the tip of the shoulder, etc.: cf. Lat. summus. [Cf. Aesch. Ag. 778 οὐκ ἀπ' ἄκρας φρενὸς εὔφρων.]

l. 243. **ἔγνω**, 'perceived,' i.e. 'recognised': cf. on 227 γίγνωσκε. **καὶ μόνη κ.τ.λ.** In Homer, Helen alone knows Odysseus. [Probably invented by Euripides; as it is unlikely that Hecuba would have allowed Odysseus to escape: see Introd., p. 6.]

l. 244. **μεμνήμεθ' ἐλθόντες**: the participle is generally preferred to the infinitive, in indirect discourse with verbs of mental action. N.B. case of ἐλθ.: when the subject of the main verb is also the subject of the subordinate verb or partic., the latter is attracted to the case of the former.

l. 246. **ὥστ' ἐνθανεῖν γε**, 'yes, till my hand was like to have (infin.) grown dead upon thy robes.' γε accepts and extends the notion of the previous question: contrast its force inf. 766 ἀνόνητά γε. [Jelf, 735. 8. ἐνθ., Schol. = νεκρωθῆναι; Musgr. suggests ἐντακῆναι. Others ἐμβαλεῖν, Odysseus grudging the admission.]

l. 247. **ἐμὸς τότε**; as I now am thine. [Ll. 247-8 are, in most MSS., transposed with ll. 249-50.]

l. 251. **οὔκουν κ.τ.λ.**, 'art thou not then a villain for these designs'; βουλ., instrumental dative.

l. 253. **δύνᾳ = δύνασαι**: [Pors. Dind.; attacked as a Doric form: but cf. ἐπίστᾳ, Aesch. Eum. 86, 581,—both in dialogue. Herm., Nauck., Kirch., δύνῃ:—a later form, on anal. of λύῃ, etc.? Hav. The MSS. read both. Cf. Eur. And. 238; Soph. Phil. 798. Some, improbably, δύνῃ = subj.]

l. 254. **δημηγόρους**: perhaps having in mind Cleon and other orators of the Agora.

l. 255. **γιγνώσκοισθε**, 'may ye not be known to me': opt. of wish.

l. 258. **ἀτὰρ κ.τ.λ.**, 'but tell me, what subtle conceit did they find in passing sentence' etc.? τοῦθ', sc. τὸ ὁρίσαι κ.τ.λ.

l. 260. **χρῆν**: the infin., Dind.: more commonly χρῆναι. χρή is prob. a noun: imperf. χρή-ῆν = χρῆν (as inf. 629), sometimes augmented on false analogy, ἐχρῆν; inf. χρή-εῖναι, = χρῆναι, or χρῆν, as here. (Hav.) [(2) the imperf. Paley. Cf. Herc. Fur. 828 τὸ χρῆν νιν ἐξέσωσεν. Scaliger suggests χρεών here; Nauck, in both, τὸ χρή.]

l. 262. **ἢ τοὺς κ.τ.λ.**: Achilles fell by the hand of Apollo.

l. 263. **τείνει**, 'directs'; met. from a bow.

l. 264. **οὐδὲν κ.τ.λ.** For the double acc. of act and patient, see sup. 236, on ἐξιστορῆσαι.   γ', emphatic: she, 'at any rate.'

15

HECUBA.

l. 265. προσφάγματα. For the plural noun in apposition to a singular, cf. Eur. Hipp. 11 Ἱππόλυτος, ἁγνοῦ Πιτθέως παιδεύματα.
l. 266. ἄγει: prob. not hist. pres., but ''tis she who brought him'; like Virg. Aen. viii. 294 Tu Cretia mactas prodigia, 'art the slayer of the Cretan monster.'
l. 268. οὐχ ἡμῶν τόδε, 'this doth not touch us'; lit. is not of us, possessive genitive.
l. 270. ηὑρέθη: found also unaugmented, εὑρ-: see on 18 sup.
ll. 271-2. μέν, the abstract and general claims of justice; δέ, the personal and particular claims of Hecuba.
l. 271. τῷ δικαίῳ, 'in the name of justice:' dat. of respect. λόγον, cogn. acc., 'I urge this plea.' τόνδ', referring to preceding words; generally to succeeding. [τῷ δικ.: Weil and the Schol. κατὰ τὸ δίκαιον; (2) 'against his claims on the score of justice' (Paley), dat. incom. after ἁμιλ.]
l. 274. προσπίτνων, parenthetic.
l. 275. σου, partit. gen., after ἀνθάπτ., as also τῶν αὐτῶν:—σχῆμα καθ' ὅλον καὶ μέρος. See on 62 sup.
l. 279. ταύτῃ, 'in her.' [The line is rejected by Kirch. and Nauck.]
l. 282. μή, not οὐ, because the relative 'distributes,' refers to a general class, i. e. contains an implicit reason or condition:—'such things as are not right'; Jelf, 743.
l. 283. εὐτυχοῦντας, not τοὺς εὐτ., but a participle agreeing with τοὺς κρατ.:—'when fortunate.'
l. 284. ἦν .. εἴμ', the verb: 'for once I lived indeed.' [Schol., Paley, Jelf, 375. 3; (2) the copula, supplying εὐτυχοῦσα from εὐτυχοῦντας, 'was happy,' etc.; Weil.]
l. 285. ἀφείλετο, for the double acc. see on 236 sup. ἐξιστορῆσαι.
l. 288. παρηγόρησον, ὡς, 'win them from their project and show them that,' etc.: παρ-, talk 'over'; ὡς, (saying) that. φθόνος, ira deorum, Nemesis: cf. Iph. Aul. 1103 θεῶν φθόνος, Musgr. [Hermann, ὡς = nam; making the subsq. words a comment of Hecuba's.]
l. 291. νόμος, probably an anachronism. The law is the Athenian law of ὕβρις. [Quoted Dem. in Mid. p. 529. For law on ὕβρις and φόνος, see Xen. de Rep. Ath. i. 10; Paley.]
l. 293. ἀξίωμα, 'thy great repute.' [λέγῃς, Kirch., following Muretus. Nauck reads λέγῃ with the MSS.; ἀξίωμα being the subject.]
l. 295. τῶν δοκούντων, i. e. τῶν εἶναί τι δοκούντων; opposed to ἄδοξοι, Schol.; cf. the Eng. 'men of repute,' i. e. of good repute, etc.
l. 297. ἥτις, = ὥστε ἐκείνη; 'that it,' etc.; cf. the Lat. qui with subj., expressing result. ['The relative with any tense of the

NOTES. LINES 265—320.

Indicative, or even with the Optative and ἄν, can be used to denote a result, where ὥστε might have been expected. This occurs chiefly after negatives, or interrogatives, implying a negative.' Goodw. M. & T. § 65. 1, note 5.]

l. 299. τῷ θυμουμένῳ, 'in (lit. 'by') thine angry spirit'; neuter; causal dative. [τῷ θυμωδεῖ μέρει τῆς ψυχῆς. For the use of the neut. partic., cf. Hippol. 248 τὸ μαινόμενον; Thuc. i. 36 τὸ δεδιός, etc.; For the law-court character of the scene, cf. note on 1132 inf.; and see Introd., p. 10.]

l. 300. δυσμενῆ ποιοῦ : 'account as hostile.' φρενί : i.e. in imagination, opposed to fact : local dative.

l. 301. τὸ μὲν σὸν σῶμα, 'thine own person'; contrasted with τὴν παῖδα 305. ηὐτύχουν, i. e. ἐσώθην : on the form see 18 sup.

l. 302. ἄλλως : not 'otherwise,' but 'idly': contrast inf. 974.

l. 303. εἰς ἅπαντας, 'before all,' 'unto all': with idea of previous motion to : cf. 190 πρὸς τύμβον : [Jelf, 625. 1. Weil, 'among all, before all, to all.' Cf. Hippol. 986 εἰς ὄχλον δοῦναι λόγον. Distinguish sup. 217 πρὸς σὲ σημανῶν ἔπος.]

l. 305. δοῦναι, 'that we should give': dandam esse, Weil. Cf. the infinitive of treaties; and the infinitive used for the imperative, generally. The infin. in such cases depends on some word of command, understood : Goodw. M. & T. § 103. εἶπον may be here regarded as containing an idea of command.'

l. 308. φέρηται; middle : 'wins for himself.'

l. 309. ἡμῖν, 'at our hands': dative of interest, almost, of agent : [Weil, and Paley. Porson, 'in our eyes': (so Jelf, 599. 1.) Cf. Alc. 434 ἀξία δέ μοι τιμῆς.]

l. 310. ἀνήρ: placed emphatically at the end.

l. 311. οὔκουν : 'not, then': distinguish οὐκοῦν, 'then.' φίλῳ χρώμεσθ', 'treat as a friend,' Musgr. [οὔκουν and οὐκοῦν, orig. the same, οὐκ οὖν : used in a negative statement or a negative interrogation. As the last often forms virtually a positive statement, οὐκ οὖν gradually assumed in it the separate existence of a positive particle, οὐκοῦν, which could be negatived by an additional οὐ or used with an imperative. Elmsl. ad Heracl. 256.]

l. 312. ὄλωλε. [Kirch. and Nauck, with most MSS. V. l., Parisian MS., ἄπεστι Dind.]

l. 318. κεἰ, 'even if'; to be distinguished from εἰ καί, 'although' (inf. 843). [In the first, καί belongs only to the εἰ; in the last, to the sentence : Jelf, 861. 2.]

ll. 319-20. τύμβον δὲ κ.τ.λ. : 'yet would I wish to see my tomb held in honour: for the gratefulness of this is lasting':

HECUBA.

taking ὁρᾶσθαι, middle, and χάρις as pleasure felt by the dead. [Others, ὁρᾶσθαι, passive ; χάρις, gratitude felt by the living.]

l. 323. ἠδέ: an Epic form, rare in tragic dialogue : but cf. Herc. Fur. 30. σέθεν, archaic form of σοῦ.

l. 326. τόλμα, 'endure.' κακῶς, with νομίζομεν,—'are wrong in our custom of,' etc.

l. 327. ἀμαθίαν ὀφλήσομεν, 'will stand condemned for ignorance' : ἀμ. cog. acc. Metaphor from the law-court,—δίκην ὀφλεῖν, 'to lose in a case': though, in metaphor, the acc. seems to represent the 'penalty,' rather than the 'case.' [Cf. Soph. Oed. Tyr. 511 οὔποτ' ὀφλήσει κακίαν.]

ll. 328-9. οἱ βάρβαροι κ.τ.λ. N.B. use of generic article with second person.

l. 330. ὡς ἄν, 'that so.' ἄν is sometimes added to ὡς, with the subj. ; in Hom. and Hdt., also with the opt. It does not affect the sense in any perceptible way : [Goodw. M. T. 44. 1, n. 2. But see Monro (§ 362): 'ἄν particularises'; Jelf (810. 1), ἄν points to a suppressed condition, and adds to the idea of purpose a further idea of result.]

l. 331. ὑμεῖς δ' κ.τ.λ., i. e. produce bad soldiers, and fail in war.

l. 332. τὸ δοῦλον. i. e. ἡ δουλεία. κακόν, ' sorry.' [πέφυκ' ἀεί : MSS. πεφυκέναι,—either (1) epexegetic, Herm.; or (2) τὸ δοῦλον πεφυκέναι.]

l. 333. τολμᾷ, 'endures'; as in 326: [Musgrave; Pal., 'ventures': v. l. τολμᾶν. νικώμενον, Kirch. and Nauck; Weil, following Stobaeus, κρατούμενον.]

l. 337. σπούδαζε, 'exert thyself.' πάσας, i. e. παντοίας. στόμα, 'like the throat of a nightingale'; i. e. 'like a full-throated nightingale.'

l. 338. ἱεῖσα. For ῑ, cf. Aesch. Theb. 488; on the other hand ῑ, inf. 367, 900: Paley. The ordinary usage is ῐ in Hom. and Ep., ῑ in Att. μὴ στερηθῆναι : infin. of purpose, rather than consequence.

l. 340. πεῖθε, 'strive to persuade him : ' see on sup. 72 ἀποπέμπομαι.

l. 341. ὥστ' ἐποικτεῖραι, 'so that he well might pity.' N. B. distinc. between ὥστε with infin. (probable result), and ὥστε with Indic. (actual result). Cf. on 246 sup. ὥστ' ἐνθανεῖν γε.

l. 342. δεξιὰν κ.τ.λ. Suppliants touched the right hand and beard of those they were addressing.

l. 344. σου, γενειάδος ; both partit. gens. after προσθίγω : cf. sup. on μου χειρός 62.

l. 345. πέφευγας κ.τ.λ., 'thou hast escaped the Zeus of my

supplications'; viz. the punishment of Ζεὺς Ἱκέσιος (Zeus, as god of suppliants), for refusing a suppliant's prayer.

l. 346. ὡς, 'since'; for. γε, 'at any rate'; emphasising ἔψομαι.

l. 350. πρῶτον βίου, 'the first point in my life';—first, i. e. in my argument, the first point that I will mention.   [Or first in time, (Weil: début); or in importance (Herm. and Paley); or both. All are supported by Schol.]

l. 351. ὕπο: ἐλπίδων being personified: 'fair hopes were my nursing-mothers.'   [Or ὕπο, of accompanying circumstances, like ὑπὸ κλαυθμῶν καταθάψομεν Aesch. Ag. 1553.]

ll. 352-3. ζῆλον κ.τ.λ., 'provoking no small rivalry for my hand, as to whose household I should come.' γάμων, objective genitive. ὅτου, interrogative pronoun, following the virtual question, contained in ζῆλον,—'rivalry, to see to whose house' etc. ἀφίξομαι, reverting, for vividness (according to the usual idiom), to present oration: the future optative would be 'grammatically correct.' [ἔχουσα, cf. Aristot. Eth. x. 1. 2 πολλὴν ἐχόντων ἀμφισβήτησιν.]

l. 355. ἀπόβλεπτος: 'conspicuous.' ἀποβλέπω, lit. to look away from one object at another. N.B. absence of caesura (distinguish the 'quasi-caesura,'—elision at end of 3rd foot, which is equiv. to caesura in 4th); and Homeric use of μετά with the dative.   [Owing to these two peculiarities, the line is sometimes considered an interpolation. For the first, however, which is not infrequent, cf. inf. 549 and 1159; for the second, Aesch. Pers. 613 λιβάσιν μέτα. Kirch. reads παρθένων ἀποβ.; for the idea, cf. ἐπίστρεπτος, Aesch. Cho. 350; and the Lat. respicio.]

l. 356. τὸ κατθανεῖν, with regard to death: acc. of respect.

l. 357. μέν, answered by ἔπειτα, l. 359.

l. 358. εἰωθός: N. B. participle used as adjective: see on 122 ἦν σπεύδων: [and cf. Hom. Il. xix. 80 ἐπισταμένῳ περ ἐόντι: Pors. The transition from the one to the other is more common in Lat., e.g. praesens, sapiens, etc.]

l. 359. ἄν .. ἄν. For the repetition of ἄν, which is here due either to the lateness of the verb or a desire to emphasise ἴσως, cf. inf. 742 ἄλγος ἂν προσθείμεθ᾽ ἄν, and 1199 οὔποτ᾽ ἂν .. γένοιτ᾽ ἄν. δεσποτῶν, ὅστις: the relative being indefinite, and so, virtually plural. ὠμῶν φρένας, 'savage of heart': φρ., acc. of respect.

l. 360. ἀργύρου, usual gen. of price. ὠνήσεται: a return to present narration, like ἀφίξομαι, sup. 353.

l. 362. προσθεὶς δ᾽ ἀνάγκην σιτοποιόν, 'laying upon me the slavery of making bread': for ἀν., cf. inf. 639 πόνων ἀνάγκαι κρείσσονες.

l. 363. κερκίσιν τ᾽ ἐφεστάναι, 'to stand at the loom.' κερκίς,

HECUBA.

really the loom-comb, radius, with which the threads of the woof (the horizontal threads) were driven up the threads of the warp (the vertical threads) : here put for ἱστός, the loom,—the upright frame from which the warp was suspended.

l. 366. τυράννων, 'deemed worthy of princes ': gen. of value.

ll. 367-8. οὐ δῆτα κ.τ.λ. : 'No; I resign this light of mine eyes, while it be free, and consecrate myself to death.' οὐ δῆτα, i.e. ἔσται τοῦτο: δῆτα emphasises. ὀμμάτων φέγγος: sight, i.e. life. ἐλεύθερον, proleptic. προστιθεῖσ', Lat. addicens. [Cf. Androm. 1016. For φέγγ., of the eyes, cf. the Homeric φάεα καλά, e.g. Od. xvi. 15 and inf. 1067 τυφλὸν φέγγος. Others, less probably, take it 'the light of day'; making ὀμμάτων gen. after ἀφίημ'.]

l. 369. διέργασαι, ' despatch ' ; cf. Lat. conficere.

l. 370. οὔτ' ἐλπίδος κ.τ.λ., 'no confidence, that hope or thought can give, that ' etc. For the omission of τοῦ with ἐλπ., cf. that of ἄλλοτε with ἐπ' ἀκταῖς, 28 sup.

l. 372. δέ : N.B. the position, common with vocatives, in turning from one thought to another. Cf. inf. 1287 'Εκάβη, σὺ δ', ὦ κ.τ.λ. μηδέν, adverbial, μηδαμῶς.

l. 373. λέγουσα, viz. μήτε λέγουσα : see on 370 sup. συμβούλου δέ μοι θανεῖν, i.e. σὺν ἐμοὶ βούλου ἐμὲ θανεῖν, Schol. [μήτε δρ. : Pors. for μηδὲ δρ. (MSS. Dind.) ; which is doubtful.]

l. 377. μᾶλλον εὐτυχέστερος, ' happier in death rather than in life ': N.B. the two comparatives : cf. Hippol. 485 μᾶλλον ἀλγίων κλύειν. [These are not necessarily redundant : perhaps, μᾶλλον goes with ἢ ζῶν, while εὐτυχέστερος may contain a comparison with some suppressed idea, e.g. rather than before. rather than not, i.e. may be virtually positive, though the influence of μᾶλλον may have attracted it from a positive form into a comparative : Herm. and Paley: Jelf, 784. 1.]

l. 378. μή, hypothetic, besides being with infin.

l. 379. δεινὸς χαρακτὴρ κ.τ.λ., 'is an impress wonderful and deeply stamped.' Paley cf. Milton's Comus, ' Reason's mintage charactered in the face.'

ll. 380-1. ἐσθλῶν, gen. of origin. κἀπὶ μεῖζον κ.τ.λ., ' and the count of noble birth, in those that are worthy of it, grows to more and more.' τοῖσιν ἀξίοις, dat. com. : [Weil. Paley, however, ' extends to something more ' ; viz. results in action. Others, again, improbably, make ἐσθλῶν γενέσθαι the subject of ἔρχεται and μεῖζον an epithet of ὄνομα.]

l. 382. ἀλλὰ τῷ καλῷ κ.τ.λ., ' yet to nobleness (or ' to thy nobleness '/ is pain attached.'

NOTES. LINES 363—407.

l. 384. ψόγον, 'blame'; viz. for not honouring Achilles: [Paley. Others, less probably, for sacrificing Polyxena.]
l. 390. ἀλλὰ τήνδ', ᾐτήσατο: see on 40 sup.
l. 391. ἀλλά, 'then.' N.B. position. ἀλλά orig. n. pl. of ἄλλος: 'otherwise.'
l. 394. εἷς, one death, that of thy daughter. [So the best MS., followed by Kirch. and Nauck. V. l., all the other MSS., σῆς.]
l. 395. μηδὲ τόνδ' ὠφείλομεν, sc. φέρειν, out of προσοιστέος: 'would that we had not to offer even this death': μηδέ, not οὐδέ, because a wish is implied; the indic., not the subj., because the wish is unattainable. Such phrases were originally apodoses with the protasis implied: [Goodw. M. & T. 49. 2, note 3 b, and 83; cf. Jelf, 856; contrast εἰ γένοιτο 836 inf.; where the apod. is implied. The two phrases are sometimes combined, εἰ and the imperf. (or second aor.) indic. of ὀφείλω being found together.— Others take ὠφείλομεν in its primary, absolute, sense of 'owe.' (According to Monro (Hom. Gram. 358), μή belongs logically to infinitive following.)]
l. 396. γε: emphasising.
l. 397. κεκτημένος: for particip. and case see on sup. 244 μεμνήμεθ' ἐλθόντες. (οἶδα, with partic., 'to know that'; with infin., 'to know how to.')
l. 398. ὁποῖα κισσὸς κ.τ.λ., 'Like ivy, I will cling to her, as to an oak'; a double comparison, whether due to intention or carelessness. δρυός, partit. gen. after a verb of touching, etc. [Herm. and Dind.: cf. Troad. 147 μάτηρ δ' ὥς τις πτανοῖς κλαγγὰν ὄρνισιν ὅπως ἐξάρξω 'γώ. Others, (2), understand some such word as ἴσθι before ὅπως (Musgr.); (3) suggest emend. to ὅμως (Pal.).]
l. 400. ὡς, sc. ἴσθι ὥς: a common ellipse: cf. Med. 609; Soph. Aj. 39, etc.
l. 401. ἀλλὰ μήν, 'well, neither will I,' etc.: ἀλλὰ μήν catches up the remark of another speaker.
l. 403. χάλα, 'bear with'; more commonly transitive, 'slacken,' with e.g. τὴν ὀργήν: a naval metaphor from slackening the sheet, Schol. τοκεῦσι, generalising plural, used for emphasis. [See on 236 sup. τοὺς ἐρωτῶντας.]
l. 404. τοῖς κρατοῦσι; see last note.
l. 406. γέροντα: for γέρων, as adj., cf. Aesch. Ag. 750 γέρων λόγος. πρὸς βίαν, 'with violence': cf. πρὸς χάριν, etc. πρός and the acc. derive their adverbial use from the idea of moving or turning towards.
l. 407. ἀσχημονῆσαι, 'to show unseemly'; not quite the Eng. 'to

HECUBA.

be disfigured.' ἕκ, 'dragged by a young arm': Ionic use of ἐκ, common in tragedy.

l. 408. ἆ πείσει, sc. ἐὰν τοῖς κρατοῦσι μάχῃ. μὴ σύ γ'. sc. τοῖς κρατ. μάχου: the imperative is often omitted in this formula. οὐ γὰρ ἄξιον, sc. τό σε πεσεῖν πρὸς οὖδας κ.τ.λ. (nom. infin.): tr., 'it is not seemly that,' etc.

l. 409. μοι, prob. eth. dat.; not dat. after φίλη.

l. 410. προσβαλεῖν, epexegetic infinitive, 'that I may lay it to mine.' See p. 64. [Or (2), object of δύς; or (3)? 'imperatival infin.': with which cf. Thuc. vi. 34 πείθεσθε καὶ παραστῆναι παντί.]

ll. 411-2. [These lines occur also Alc. 207-8.]

l. 413. δέχει: N.B. mood. [V. l. δέχου.]

l. 416. ἄνυμφος, referred to ἄπειμι, 414. ὧν: gen. after τυχ. The antecedents are νυμφεύματα and ὑμέναιος, contained in ἄνυμφος and ἀνυμέναιος.

l. 417. τέκνον. [Others take it as nom., destroying the comma; cf. Eur. Tro. 735 τιμηθεὶς τέκνον; Hom. Od. ii. 363 φίλε τέκνον.]

l. 418. ἐκεῖ: often used alone for ἐν Ἀΐδου; e.g. Med. 1073 εὐδαιμονοῖτον, ἀλλ' ἐκεῖ. See 1270 inf. ἐνθάδ', 'on earth.' ἐν Ἀΐδου, sc. δόμῳ: cf. Lat. ad Vestae, etc.

l. 419. ποῖ, pregnant, containing a notion of previous motion to: 'to what end will my life come?' δράσω, τελευτήσω: perhaps delib. conj., as inf. 422 εἴπω. [See on 88 sup.]

l. 421. πεντήκοντα. According to the ordinary account, Priam had fifty children, Hecuba only nineteen. τέκνων, privative gen., after ἄμμοροι.

l. 422. τί κ.τ.λ., 'what wouldst thou that I am to say?' σοι, eth. dat. πρὸς Ἕκτορ' εἴπω: see on 217 sup. πρὸς σὲ σημανῶν ἔπος. εἴπω. delib. conj.

l. 423. ἐμέ. The addition of the participle οὖσαν would be more usual.

l. 425. ὦ τῆς ἀώρου κ.τ.λ.; descriptive, rather than causal, genitive. See on 199 sup. ὦ δυστάνου μᾶτερ βιοτᾶς. [ἀθλίας; MSS. followed by Herm., Kirch., Nauck. Markland emend. ἀθλία. Dind.]

l. 426. τε. N.B. position.

l. 427. χαίρουσιν, 'they do fare well': recovering the actual meaning of the word, which χαῖρε, like the Eng. 'fare-well' and 'good-bye,' (= God be with you), has almost lost. τόδε, sc. τὸ χαίρειν.

l. 430. ζῇ κ.τ.λ., 'Sophoclean irony,' the irony of fate; which is unconscious: cf. Soph. O. T. 236, 260; Electr. 1448, etc. Distinguish the simple irony of inf. 990, etc. θανούσης, agreeing, κατὰ

NOTES. LINES 407—446.

σύνεσιν, with σου contained in τὸ σόν: cf. Soph. O. C. 344 τἀμὰ
δυστήνου κακά; Ov. Her. 5. 45 nostros vidisti flentis ocellos.
l. 432. ἀμφιθείς, lit. 'put round': here = 'covering,' καλύπτων:
cf. Lat. circumdo. μ'...κάρα, both accs. after ἀμφ., by the σχῆμα
καθ' ὅλον καὶ μέρος: see on 62 sup. μου χειρός.
ll. 433-4. γ', 'even,' before my sacrifice. ἐκτέτηκα, ἐκτήκω:
N.B. the perf. intrans.; the pres. trans.: as with several verbs, e.g.
ἕστηκα, ἵστημι.
l. 436. μέτεστι, viz., μοι..σου: 'no more part have I in thee.'
χρόνον, acc. of dur.
l. 437. μεταξύ, ' before '; lit. ' between,' i.e. ' between ' this and the
sword-and-pyre: [Herm., Dind.; for μεταξύ, referring to one only of
two limits, cf. Aristoph. Acharn. 433 κεῖται δ' ἄνωθεν τῶν Θυεστείων
ῥακῶν, μεταξὺ τῶν Ἰνοῦς. Weil, less probably, between the sword
and the pyre; as a hyperbole.]
l. 438. προλείπω, 'I faint': intrans.; usually trans., 'to leave.'
λυέται, N.B. ῠ.
ll. 441-3. ὥς, for οὕτως, ' thus '; i.e. in the same state as Polyxena:
Herm. εἷλε, with play on 'Ελένην: cf. Aesch. Agam. 689 ἑλέναυς,
ἕλανδρος, ἑλέπτολις. The Epic ὥς is, however, rare in Tragedy; [and
all the three lines, 441-3, are unlikely, (if προλείπω, 438, is empha-
sised), and, at any rate, unnatural, in the mouth of Hecuba. Herm.,
therefore, gives them to the Chorus; others bracket them as
spurious.]

(While Hecuba lies fainting upon the stage, the Chorus sing the
First Stasimon.—On the 'Stasimon,' with its ' Strophe ' and ' Antistrophe,' see Introd., p. 12.)

FIRST STASIMON, 444-483. **The Chorus lament their
captivity.**

First Strophe, 444-454. *Sea-breeze, whither wilt thou carry
me to captivity? To the Dorian land? Or the Phthiotid, watered by
Apidanus?*

First Antistrophe, 455-465. *Or to Delos, birth-place of the
palm and bay-tree, where, with the Delian maids, I shall sing the
praises of Artemis?*

Second Strophe, 466-474. *Or to Athens, where I shall em-
broider Athene's saffron robe with the picture of the goddess in her
chariot, or of the victory over the Titans?*

Second Antistrophe, 475-483. *Alas, for the land of my fathers,
which lies in its smoke; while I am carried into captivity worse
than death.*

ll. 444-6. αὔρα κ.τ.λ., 'breeze, breeze of the sea, that conveyest the

23

HECUBA.

swift sea-faring barks over the swelling mere.' ποντιάς, fem. adj. ἀκάτους, = in prose, 'skiffs.' [Paley remarks that the fate of Polyxena would be a more appropriate subject for this ode. See Introd., p. 10.]

l. 448. τῷ δουλόσυνος κτηθεῖσ᾽, together: τίνι δουλεύουσα: trans. 'to whose house, gotten for slavery, shall I be brought?' [τῷ is otherwise taken as a dat. com., with the whole sentence.— Contrast sup. 101 sqq., where the Chorus have already been allotted to different masters: Weil.]

l. 450. Δωρίδος αἴας, the Peloponnese. ὅρμον, acc. of motion to, after ἀφίξομαι: [or, Weil, after με πορεύσεις. Δωρ. αἴ.: cf. Soph. O. C. 695 ἐν τᾷ μεγάλᾳ Δωρίδι νάσῳ Πέλοπος.]

l. 451. Φθιάδος. Phthias, or Pthiotis, was a district in Thessaly. from which Achilles came. [ὑδ. πατ., cf. Bacch. 573.]

l. 454. γύας: from γύης, masc.: [Elms. ad Heracl. 839. γύας. Herm., Dind.; Kirch., Nauck, πεδία.]

l. 455. νάσων. after ὅρμον.

l. 456. πεμπομέναν may be explained as reverting to με in l. 447.

l. 457. οἴκοις. The 'local dative' is poetic: except in adverbs and names of places which have become adverbial; these being usually locative forms.

l. 458. ἔνθα, sc. Delos; where Leto gave birth to Apollo and Artemis. Zeus caused a palm and a bay-tree to spring up in support or honour of her travail. πρωτόγονος, 'first-born': i.e. first produced at the birth of Apollo. In 425–424 B. C., about the probable date of this play, Delos was again purified by the Athenians, and the Delian festival renewed. [Thuc. iii. 104; see Introd., p. 5, on date of play. For the legend of Leto's travail, see Homeric Hymn to Apollo and Artemis, and Hymn of Callimachus to Artemis.]

l. 460. Λατοῖ φίλᾳ, dat. com.

l. 461. ἄγαλμα, acc. in appos. to the sentence: 'in honour of.' Δίας, 'of Zeus': δίας, 'divine'.

l. 463. Ἀρτέμιδός τε: τε, placed early; should follow χρυσέαν.

l. 466. Παλλάδος ἐν πόλει, Athens.

ll. 467-8. καλλιδίφρου, πέπλῳ. At the festival of the Greater Panathenaea, which took place the third year of each Olympiad viz. every four years, an embroidered saffron robe was carried in solemn procession to the temple of Athena on the Acropolis. The robe was often ornamented with a representation of Athene herself, in her chariot, fighting against the giants. [θεᾶς ναίουσ᾽, Nauck: Kirchhoff, Dind., Ἀθαναίας.]

l. 469. ζεύξομαι, 'I will yoke': i.e. will depict as yoked. ἆρα, generally before the verb. [ζεύξ., cf. Verg. Ecl. vi. 63 solo proceras erigit alnos; i. e. erectas canit. ἄρα, Kirch. and Nauck; Dind. ἅρματι.]

l. 470. δαιδαλέαισι: of embroidery. [Dind. δαιδαλταῖσι.]

l. 471. ἀνθοκρόκοισι, 'saffron-flowered'; from κρόκος, saffron. [Or (2) 'flower-inwoven'; from κρόκη, a woof.]

l. 473. τάν, the article used as relative; cf. 636 inf. τὰν καλλίσταν, and Aesch. Ag. 642 διπλῇ μάστιγι τὴν Ἄρης φιλεῖ. The article and relative were originally the same, viz. a demonstrative pronoun. ἀμφιπύρῳ: lit. 'with fire at each end'; referring to the two points of the thunderbolt.

l. 474. κοιμίζει, not historic present, but 'is laying to sleep,' i. e. in the picture.

l. 475. τεκέων, gen. of cause; cf. 183 sup. αἰαῖ, σᾶς ψυχᾶς.

l. 476. πατέρων, 'forefathers'; as the Chorus speak of themselves in the singular, Weil. See Introd., p. 12.

l. 477. καπνῷ κατερείπεται τυφομένα, 'lies in ruins, smouldering with smoke.'

l. 479. Ἀργείων, possessive genitive after the idea of κτῆμα in δορίκτητος: 'spear-possessed of the Argives:' [Weil. πρὸς Ἀργείων, Dind.; ὑπ' Ἀργείων, Herm., Paley. δορικ., Kirch. and Nauck; v. l. δορίληπτος, Herm., Dind.]

ll. 481-3. λιποῦσ' Ἀσίαν κ.τ.λ.: 'leaving Asia, the hand-maid of Europe, getting, in exchange for her, the chambers of death.' Εὐρώπας θεράπναν, referring to the capture of Troy, and enslavement of the Chorus, by the Greeks: θεράπ. contracted for θεράπαιναν? ἀλλάξασ': the active usually means to give, the middle, to take, in exchange. Ἅιδα θαλάμους, i. e. the tents of slavery: Ἅιδα, Doric gen. [2) 'receiving the bridal chamber in exchange for death,' i.e. the Greeks spared the women from death to make them concubines; 3) 'giving the bridal chamber in exchange for death'; (4) 'exchanging the chambers of death,' i.e. for slavery, τοῦ δούλα κεκλῆσθαι, Dind. θεράπνα, according to some, is always used by Euripides of 'abode' (Troad. 211, 1070; Bacch. 1043; Herc. Fur. 370; Iph. Aul. 1499. In this case the passage might mean (5) 'receiving, in exchange, abode in Europe, even the chambers of death,' Weil.]

SECOND EPEISODION, 484-625. **Talthybius describes the noble death of Polyxena, and Hecuba prepares for her burial.**

(Talthybius enters by the right-hand side-door: see Introd., p. 12.)

l. 484. Talthybius was the herald of Agamemnon. δή ποτε, 'so lately': sometimes written as one word, δήποτε.

l. 485. ἂν ἐξεύροιμι; 'where should I find?' The optative with

HECUBA.

ἄν is often used as a milder form of future: it is explained as the apodosis of a suppressed protasis. Goodw. M. & T. 52. 2.

l. 486. νῶτ' ἔχουσα, 'with her back upon the earth': cf. sup. 35 ναῦς ἔχοντες.

l. 487. συγκεκλημένη, 'huddled.'

l. 488. ὁρᾶν, 'regard.'

l. 489. ἄλλως .. μάτην .. ψευδῆ, emphatic pleonasm. κεκτῆσθαι. ἀνθρώπους, the object of ὁρᾶν, becomes the subject of κεκτ. [Weil keeps the subject by translating δόξαν, 'reputation,' and bracketing the next line: Reiske and Musgrave, by suggesting αὐτοῖς for ἄλλως. ἄλλ. μ. ψ., cf. Ovid, Trist. i. 2. 13 verba miser frustra non proficientia perdo.]

l. 491. ἐπισκοπεῖν, 'is overseer of': Eng. 'bishop' = Gk. ἐπίσκοπος, 'overseer.')

l. 494. ἀνέστηκεν, 'has been dispeopled': the regular word. Cf. ἀνάστατος, of a people 'made to get up and depart'; e.g. Hdt. i. 177, iii. 118.

l. 495. αὐτή. [Elmsley, for MSS. αὕτη.]

l. 496. φύρουσα, 'defiling': usually of mixing a dry thing with a moist.

l. 497. γέρων μέν εἰμ': and life is more precious to the aged.

l. 498. περιπεσεῖν, 'fall on' (lit. 'about,' 'in the way of,') any shameful chance.

l. 499. μετάρσιον, predicate: represented in Eng. by adverb.

l. 501. τίς οὗτος, 'who art thou that,' etc.

l. 504. πέμψαντος μέτα, i.e. πέμψαντος ἐμὲ μετὰ σέ. The ellipse after the preposition is remarkable: but cf. Aesch. Ag. 1359 τοῦ δρῶντός ἐστι καὶ τὸ βουλεῦσαι πέρι. [(2) Herm. considers the phrase as tmesis, μεταπέμψαντος, sc. σε: comparing for the absence of object, Thuc. i. 112 Ἀμυρταίου μεταπέμποντος.]

l. 505. ὦ φίλτατ': as if Talthybius was bringing good news.

l. 506. δοκοῦν, acc. absol.: 'because it seemeth good'; cf. on δοκοῦν, sup. 121. ὡς, not causal, 'since' (Weil), but exclamatory, 'how.' ἂν λέγοις, sc. εἰ λέγοις ἐλθεῖν, κ.τ.λ.

l. 510. Ἀτρεῖδαι, Agamemnon and Menelaus. λεώς. In these heroic times, however, the people's assembly (the ἀγορά) met only to receive from the King the result of discussions with his advisers (the βουλή).

l. 511. τί λέξεις; sudden fut. for pres., (cf. Gk. aor., e.g. 583 ἐπέζεσε, 'what sayest thou?' as if anticipating what she had just heard, or expecting its confirmation (Weil, on Hipp. 353): cf. on 1124 inf. ὡς θανουμένους, 'that I may die': lit. 'as doomed

NOTES. LINES 485—532.

to die.' For gender and number, see on sup. 237 τοὺς ἐρωτῶντας. σημανῶν, 'to tell me.' Purpose may be expressed by fut. partic., with or without ὡς: cf. inf. 634 ναυστολήσων; 731 ἀποστελῶν; 1202 κηδεύσων. [τί λέξ.: others keep future sense: as if worse were to come.]

l. 514. τοὐπὶ σ', 'so far as toucheth thee': τό, adverbial acc., cf. inf. 989 τοὐκείνου μέρος; ἐπὶ σέ, 'in reference to thee': [σέ being viewed 'as the aim of the action or state': Jelf, 635. 3 c.— Cf. Soph. Ant 889 ἡμεῖς γὰρ ἁγνοὶ τοὐπὶ τήνδε τὴν κόρην.]

l. 515. πῶς καί, 'how then'; πῶς being strengthened by καί, Jelf, 760. 2; cf. ποῖ καί 1064 inf. Contrast καὶ πῶς inf. 883, which is incredulous. ἐξεπράξατ', 'despatch': cf. sup. 369 διέργασαι. αἰδούμενοι, 'reverently.'

l. 516. πρὸς τὸ δεινὸν ἤλθεθ', 'did ye proceed to cruelty?' [Others, 'to the cruel deed.']

l. 518. διπλᾶ κ.τ.λ., 'thou wouldst have me reap a double profit of tears.' [Others, e.g. Jelf (583), take με as object of κερδ. ('win from me'); which seems unsupported.]

l. 519. παιδός, objective genitive.

l. 520. πρὸς τάφῳ θ', viz. ἔτεγξα.

l. 522. πρὸ τύμβου; see note on 37 sup. ἐπὶ σφαγάς, 'for the sacrifice': the acc., because παρῆν contains an idea of motion to.

l. 523. -έως=ηως; see sup. 24. χερός, 'by the hand'; partitive genitive; as in 543 inf. κώπης φάσγανον λαβών, and, though less directly, 1166 κόμης κατεῖχον.

l. 524. ἐγώ, sc. ἔστην (intrans.), out of ἔστησ' (trans.): cf. 520 πρὸς τάφῳ θ'. (The pres., fut., imperf., and 1st aor. of ἵστημι are trans.; the other tenses intrans.)

l. 526. μόσχου, cf. μόσχον 205 sup.; and πῶλον 144.

l. 528. αἴρει, 'raises aloft.' παῖς 'Ἀχιλλέως, Pyrrhus: called also Neoptolemus. [αἴρει: Kirchhoff, from the Marcianus. Vulg. ἔρρει: in the sense of χέω: for which Barnes cf. two senses of ruo: but the phrase seems really unsupportable. (N.B. ῥεῖ γάλα, etc., of a river, cannot be considered parallel.) ἐκχεῖ and αἱρεῖ have been suggested: Dind. ἐξέρραινε.]

l. 529. χοάς, acc. in appos. to sentence: [Weil, to δέπας. Others separate λαβ., δεπ., and αἴρ. χο.]

l. 530. σιγὴν κηρῦξαι, 'to command their silence.'

l. 531. παραστάς, 'standing forth': cf. παρα-βαίνω. [V. l., Vat. MS., καταστάς; Nauck, Weil.]

l. 532. σῖγα, the adverb; N.B. the accent: (σίγα, next line, the imperative.) ἔχω is more common than εἰμί with adverbs: but cf. inf. 732 ἐστὶν καλῶς.

l. 533. νήνεμον, proleptic: 'and I made the host stand breathless.'

l. 534. πατὴρ δ' ἐμός: cf. on 1127 inf. οὗτος. The nominative, with or without the article, is not infrequently used in a vocative sense, especially in commands.

l. 535. μοι, prob. not eth. dat., but dat. of person at whose hand a thing is received: [Pors.; cf. Hom. Il. ii. 186 δέξατό οἱ σκῆπτρον: a common Homeric construction. V. l. μου.]

l. 536. νεκρῶν ἀγωγούς, 'that evoke the dead'; νεκ., objective genitive: cf. καρδίας δηκτήρια 235 sup.

l. 537. ἀκραιφνές, 'virgin': derived from ἀκέραιος, ('unmixed'). Cf. Iph. Aul. 1574.

l. 539. λῦσαι, infinitive as acc. subs.,—object of δύς: see Appendix, p. 64. It goes, in slightly different ways, with πρυμ. and χαλ.; or, rather, these almost form one expression, a hendiadys. χαλινωτήρια, sc. ὅπλα, the hawsers that reined them in: poetical for πρυμνήσια, the stern-cables that fastened the ship ashore. [Cf. Pind. Pyth. iv. 25 θοᾶς Ἀργοῦς χαλινόν. Weil.]

l. 541. τυχόντας: acc., in spite of dat. ἡμῖν, because τυχ. really belongs to the infin., μολεῖν, which is a subs. in the acc. after δύς: τὸ τυχόντας μολεῖν = τὸ τυχεῖν καὶ μολεῖν. This 'attraction' of the participle is regular: but N.B. if the subject of the infin. be the subject of the main verb, the participle is nom. Cf. on ἐλθόντες. 244 sup.

l. 542. ἐπηύξατο: ἐπι- 'after him' (Neoptolemus): [cf. Hom. Il. xxii. 429 ὣς ἔφατο κλαίαν, ἐπὶ δὲ στενάχοντο πολῖται. V. l. ἐπεύξατο, see on sup. 18 ηὐτύχει.]

l. 543. κώπης, 'by the hilt': partit. gen.: cf. on 523 sup. χερός.

l. 546. ἐφράσθη, 'when she was ware of it,' 'noted it.' The middle form ἐφρασάμην is perhaps more common.

l. 549. παρέξω γάρ: on the absence of caesura (γάρ makes one word with παρέξω), see sup. 355.

l. 551. θεῶν, as one syll., θуῶν: see sup. 24 Ἀχιλλέως.

l. 552. κεκλῆσθαι. N. B. the infinitive: the participle would mean she actually was called.

l. 553. ἐπερρόθησαν, 'roared applause': metaphor from the waves on the shore. ἐπι-, lit. 'thereto': cf. sup. 542 ἐπ-ηύξατο.

ll. 555–6. ὑστάτην ὄπα, viz. μεθεῖναι παρθένον. οὗπερ, relative to ἐκείνου understood; which is genitive after ὄπα. [The lines are said to be spurious, from the resemblance to the Homeric οὗ κράτος ἐστὶ μέγιστον, and the unnatural position of οὗπερ.]

NOTES. LINES 532—583.

l. 558. λαβοῦσα κ.τ.λ., 'she took her robes and rent them from the top of the shoulder to the middle of her waist by the navel.'

l. 560. ὡς ἀγάλματος. [Cf. Aesch. Ag. 241 πρέπουσά θ' ὡς ἐν γραφαῖς.]

l. 562. πάντων τλημονέστατον, 'bravest words of all': i.e. bravest in the world; [or braver than all she had said or done before. τλ. (2) = ἀθλιώτατον, Schol.]

l. 563. τόδ', after παῖσον, Paley.

ll. 564-5. αὐχήν, 'neck'; λαιμός, 'throat.'

l. 566. οἴκτῳ κόρης : explaining how οὐ θέλων τε καὶ θέλων.

l. 567. πνεύματος διαρροάς, 'the channels of her breath.'

l. 568. κρουνοὶ δ' ἐχώρουν, 'and the springs of blood flowed': κρ. sc. αἵματος. ἡ δὲ κ.τ.λ.: cf. the death of Lucrece in Ovid, Fast. ii. 833 tum quoque jam moriens, ne non procumbat honeste, respicit: haec etiam cura cadentis erat.

l. 570. ἃ κρύπτειν ὄμμαϊ'. For the double acc. with κρύπτω, cf. Aesch. Prom. Vinc. 625 μή με κρύψῃς τοῦτο. Both are in a way direct accs.: cf. Lat. celo.

l. 571. ἀφῆκε πνεῦμα, 'had yielded up her breath.'

l. 574. φύλλοις ἔβαλλον, 'strewed her with leaves.' φυλλοβολία: especially of decking with leaves a winner in the games: perhaps referred to here: Schol. οἱ δὲ πληροῦσιν, 'others pile up:' [Kirchhoff. οἱ δ' ἐπληροῦσαν (Nauck); a form of the 1st aor. found only in O.T. and modern Greek.]

l. 575. ὁ δ' οὐ φέρων. οὐ is used where the article and participle refer to definite persons; μή, where to indefinite: the last being virtually hypothetic. Thus ὁ οὐ φέρων, the particular man who did not bear; ὁ μή τι δρῶν κακόν (inf. 608), anyone who (= if anyone) does no evil.

l. 576. τοιάδ' ἤκουεν κακά, 'received reproaches such as these.' κλύω and Lat. audio are also used in this sense, 'to be spoken of': cf. Hor. Sat. ii. 6. 20 matutine pater seu Jane libentius audis.

l. 577. ἕστηκας, 'dost thou stand still.'

l. 579. εἶ; not from εἰμί, 'I am,' but from εἶμι, 'I go.' εἰμί, I am,' the copula, is used analytically with the present, aorist, or perfect participle; but perhaps not with the future. Cf. on inf. 668 εἶ βλέπουσα.

l. 583. ἐπέζεσε, 'surges and boils against the house of Priam': ἐπιζέω, to 'boil over.' N. B. aor.; present momentary action, represented as past (Goodw. M. & T. § 19, n. 5): especially common with certain forms, e.g. ἐπῄνεσα. Cf. ἀπέπτυσ' inf. 1276, and

HECUBA.

see on sup. 511 τί λέξεις; [Or (2), as perf., 'hath surged up against';—on aor. used with perf. and pluperf. force, see Goodw. M. & T. § 19, note 4.]

l. 584. θεῶν ἀναγκαῖον τόδε, 'this is an unavoidable doom of the gods': θ. gen. of origin or cause,—almost ἐκ θεῶν: Weil. [Kirch. and Nauck, following Schol., destroy colon after τήμῇ.]

l. 586. ἦν γὰρ κ.τ.λ. ' If I put my hand to one evil, another doth not suffer me, and from that again some other grief calls me aside, bringing succession of new ills to old ': διάδοχος here having an almost active sense and being followed by an objective genitive, like καρδίας δηκτήρια 235 sup. [Cf. Suppl. 71 ἀγὼν . . γόων γ'οις διάδοχος.]

l. 589. τὸ μὲν σὸν κ.τ.λ.: lit. 'I cannot indeed wipe out thy sad fate from my heart so far as not to bewail it.' In sense, μέν belongs rather to μὴ στένειν, which is contrasted with λίαν (στένειν) 591.

l. 590. ἂν δυναίμην: see on 485 sup. ἂν ἐξεύροιμι.

l. 591. τὸ λίαν, sc. στένειν. παρεῖλες: παραιρέω, lit. 'take away from beside.'

ll. 592-602. [For the doctrine of φυσικὴ ἀρετή, given in ll. 592-8, and modified in ll. 599-602, cf. Aristot. Eth. vi. 13, where innate virtue is said to be useless, or even harmful, except in conjunction with prudence ,φρόνησις) ; for the unchanging character of the good man, ll. 597-8, cf. Arist. Eth. i. 10, 13 ; for the importance of early training, 600-1, cf. Eth. passim, e. g. x. 9 ; and for the theory that knowledge of evil may be acquired by exclusive study of the good, l. 602. cf. Plat. Rep. 409 E ἀρετὴ δὲ φύσεως παιδευομένης χρόνῳ ἅμα αὐτῆς τε καὶ πονηρίας ἐπιστήμην λήψεται. On the doctrines of Euripides as a moral teacher, and their relation to the charge of sophistry brought against him by Aristophanes, see Introd. p. 10.]

ll. 592-8. Divinely-ordered circumstance may change the produce of a soil, never the conduct of a man.

l. 592. δεινόν, ' a strange thing.'

l. 595. ἄνθρωποι δ' ἀεί: ' but ever with man,' etc.: broken up into two singulars, each followed by a singular verb. [ἄνθρωποι, Herm. emend.; Kirch. and Nauck. Others, ἐν βροτοῖς. MSS. ἀνθρώποις, local dat. 'among,' Jelf, 605. 2 : cf. on Θρῃξί inf. 1267.]

l. 598. διέφθειρε, gnomic aorist: cf. inf. 1194 ἀπώλοντ'.

l. 599. διαφέρουσιν: 'make the difference.' τροφαί, sc. αἱ τροφαί. [διαφ. (2) 'have they more weight '; ἤ, 'than.' The comparative value of heredity and early training is still disputed.]

30

NOTES. LINES 583—620.

l. 600. ἔχει δίδαξιν ἐσθλοῦ, 'containeth instruction of good.'

l. 602. κανόνι τοῦ καλοῦ μαθών, 'having learnt it by the standard of right': i.e. knowledge of a rule implies knowledge of what deviates from that rule. Cf. N.T., 'without the law I had not known sin.'

l. 603. καὶ ταῦτα κ.τ.λ.: Philosophy will not help me now.

l. 605. μοι, eth. dat. μηδένα: on the acc. following 'Ἀργείοις, see on τυχόντας 541 sup. εἴργειν: the subject is αὐτούς understood.

l. 607. ναυτική τ' ἀναρχία κ.τ.λ.: attacking, perhaps, extreme Athenian democracy: which was closely connected with the nautical population of the Piraeus.

l. 608. κακός, i.e. in the eyes of the lawless multitude. μή. see on 575 sup. ὁ δ' οὐ φέρων.

l. 610. ποντίας ἁλός, 'bring hither of the salt sea-water': partit. gen. [Weil, with βάψασα: 'dipped it in the sea.']

l. 612. νύμφην τ' κ.τ.λ., 'a bride unwedded and a wedded maid': i.e. as wedded to a dead man in her sacrifice to him; with no reference to any previous betrothal to Achilles: see on sup. 40. For the 'oxymoron,' cf. γάμος ἄγαμος Hel. 690, etc. [Cf. Seneca's Troy, desponsa nostris cineribus Polyxena: Weil. (2) As wedded to death; cf. sup. 368 "Ἀιδῃ προστιθεῖσ' ἐμὸν δέμας: (3) Dind., Matthiae, simply 'virgo infelix.']

l. 613. προθῶμαι, 'lay out.' In later Greece, the πρόθεσις was a fixed ceremony: the dead body was laid, richly dressed, on a bed, and the relations stood round, the women lamenting over it. ὡς μὲν ἀξία κ.τ.λ., 'as she deserveth, wherewithal? indeed I could not: but as best I can: what else is left to me?'

l. 614. πάθω, almost δράσω, but containing less personal agency.

l. 615. κόσμον, 'bravery.' τε, coupling κόσμον ἀγείρασ' to λαβοῦσα τεῦχος, sup. 609: [Pors., Weil; or to an idea of αὐτὴ διδοῦσα οἷα ἔχω in ὡς ἔχω, 614. τ': v.l. γ', Dind.; explaining ὡς ἔχω.]

l. 618. τι κλέμμα, 'somewhat stolen from,' etc.

l. 619. ὦ σχήματ' οἴκων, 'O stately halls.' Adjectival substantive: see on 21 sup. "Ἕκτορος ψυχή. [Paley, less probably, 'my own familiar home.']

l. 620. ὦ πλεῖστ' ἔχων κ.τ.λ. 'possessed of greatest, fairest, wealth; most blessed in thy children': [Herm.; or, not improbably, (2) destroying the comma; πλεῖστα κάλλιστά τ', sc. τέκνα, forming one idea with εὐτεκνώτατε, Weil; or (3) κάλλιστα alone qualifying εὐτεκνώτατε, Pors. Dind.: cf. Med. 1320 μέγιστον ἐχθίστῃ. V.l. 'Α,' κάλλιστα κευτεκνώτατε: Kirch.]

HECUBA.

l. 622. **ἐς τὸ μηδέν**, 'to naught': cf. Soph. Elect. 1000 κἀπὶ μηδὲν ἔρχεται. **φρονήματος**, 'proud estate': priv. gen. [τὸ μηδέν : cf. ὁ, ἡ, μηδέν, ὁ μηδείς, ὁ μὴ ὤν, etc. In these phrases μή may be more indefinite in grammar and more metaphorical in sense than οὐ; cf. Ant. 1325 τὸν οὐκ ὄντα μᾶλλον ἢ μηδένα (i.e. τὸν μὴ ὄντα), and the common μηδὲν εἶναι of the dead. But the two seem generally to be used indifferently; the choice between them being settled by mere sound, avoidance of hiatus, etc. Thus, in Aj. 1231 ὅτ' οὐδὲν ὢν τοῦ μηδὲν ἀντέστης ὕπερ, οὐδέν bears the sense of μηδέν here. See Jebb ad loc., and on Elect. 1166.]

l. 623. **εἶτα δῆτ' ὀγκούμεθα**, 'and then we are puffed up':—'we,' i.e. human beings; becoming general in statement.

l. 624. **ἐν**, like ἐπί, 'at,' 'because of': [Weil; or, perhaps, 'as living in.']

l. 626. **τὰ δ'**, viz. τιμή and πλοῦτος. **ἄλλως**, sc. ἔχει: 'are idle.'

l. 627. **κεῖνος** κ.τ.λ. [Cf. Ennius (?) ap. Cic. de Fin. ii. 13 nimium boni est, cui nihil est mali. Plato (Phileb. 43 d) discusses the question whether pleasure is the absence of pain; and Epicurus makes pleasure amount nearly to absence of pain: pleasure, in both contexts, being equivalent to happiness.]

l. 628. **μηδέν**, not οὐδέν, because ὅτῳ is indefinite, or contains a condition: cf. on sup. 282 & μὴ χρεών.

SECOND STASIMON, 629-657. **The Chorus bewail the judgment of Paris.**

Strophe, 629-637. *It was fated then that sorrow should befal me, when Paris prepared to sail over the sea for Helen, the fairest of women on whom the golden sun doth look.*

Antistrophe, 638-648. *Sorrow or worse slavery came to the whole land of the Simois from the folly of one Trojan, and the spears of the stranger. The judgment of the shepherd on Ida.*

Epode, 647-657, *has ended in death and ruin for me; while many a Spartan damsel, also, mourns therefrom, and many a Spartan mother smites her white head and tears her cheek for her sons that have perished.*

l. 629. **χρῆν**, 'it was fated': imperf. indic.: for the form see on 260 sup.

l. 631. **Ἰδαίαν**. Ida was a mountain near Troy.

l. 632. **Ἀλέξανδρος**. Alexander was a name given to Paris for his courageous protection of the shepherds on Mount Ida, with whom he was brought up. (ἀλέξω, with dat.. = to defend.

l. 634. **ναυστολήσων**. For the fut. partic., expressing purpose, see on 511 sup. ὡς θανουμένους.

NOTES. LINES 622—656.

l. 635. ἐπί, 'in quest of': [as in Hom. Od. v. 149 ἐπ' Ὀδυσσῆα ἤϊε.] τάν, sc. ἥν: see on sup. 473 γενεὰν τὰν κ.τ.λ. καλλίσταν, in translation, would appear in the main clause, agreeing with Ἑλένας.

l. 639. ἀνάγκαι, 'drudgeries,' or, 'evils of slavery': cf. on sup. 362 ἀνάγκαν σιτοποιόν.

l. 640. κοινόν, ἰδίας, 'evil for all from the folly of one.' [Herm. opposes ἰδίας, as 'domestic.' to ἀπ' ἄλλων, 'foreign.']

l. 641. Σιμουντίδι. The Simois and Scamander flow from Mount Ida, and meet in the Trojan plain.

l. 643. ἄλλων, the Greeks.

ll. 644-5. ἐκρίθη δ' ἔρις, ἃν κ.τ.λ.: 'the rivalry was decided, wherein,' etc. ἃν, cog. acc.; making, with κρίνει, one expression, which governs the direct accusative παῖδας. κρίνει, historic present. μακάρων παῖδας, 'daughters of the gods'; like υἷες Ἀχαιῶν, 'the sons of men,' etc. Eris, goddess of strife, not being invited to the marriage of Peleus and Thetis, avenged herself by throwing down among the assembled goddesses a golden apple, inscribed with the words, 'to the most fair.' Hera, Athena, and Aphrodite claimed the apple; and the herdsman, Paris, was selected to decide between them. He awarded it to Aphrodite, who in return enabled him to carry away Helen, the wife of Menelaus, from Sparta.

l. 647. ἐπί, a judgment 'fraught with,' etc. :—cf. inf. 842 ἐπ' αἰσχροῖς. ἐπί with the dative, of accompanying circumstances: here = result; more often = purpose.

l. 649. καί, viz. as well as the Trojans.—This passage is said to be an allusion to the capture of the Spartan hoplites in Sphacteria by Demosthenes and Cleon, 425 B.C.: see Introd., p. 5, on date of play. τις, 'many an one': [like the English colloquial 'one or two': cf. Hom. Od. xiii. 394 καί τιν' ᾧω αἵματί τ' ἐγκεφάλῳ τε παλάξεμεν ἄσπετον οὖδας.]

l. 650. Εὐρώταν. The Eurotas was the chief river in Laconia.

l. 653. τέκνων θανόντων, 'for her sons that are dead': gen. of cause, rather than gen. abs.

l. 656. δίαιμον τιθεμένα, i. e. αἱματοῦσα: for the periphrasis see on 111 sup., σφάγιον θέσθαι. N.B. middle, of self: contrast active, inf. 869 θήσω σε ἐλεύθερον, of someone else.

THIRD EPEISODION, 658-904. **The dead body of Polydorus is brought on the stage. Hecuba prepares for vengeance on Polymestor.**

(The attendant enters by the left-hand side-entrance: see Introd. p. 12.)

C   33

HECUBA.

l. 658. ΘΕΡ.: see sup. 609.
l. 659. θῆλυν: adjectives in -υs are sometimes of two terminations: cf. Il. xix. 97 "Ηρη, θῆλυς ἐοῦσα. Cf. ἥμισυς.
l. 660. στέφανον, 'the palm.'
l. 661. τί δέ; 'how now?' βοῆς, caus. gen. after τάλαινα.
l. 662. σου: as a fact the previous tidings had been brought by Talthybius: see sup. 484.
l. 663. Ἑκάβῃ: οὐχ ὑμῖν, whom it does not concern.
l. 664. εὐφημεῖν στόμα, 'to keep ill-sayings from their lips': στόμα, acc. of respect. [The meaning of εὐφημέω is best given in the line, σιγᾶν θ' ὅπου δεῖ καὶ λέγειν τὰ καίρια Aesch. Cho. 582. Cf. Hor. Od. iii. 1. 2 favete linguis; and ib. iii. 14. 11 male ominatis parcite verbis.]
l. 665. ὕπο, 'from within': cf. 53 sup. ὑπὸ σκηνῆς.   [One MS. as a variant: Dind. V. ll. ἄπο (most MSS., and ὕπερ; Pors., Herm., Nauck, Kirch., the last,—translated by some 'from within,' by others 'beyond the limit of.']
l. 666. ἐς καιρόν, sc. καιρίως: adverbial: cf. εἰς τάχος, etc. [See on πρὸς βίαν sup. 406.]
l. 667. κᾶτι μᾶλλον ἢ λέγω, 'nay, more than all-wretched.'
l. 668. εἰ βλέπουσα, sc. βλέπεις: εἰ, the copula; for the analytic tenses, see on εἰ δώσων sup. 579.   [.2) Schol. Herm., εἰ, the verb: 'no longer art thou alive, though thou seest the light'; cf. 683 inf. οὐκέτ' εἰμὶ δή. N.B. Difficulty in Greek from the same word doing duty as copula and verb of existence.]
l. 672. ἧς ἀπηγγέλθη κ.τ.λ.: 'whose burial, it was announced, was being busily prepared at the hand of all the Achaeans.'
l. 673. διὰ χερός, lit. 'by means of the hand,' almost χερί: cf. Soph. O. C. 470 δι' ὁσίων χειρῶν θιγών.   σπουδὴν ἔχειν, i. e. σπουδάζεσθαι.
l. 674. μοι, probably not dative of person addressed, but ethic dat.: 'ah me.'
l. 676. τὸ βακχεῖον κάρα, 'the inspired person.' For the periphrasis, see on sup. 21 "Εκτορος ψυχή.
l. 678. ζῶσαν λέλακας, 'she is alive whom thou bewailest'; λάσκω, lit. of a loud crashing or ringing sound: the perf. often appears to have almost a present signification. Cf. 1110 "Ηχω λέλακε.   ζῶσαν: the acc. is on the analogy of acc. after θρηνέω, etc. [Or, 'whose name has rung from thy lips.']
l. 679. γυμνωθέν, 'laid bare,' i. e. by the attendant, as is shown by 734 inf.
l. 680. εἰ, 'and see if.'

NOTES. LINES 658—717.

l. 682. οἴκοις, dat. of place: see on sup. 457 οἴκοις.

l. 683. οὐκέτ' εἰμὶ δή. 'all my life is gone from me': εἰμί, the verb. [See on 668 sup. οὐκέτ' εἰ βλέπουσα φῶς.]

ll. 685-7. κατάρχομαι νόμον κ.τ.λ., 'I lead off a Bacchic measure, lately instructed in my sorrows by the tormentor': κατάρχομαι: more often with genitive, but cf. Orest. 960 κατάρχομαι στεναγμόν. · βακχεῖον, i. e. frenzied. ἀλάστορος, i. e. the ghost of Polydorus: ἀλάστωρ, orig.=an avenging deity,—often with δαίμων. κακῶν, objective genitive: see on 235 sup. καρδίας δηκτήρια. [ἀλάστ.. Polyd.:—Schol.: cf. sup. 54 φάντασμα δειμαίνουσ' ἐμόν; 75 δι' ὀνείρων φοβερὰν ὄψιν ἔμαθον; and see l. 688. (2)=κακοῦ δαίμονος, Schol., Weil; 3)=ἐκ Πολυμήστορος, Schol. (with κακῶν? .]

l. 688. γάρ, 'what!', or 'then.'

l. 689. καινά, 'strange'; rather than 'new': cf. inf. 1038.

l. 691. οὐδέποτ' κ.τ.λ., i. e. οὐδέποτε στόνων καὶ δακρύων ἐπισχήσει: 'the day of my life will never be free from groans and tears': the verb being intrans., and the adjs. proleptic. [Others sc. με,—either (2) 'will dawn upon me'; or (3 v. ll. ἀστένακτον ἀδάκρυτον,—again proleptic,—'will stay me from groans and tears'; ἐπισχ. being trans.—MSS. ἁμέρα μ'.]

l. 695. θνήσκεις, not historic present, but 'what is the death you died?': cf. sup. on ἄγει 266.

l. 699. πέσημα: cf. Lat. cadaver.

l. 701. πόντου νιν κ.τ.λ., 'a sea-wave cast him up from the deep': πόντου after ἐξ-.

l. 702. ἔμαθον, 'I perceived'; i.e. at the time of the vision past, like παρέβα. [Others, 'I have learnt,' 'I know':—present the next words being parenthetic: Weil.]

l. 703. παρέβα, 'escaped me.'

l. 706. ἄν, ὄψιν.

l. 707. Διὸς ἐν φάει, 'in the light of day': cf. Lat. sub Jove, sub Divo.

l. 708. ὀνειρόφρων, 'from thy dream-wisdom.' [Cf. Aesch. Pers. 224 θυμόμαντις.]

l. 711. ἵν', either 'with whom'; or 'where,' i. e. in Thrace.

l. 713. τί λέξεις; 'what sayest thou?': cf. on sup. 511. [ἔχοι, Nauck; v.l. ἔχῃ, Dind.: for which see on 27 sup. ἔχῃ.]

l. 715. ξένων, 'between friends': i.e. genitive both subjective and objective. [Others, one or the other, alone:—'on the part of friends,' or 'towards friends.']

l. 717. κατάρατ' ἀνδρῶν, 'accursed among men': the genitive giving a superlative force to the adj.: cf. on sup. 193 ἀμέγαρτα κακῶν.

C 2   35

HECUBA.

l. 722. ὅστις ἐστί σοι βαρύς, 'whoever it be whose hand weigheth hard on thee.'

l. 724. ἀλλά, γάρ: ἀλλά, with τοὐνθένδε κ.τ.λ.; γάρ, with εἰσορῶ κ.τ.λ. (The ἀλλά clause is often omitted, so that ἀλλὰ γάρ seem to form one expression. The phrase is then rightly explained as an aposiopesis.) δέμας, 'form.' On periphr. see sup. 21 "Ἕκτορος ψυχή. [Cf. Orest. 107 Ἑρμιόνης δέμας; and Virg. Aen. vii. 650 quo pulchrior alter non fuit, excepto Laurentis corpore Turni.]

l. 725. τοὐνθένδε: crasis, τὸ ἐνθένδε, 'forthwith': lit. 'from here,' 'from now': for acc. see on τοὐπὶ σέ 514.

l. 726. μέλλεις, 'delayest.' [On the artistic point of Agamemnon's coming, see Introd., p. 10.]

ll. 727-8. ἐφ' οἷσπερ κ.τ.λ., 'in accordance with the message which Talthybius brought to me, that none of the Argives should lay hand on thy daughter': ἐφ' οἷσπερ = ἐπ' ἐκείνοις ἅπερ.

l. 729. μὲν οὖν, 'then': μέν answered by δέ; οὖν separate:—distinguish μὲν οὖν inf. 1261. οὐδὲ ψαύομεν.—N.B. violation of the cretic pause.—When a word ends in the middle of the fifth foot, that word must either (a) end in a short syllable (short, i. e. both by nature and position); or (b) be a monosyllable going closely with the subsequent word. [Cf. Ion 1. MSS. Ἄτλας, ὁ χαλκέοισι νώτοις οὐρανόν. Nauck conj. εἴωμεν οὐδ' ἐψαύομεν.]

l. 731. ἀποστελῶν: see on sup. 511 ὡς θανουμένους. τἀκεῖθεν, 'things there'; lit. 'from there.' i. e. what would come from there,' Weil. Cf. Lat. ex illa parte, ' on that side.'

l. 732. ἐστὶν καλῶς: on εἰμί with adverb, cf. on 532 σῖγα ἔστω. But καλῶς is, perhaps, partly an echo of εὖ. ['The word "well" cannot apply to sad things': Weil.]

l. 733. ἔα, 'ha!' ἐπὶ σκηναῖς, 'at,' i.e. 'near,' the tent.

l. 734. οὐ γὰρ Ἀργεῖον, sc. ὄντα. [V. l. Ἀργείων, Dind.; Herm., Ἀργεῖοι.]

l. 736. δύστην', addressing herself: δύστ. of two terminations. ἐμαυτὴν γάρ κ.τ.λ., viz. not Agamemnon or Polydorus. [v.2 Hecuba addresses Polydorus in δύστην', then turns the address on herself: Schol., Herm.]

ll. 737-8. δράσω: returning to the first person at once, as usual in Greek: cf. Eur. Med. 872, Soph. Aj. 864, etc. προσπέσω, φέρω, delib. conj. δράσω, prob. fut. indic. . γόνυ, after προσ-.

l. 739. μοι, eth. dat. ἐγκλίνασα κ.τ.λ., 'turning thy back upon our face.'

l. 740. δύρει: δύρομαι, poet. for ὀδύρομαι: cf. κέλλω and ὀκέλλω,

36

NOTES. LINES 722—767.

etc. [τίς ἔσθ' ὅδε; Dind. makes this an indirect question, explanatory of τὸ πραχθέν.]

l. 742. ἄν..ἄν. The repetition gives emphasis. It is not usual in so short a sentence. [Kirch., Nauck : one brings out ἄλγ., the other προσ., Weil. V. l. ἂν προσθείμεθα: Brunck, αὖ προσθείμεθ' ἄν. (Dind.,.]

l. 743. μή, hypoth.; with κλύων.

l. 744. ἐξιστορῆσαι, 'search out.' ὁδόν, 'drift,' 'course.'

l. 745. ἆρ' ἐκλογίζομαί γε κ.τ.λ., 'am I not too far accounting as hostile?': lit. putting down on the side of hostility: cf. 806 inf. ἐν αἰσχρῷ θέμενος: γε strengthens the question,—'can it be that.' [Or μᾶλλον, 'rather,' i.e. than on the side of friendship, a virtual positive: cf. on sup. 377 μᾶλλον εὐτυχέστερος.]

l. 748. ἐς ταὐτὸν ἥκεις, sc. ἐμοί: 'thou art at one with me:' cf. Orest. 1280. ἐγώ, sc. βούλομαι.

l. 750. τέκνοισι, dat. com. after τιμωρεῖν : Jelf 596. 1. (τιμ., act. or mid.: with acc., 'to punish' (see 756, 882,; with dat., 'to avenge.') στρέφω: 'why do I revolve these thoughts?': cf. Lat. volvo. [τί: Nauck, ποῖ, 'to what result.']

l. 752. γουνάτων, ' by thy knees': supplicatory genitive of cause: often preceded by πρός : [(2) partitive genitive, of the part touched in supplication : Jelf 536. obs. 5.]

l. 754. μῶν ἐλεύθερον αἰῶνα θέσθαι, 'to have thy life made free': N. B. the middle : contrast its force in 656 sup. δίαιμον τιθεμένα. μῶν, = μὴ οὖν, expecting negative answer: cf. Lat. num.

l. 755. ῥᾴδιον, τὸ τούτου τυχεῖν. In what way is not quite clear. Some, improbably, suggest, by suicide. Perhaps Agamemnon was ready to give her liberty, for the sake of Cassandra, or from respect to her own sorrows or old age.

l. 756. τιμωρουμένη, hypothetic, ' if I avenge myself on.' See sup. 749. [Nauck and Kirchhoff bracket 756-8 : they are wanting in two good MSS.]

l. 760. οὗ, causal genitive: 'for whom.' καταστάζω, trans.. ' drop'; contrast 241 sup. κατέσταζον, intrans., 'drip.'

l. 761. τὸ μέλλον, ' what thou art about to say': cf. the Eng. colloquialism, 'what is coming.'

l. 762. τοῦτόν ποτ' κ.τ.λ. : 'him I once brought forth and bare in my womb,' lit. 'beneath my girdle': a ὕστερον πρότερον.

l. 766. ἀνόνητά γ', 'yes, but (γε) to no profit.' Cf. sup. 246.

l. 767. πτόλις, the epic form of πόλις: cf. πτόλεμος. The explan. of the πτ. is doubtful.

HECUBA.

l. 768. ὀρρωδῶν θανεῖν, i.e. τὸ θανεῖν: 'dreading his own death.' Verbs of fearing are generally constructed with μή and the conj.

l. 770. ηὑρέθη: also εὑρέθη: see sup. 18 ηὐτύχει.

l. 771. Πολυμήστωρ: attracted into the relative clause: cf. inf. 987 Πολύδωρον. (Distinguish 'inverse attraction,'—the attraction of the case of the antecedent, which still remains in its own clause, into the case of the relative: e. g. ? Virg. Aen. i. 573 urbem quam statuo vestra est. Jebb, ad Soph. O. C. 1227, denies its existence.)

l. 772. πικροτάτου, 'most cruel.'

l. 776. τοιαῦτ', 'even so.' ἐπειδὴ κ.τ.λ.: i. e. because he would then be required to give up the gold ,see sup. 11, 12 ; or because he could then safely take it.

l. 779. ἄλλον πόνον, cog. acc.: of. ἂν κρίνει 644 sup.

l. 782. θαλασσόπλαγκτόν γ': proleptic: 'yes, to be tossed by the sea.'

l. 783. πόνων, for causal gen., cf. sup. 661 τάλαινα βοῆς.

l. 784. λοιπόν, 'left unborne.'

ll. 785-6. δυστυχής, τύχην: τύχην, i.e. δυστυχίαν. [Cf. Trabea, ap. Cic. Tusc. Disp. in. 31 fortunam ipsam anteibo fortunis meis: Weil.]

l. 789. στέργοιμ' ἄν, 'I will be content': mild future. [Lit., 'would be content,' referring to an implied protasis εἰ ταῦτα πάσχοιμι: while the protasis εἰ δοκῶ 'belongs as a condition to the expressed apodosis *with* its implied protasis': Goodw. M. & T. 54. 1 a. See on sup. 485.]

l. 790. ἀνδρός, added in aversion: cf. the Lat. homo.

ll. 793-4. κοινῆς τραπέζης κ.τ.λ., 'though he often received hospitality from me, and entertainment, first in account, of all my friends.' ἐμοί: dat. of giver, like μοι 535: rather than after κοιν. τραπ. ξενίας, part. gen. after τυχών. πρῶτα: adverbial; cf. Hom. Od. xvii. 155 πρῶτα θεῶν. [So Wakefield. Others ξεν. after ἀριθ. : and some, even, πρῶτα acc. after τυχ. Pors. emend. πρῶτος ὤν. From the redundancy and peculiarity of these ,lines, some reject 793-4; others 794-5; others, the whole passage, 794 7.]

l. 795. λαβὼν προμηθίαν, 'taking forethought': see inf. 1136 ἔκτεινά νιν σοφῇ προμηθίᾳ. [And cf. Aesch. Suppl. 178. Others, 2 , 'having received all care.' Herm., προθυμίαν.]

l. 796. εἰ κτανεῖν ἐβούλετο, i.e. 'as he should, if he wished to kill him.'

l. 798. ἴσως, 'it may be.'

ll. 799-801. ἀλλ' οἱ θεοὶ κ.τ.λ., 'but the gods are strong, and their all-powerful law: for it is by the law we show our belief in the gods: we define for ourselves justice and injustice, and so live.' κείνων: subj. gen. νόμῳ: dat. of means or manner. ἡγούμεθα,

NOTES. LINES 768—818.

'believe in,' 'acknowledge': often with εἶναι: cf. νομίζω.   ζῶμεν becomes, in transl., subordinate.   ὡρισμένοι : in middle sense.   [So Schol. and Weil, practically : though Schol., sc. κρατεῖν or σθένειν with τοὺς θεούς; Weil, κείνων, objec. gen. ('the law governs the gods, because it is the basis upon which depends our belief in the gods.')— Paley, however, νόμος, 'convention' (κειν. obj. gen.): referring to the sophistic theory that religion is a state-matter, conventional and subjective; for which cf. Plat. Theaet., Aristot. Eth. v. 7; also, Pindar, ap. Hdt. iii. 38 νόμος πάντων βασιλεύς.]

l. 802. ὅς, sc. ὁ νόμος.   εἰς σ' ἀνελθών : not merely 'when referred to thee,' but 'when it comes up before thee,'—for judgment or for mercy.   διαφθαρήσεται, 'it shall be impaired.'

l. 804. φέρειν, 'carry off what is sacred to the gods'; the robbery of a friend's deposit being compared to robbery of temple-treasure. [Others, merely, 'violate,' etc., of sacrilege generally (Weil).— Hermann imagines a reference to some particular event of the day.]

l. 805. ἴσον, 'just ': lit. 'equal,' referring to equality of offence and punishment.

l. 806. ἐν αἰσχρῷ θέμενος, 'accounting them disgraceful': placing them in the class of disgraceful things : cf. 745 sup. ἐκλογίζομαι πρὸς τὸ δυσμενές.

l. 807. ἀποσταθείς, 'standing back, for a general view': with γραφεύς.   [Eur. is said to have studied painting (Suidas); but there is not much support for the statement : Weil.]

l. 809. ἀλλὰ νῦν, sc. εἰμί. The final verb is varied in the next line by a participle.

l. 812. ποῖ μ' κ.τ.λ., 'whither dost thou withdraw thy foot from me?' με acc., κατὰ σύνεσιν, after ὑπ. ποδ., which together make one expression, equivalent to φεύγεις: [Herm. Porson, improbably, quo meum pedem subducis?, i. e. quo me cogis te sequi?]

l. 813. ἔοικα πράξειν οὐδέν, 'methinks I shall effect nothing.'

l. 814. μαθήματα, cog. acc.

l. 816. πειθώ, acc. after μανθάνειν.   τὴν τύραννον μόνην : N.B. irregular position of the article, which should precede μόνην: see Jebb on Ajax 573 ὁ λυμεὼν ἐμός.   ἀνθρώποις, possessive dative : cf. on 1267 inf. ὁ Θρῃξὶ μάντις.   [τύραννον : especially in democracies.   Cf. o flexanima atque omnium regina oratio Cic. Or. ii. 44, quoting from the Hermione of Pacuvius.]

l. 817. ἐς τέλος, 'unto perfection': τελέως : with μανθ. Cf. inf. 1193 διὰ τέλους.

l. 818. μισθοὺς διδόντες μανθάνειν, referring to the later schools of the sophists, some of whom, e. g. Gorgias, Antiphon, taught

HECUBA.

rhetoric. Euripides himself studied under the rhetorician Prodicus. ἵν' ἦν, 'that so a man might': the indic. implies impossibility of fulfilment; cf. Hippol. 647 ἵν' εἶχον μήτε προσφωνεῖν τινα. [ἵν' ἦν: Elmsley conject. for MS. ἵν' ᾖ. 'The secondary tenses of the indic., after ἵνα, denote that the end or object is dependent on some unfulfilled condition, and, therefore, is not or was not attained': Goodw. M. & T. 44. 3.]

l. 819. βούλοιτο, optat. of indefinite scope or frequency.   τυγχάνειν, ' to win his point.'

l. 820. τις, ' one ': i. e. I ; as in colloquial English.   ἐλπίσαι: the form in -ειε is more common in Attic Greek.

l. 821. οἱ μὲν γὰρ ὄντες, ' the children who were ':   [Kirch., Nauck.—V. l. οἱ μὲν τοσοῦτοι (Dind. , ' my noble children,' or, ' all my children.' Perhaps, οἱ μέν ποτ' ὄντες (Weil); or οἱ μὲν τότ' ὄντες: cf. sup. 769 τῶν τότ' ὄντων τέκνων.]

l. 822. ἐπ' αἰσχροῖς, ' for unseemly offices '; or ' to my disgrace ': cf. sup. on 647 ἐπὶ λώβᾳ.   οἴχομαι, ' am lost,' ' undone.'

l. 823. τόνδ', ' yonder.'   Troy was less than twenty miles from the nearest point of the Thracian Chersonese.

ll. 824-5. καὶ μὴν κ.τ.λ., ' moreover—this, perhaps, is a vain point in my discourse   to bring forward the plea of love, but yet—': καὶ μήν, with πρὸς σοῖσι κ.τ.λ.: the words between being parenthetic.

l. 827. ἣν καλοῦσι κ.τ.λ., not necessarily implying that she had another name among the Greeks, like Pyrrhus (Neoptolemus) or Paris (Alexander); but perhaps merely a tragic periphrasis—due to her divine character, and, possibly, met. grat.—for Cassandra. [Herm. emend. Κασάνδρα, ' Cassandra, as the Phrygians call her.'— The Schol., quoting Lycophron, says that she was originally called Alexandra, and that Cassandra was a later name, given in honour of the nobleness of her brother Hector.]

l. 828. ποῦ, ' wherein ': almost πῶς.   δείξεις, ' will you recognise,' ' acknowledge ': like the colloquial, ' what have you to show for?'

l. 830. χάριν, ' profit,' ' thanks.'   ἕξει, ' receive ' : generally χάριν ἔχειν = to feel gratitude.

ll. 831-2. φίλτρων, ' charms of love.'   χάρις, prob. i. e. 'thanks.' as sup. 830 ; not ' delight.'   [τῶν τε κ.τ.λ., (1) v. l. τῶν τε νυκτέρων πάνυ, (Dind.); πάνυ, either adjectival with φίλτρων, or adverbial with μεγίστη; (2) τῶν τε νυκτερησίων: Nauck conj., Weil; (3) νυκτέρων τ' ἀσπασμάτων, Dind. conj., φιλτρ., with χαρ.). Kirch. and Nauck reject the lines as spurious.]

NOTES. LINES 818—847.

l. 834. κηδεστήν: as brother of Cassandra.
l. 835. δράσεις, sc. καλῶς. ἑνός, 'one thing yet': privative genitive.
l. 836. εἴ μοι, 'would that': cf. the Eng. 'if only,' and Lat. si modo.—Such phrases 'were originally protases with the apodosis suppressed': Goodw. 83 Remark. Contrast ὠφείλομεν sup. 395, where the protasis is implied.
l. 837. κόμαισι: perhaps 'my grey hair': [Herm. Musgr. conj. κνήμαισι; Wakefield, κύραισι.]
l. 838. Δαιδάλου τέχναισιν: cf. Hor. Od. iv. 2. 2 ope Daedalea. Daedalus was said to have made wooden automata which moved and spoke: cf. Eur. Eurysth. frag. τὰ Δαιδάλεια πάντα κινεῖσθαι δοκεῖ βλέπειν τ' ἀγάλματα; but he is perhaps only mentioned here as the personification of mechanical craft: being chiefly known in mythology for the construction of the Cnossian labyrinth, in which the Minotaur was kept, and for the manufacture of wings for himself and his son Icarus. [The story of the wooden figures was a myth originating in the fact that Daedalus was the first to open the eyes and separate the limbs of statuary: Schol., Weil.]
l. 839. ἔχοιντο: optat., attracted to γένοιτο: [Jelf 808.— 'The subjunctive (or future indicative) is generally used when the leading verb is an optative referring to the future': Goodw. M. &. T. 34. 2.]
l. 840. ἐπισκήπτοντα κ.τ.λ., 'urging every plea upon thee.'
l. 842. παράσχες [Brunck. Most MSS. παράσχε: cf. Herc. Fur. 1211 κατάσχε. Both forms seem admissible, esp. in compounds. See Veitch: sub ἔχω.]
l. 843. εἰ καί, 'though she be nought': see on sup. 318 κεί. ἀλλ' ὅμως, sc. πίθου: cf. the English aposiopesis, 'but still,'— which, however, is not generally used in imperatival sentences.
l. 844. ἐσθλοῦ ἀνδρός: 'it is the part of a good man': possessive gen.
ll. 846-7. δεινόν γε κ.τ.λ., 'it is strange how all things fall out with men, and the laws determine the necessities of a case.' συμπίτνει, cf. συμβαίνει. τὰς ἀνάγκας: 'forced situations,' Weil: what we must do: e. g. that Hec. must appeal to her enemy, Ag., against her friend, Polym.: and that Ag. must help her. οἱ νόμοι, e. g. that a murderer, like Polymestor, should be punished, or that a man should regard the interests of his wife or concubine, as Agamemnon those of Cassandra (Weil). διώρισαν, gnomic aorist. [συμπ.: (2) 'fall in with one another,' Paley; (3) 'clash

HECUBA.

together;' (4) collabuntur, Herm. τὰς ἄν. (2) ties of affection: Lat. necessitudines. οἱ νόμ.: Brunck, Musgr., οἱ χρόνοι.]
l. 848. τοὺς τε. For the lateness of τε, cf. on inf. 854 σοί τ' ἔχειν: [and the position of 'que' in the Latin pentameter, e.g. Ov. Fast. iv. 178 ante oculos opposuitque manum. V. l. γε, Herm.]
l. 849. ποιούμενοι, 'making,' rather than 'regarding.'
l. 851. δι' οἴκτου ἔχω, 'I regard with pity': cf. δι' αἰσχύνης ἔχω Iph. Taur. 683.
l. 852. θεῶν, monosyl. by syniz., θyῶν: see sup. 24 'Ἀχιλλέως.
ll. 854-5. εἴ πως φανείη γ' κ.τ.λ., 'if by any means a way were open to satisfy you, and I should not be thought,' i.e. without my being thought, etc., γε corrects and limits the previous statement. φανείη, δόξαιμι, as if βουληθείην ἄν had preceded. The optatives express a sudden doubt. ὥστε: Agamemnon is thinking of the result (if in any way it should seem possible that). τε, as if ἐμὲ δύξαι were to follow, to which σοί ἔχειν would thus be coupled: as the lines stand, τε would naturally follow φανείη.
l. 857. ἔστιν γὰρ ᾗ, 'for there is a point in which' etc. ἔστιν may be combined with a relative to form one absolute expression, regardless of time or number, e.g. ἔστιν οἵ, ἔστιν οὕς, etc.
l. 859. εἰ δὲ σοί: [Dind. Elmsley conjectures εἰ δ' ἐμοί: followed by Nauck, Kirch.]
l. 860. χωρὶς τοῦτο, 'this is apart,' a private matter.
l. 861. πρὸς ταῦτα, 'looking to this,' 'on this idea.'
l. 863. 'Ἀχαιοῖς: dat. of agent. διαβληθήσομαι, though future in tense, implies a present necessity, 'if I am to be'; and so is joined with the present ἔχεις: Goodw. M. & T. 49. 1, n. 3.
l. 864. θνητῶν, partit. gen., not after a supposed τις, but after ὅστις κ.τ.λ. The antecedent, in such cases, is not understood, but is contained in the relative clause, which has become a substantive: Goodw. G. G. 152. ὅστις: indefinite: cf. Lat. nemo est qui, and subj.
l. 866. πόλεος: poet. for πολέως. νόμων γραφαί, probably not a reference (Paley) to the γραφὴ παρανόμων (law against unconstitutional measures), but merely equivalent to οἱ γεγραμμένοι νόμοι.
l. 867. εἴργουσι κ.τ.λ., 'constrain him to order his goings contrary to his judgment': εἴργ., lit. hinder him so that he does. χρῆσθαι τρόποις, 'adopt a line of action,' or, perhaps, 'a temper.' [Others consider μή the usual 'redundant negative' with the infinitive after verbs of preventing: but this, from its position, is unnatural.]

NOTES. LINES 847—898.

l. 868. πλέον νέμεις, 'pay too much heed,' 'tribute': nimium tribuis.
l. 869. θήσω ἐλεύθερον, the Eng. 'set free:' see on 656 δίαιμον τιθεμένα. φόβου, priv. gen. after ἐλεύθ.
l. 870. ξύνισθι, 'be privy to it.'
l. 872. ἐπικουρία: not necessarily as a Greek ally: Paley.
l. 874. εἶργε κ.τ.λ., 'stay it, but appear not to do it for my sake': μή, not οὐ, because the participle continues the imperatival notion: ἀλλὰ μὴ δόξῃς. ἐμὴν χάριν, adverb. acc.: cp. 1243;—ἐμήν, objective, sc. ἐμοῦ.
l. 878. τίνι, interrog. N.B. accent: (enclyt. = τινί.)
l. 880. κεκεύθασι, 'hide'; lit. have taken into hiding. The 'perfects with present signification' may often be so explained: e. g. novi, οἶδα.
l. 881. εἶπας: momentary aorist: see on sup. 583 ἐπέζεσε.
l. 882. φονέα: N.B. ᾱ: acc. of words in -ευς generally being ᾱ: but cf. φονέᾱ Eur. Electr. 599, 763. τιμωρήσομαι: with acc., see on 756 sup.
l. 883. καὶ πῶς, exactly the Eng. incredulous 'and how': contrast πῶς καί 515, emphatic. ἀρσένων, prob. objective gen., 'power over'; not subjective, 'power of.'
l. 885. μέμφομαι, 'I think not highly of.' μέμφομαί τινί τι is a more common construction.
l. 886. εἶλον, 'killed'; as often in Homer. The fifty sons of Aegyptus were put to death by their brides, the daughters of Danaus, on the bridal-night. Only Lynceus was spared,—by Hypermnaestra, the 'splendide mendax' of Hor. Od. iii. 11. 35.
l. 887. καὶ Λῆμνον κ.τ.λ. When the Argonauts landed at Lemnos, they found it peopled only by women: these had put to death their husbands and fathers for marrying Thracian wives. The crime afterwards became proverbial: [cf. Aesch. Cho. 633 ἤκασεν δέ τις τὸ δεινὸν αὖ Λημνίοισι πήμασι; and Hdt. ii. 138 νενόμισται ἀνὰ τὴν Ἑλλάδα τὰ σχέτλια ἔργα πάντα Λήμνια καλέεσθαι.]
l. 888. ὣς, 'so be it,' οὕτως: mostly in Hom. and Hdt.; but cf. 441 sup.
l. 889. μοι, ethic dat.: 'I pray thee give safe conduct' etc.
l. 890. καὶ σύ: addressing the γυναῖκα,—prob. the same as in 657 sup., who has never quitted the scene: Weil. πλαθεῖσα, 'drawing near': from πλάθω, collat. form of πελάω.
l. 892. χρέος, adverb. acc.; cf. sup. 874 ἐμὴν χάριν.
l. 895. ἐπίσχες, 'delay': here trans.; often intrans.
l. 897. μέριμνα: abstract for concrete. μητρί: eth. dat.
l. 898. καὶ γάρ: 'for surely': καί emphasises what follows γάρ: Jelf 786, obs. 8.

HECUBA.

l. 900. νῦν δ', 'but now,' i. e. but as it is; argumentative, not temporal.

l. 901. πλοῦν ἐρῶντας ἥσυχον, 'watching for a quiet voyage.' But ὁράω, in this sense, is strange; and ἥσυχος is rarely used of things. [Some, therefore, regard ἥσυχον as an adverb, 'inactively'; Hartung suggests ἡσύχους; Hermann, ὁρῶντά μ'. Perhaps, πλοῦν ὁρῶντ' ἀμήχανον: though the ellipse of the participle is doubtful.]

l. 902. κοινόν, 'a thing that toucheth all.' πᾶσι: eth. dat.

THIRD STASIMON, 905-952. **The Chorus describe the fall of Troy.**

First Strophe, 905-913. *City of Troy, no longer shalt thou be numbered among the untaken: so great a cloud of spears covers thee about. Thou hast been shorn of thy coronet of battlements and smirched with smoke. Alas, never again shall I set foot in thee.*

First Antistrophe, 914-922. *It befel at midnight. My lord, ceasing from feast and song and sacrifice, lay in the chamber: for he saw no longer the host of the invader.*

Second Strophe, 923-932. *And I was tiring my hair for rest before the golden mirror, when, lo, a tumult rose in the city, and a cry, 'Children of Hellas, when will ye capture Ilium and return home?'*

Second Antistrophe, 933-942. *And I left my bed, single-robed, vainly entreating Artemis; and was carried away captive over the sea, fainting with grief.*

Epode, 943-952. *Cursed be Helen and Paris, whose unholy marriage has exiled me from home.—May Helen never return to the house of her fathers!*

l. 906. τῶν ἀπορθήτων κ.τ.λ. Troy, being built by the divine hands of Poseidon, was considered impregnable. A reference is perhaps intended to Athens, 'the uncaptured': cf. Aesch. Pr. 350, Med. 827, Soph. Oed. Col. 702; Paley. ἀπορθήτων, partit. gen.; sc. πολέων: which would be expected for πόλις. λέξει. N.B. fut. mid. in passive sense: admissible only in certain verbs; cf. τιμήσεσθαι, ἀδικήσεσθαι.

l. 907. νέφος: for the metaphor, which is here further expanded in κρύπτει, cf. the Eng. phrase, 'a cloud of cavalry.' ἀμφὶ κρύπτει, tmesis.

l. 910. ἀπό . . κέκαρσαι: tmesis. στεφάναν, acc. after ἀποκ., corresponding to the direct accusative after an active verb.

l. 911. πύργων, battlements, or walls, rather than towers. Cf. στεφάνωμα πύργων Soph. Ant. 124.

ll. 911-12. κατὰ . . κέχρωσαι: tmesis. κηλίδα: cog. acc.: cf., in

44

NOTES. LINES 900—927.

Eng., to be painted a colour. (Distinguish from the acc. στεφάναν sup. 910.) [Vulg. οἰκτροτάτᾳ:—κηλῖδ', i.e. κηλῖδι; but it is doubtful if the final ι of the dative can be elided.]

l. 914. ὠλλύμαν, like ὄλωλα (and 'pereo' in Plautus), in metaphorical sense: used especially of captivity. [μέσον.: on capture of Troy at night, cf. Schol., from the 'Lesser Iliad' of Lesches, νὺξ μὲν ἔην μέσση, λαμπρὰ δ' ἐπέτελλε σελήνη: Paley.]

l. 915. ἦμος, Homeric. ἐκ, 'after': cf. on 55 sup. ἐκ τυραννικῶν δόμων.

l. 916. ἄπο: παύω usually takes genitive alone. καταπαύσας, in middle sense of καταπαυσάμενος: cf. 1061 inf. ἐξαλλάξω. θυσιᾶν, i.e. perhaps for end of war: -ᾶν, Doric form of gen. plur. of fem. nouns of 1st decl., -ῶν. [ἄπο: cf. Xen. Lac. 3. 1 παύειν τινα ἀπὸ παιδαγωγῶν; and, with ἐκ, Soph. El. 987 παῦσον ἐκ κακῶν ἐμέ. Some confine καταπ. to θυσ., regarding ἄπο as equiv. to ἀναχωρήσας; some, improbably, make καταπ. trans., sc. ἐμέ. V. l. χαροποιὸν θυσίαν. Nauck, Kirch.: prob. alone with καταπ., Weil ἄπο, as sup., ἀναχωρήσας). V. l. Dind. χοροποιῶν.]

l. 920. ξυστὸν κ.τ.λ., 'his spear-shaft on the peg': parenthetic: sc. ἦν, Schol., Weil.

l. 921. ναύταν κ.τ.λ., 'no longer beholding the sea-man company that had set foot in Ilian Troy.'—The Greek fleet had retired to Tenedos, leaving behind them only the wooden horse, with the body of men concealed in it. ναύταν, adjectival: cf. δούλων σφαγίων 137 sup., and Virg. Georg. ii. 145 bellator equus. Τροίαν 'Ιλιάδ', the district: generally Ἴλιος, or Τροία, the town; Τρωάς, the district. [ὁρῶν, (2) 'looking for': see on ὁρῶντας 901. sup. ἐμβεβῶτα, (2) pred.: praesentem, Paley; perhaps (3) 'which had all the while set foot in Troy,' i.e. in the town, by means of the wooden horse.]

ll. 923-6. ἐγὼ δὲ κ.τ.λ., 'I was tiring my tresses in the bands of my snood, gazing into the glittering depths of the golden mirror.' ἀναδέτοις, probably active, 'binding up the hair'; not passive, 'bound on' (i.e. tied under the chin, Paley): though the last conforms better to the use of verbals in -τος. μίτραισιν: cf. Ar. Thesm. 257 μίτρας, ἣν ἐγὼ νύκτωρ φορῶ: where it is used in the singular. ἀτέρμονας αὐγάς: lit. limitless rays, i.e. deep vista: [the words seem to suggest both the actual multiplying of objects in a mirror and the imaginary infinity of a through-the-looking-glass world. Schol., ἀτέρμ., because the ἔνοπτρον was κυκλοτερές; Herm., because of the brightness of the metal.]

l. 927. ἐπιδέμνιος, 'couched'; proleptic. [Pors., ἐπιδέμνιον, 'my cushioned bed.']

HECUBA.

l. 928. ἀνά, with ἔμολε, by tmesis, ἀνέμολε; like ἐκ δὲ πηδήσας 1172 inf.

l. 931. τὰν Ἰλιάδα σκοπιάν, Pergamus, the acropolis of Troy.

l. 933. μονόπεπλος, 'single-robed.' The πέπλος was strictly a woman's outer garment, corresponding to the man's ἱμάτιον; but see next note. [The scene is described by Q. Smyrnaeus, xiii. 109 sqq.]

l. 934. Δωρὶς ὡς κόρα. The Spartan damsels wore a Doric χιτών, with no other dress over it. The χιτών was really an undergarment: the Ionian being a long linen dress with sleeves; the Dorian short, woollen, and without sleeves.

l. 935. προσίζουσ', 'sitting down before holy Artemis'; i.e. in supplication, at her temple, to which the Trojan women had fled for refuge.

l. 936. οὐκ ἤνυσ', 'effected nothing by my prayer': cf. inf. 1167 οὐδὲν ἤνυον. Ἄρτεμιν: Artemis, with Apollo, took the side of the Trojans in the Trojan war. [Ἄρτ.; as patroness of women; Paley. Dind., following Schol., imagines further allusion to the Dorian women, who especially worshipped Artemis.]

l. 939. τ', coupling ἄγομαι and ἀπεῖπον: [Paley; (2) ἰδοῦσ' and ἀπόσκ. Herm., Matthiae, Weil, consider τάλαιν', ἀπεῖπον ἄλγει parenthetic.]

l. 940. πόδα, prob. not technical, 'sheet' (Lat. pes); but metaphorical, 'foot': 'stirred its returning steps,' Weil. See on inf. 1020 λῦσαι πόδα.

l. 942. ἀπεῖπον, 'I fainted for grief': ἀπ. intrans.; gen. trans., deny, renounce, 'give up.'

l. 943. τοῖν Διοσκόροιν, Castor and Pollux, born from one of Leda's two eggs; Helen being born from the other.

l. 945. αἰνόπαριν: cf. Hom. Il. iii. 39 δύσπαρι. κατάρᾳ διδοῦσ', 'devoting to curses.'

l. 946. ἐπεί, 'seeing that.' 'since.'

l. 947. ἀπώλεσεν, in pregnant sense: 'drave me, ruined, from,' etc.

l. 948. γάμος, οὐ γάμος κ.τ.λ.: cf. inf. 1121 ἀπώλεσ', οὐκ ἀπώλεσ', ἀλλὰ μειζόνως.

l. 950. ἄν. sc. Ἑλέναν; becoming, with ἴκοιτο, ἥ.

EXODUS, ll. 953-1295. **Hecuba murders Polymestor's children and puts out his eyes. Polymestor is exiled by Agamemnon to a desert island.**

(Polym. enters by the left-hand side-door: see Introd., p. 12.)

l. 953. Πρίαμε. N.B. the address to the dead Priam. [Nauck regards it as unnatural, and condemns the verse.]

NOTES. LINES 928—976.

ll. 956-7. οὐκ ἔστιν οὐδέν κ.τ.λ., 'nothing is certain, neither good repute, nor yet that when a man fares well he shall not some time in turn fare ill.' οὐκ, οὐδέν form one strong negative. καλῶς πράσσοντα κ.τ.λ., sc. τὸ καλ. πράσ. κ.τ.λ., 'the idea that' etc.: nom. infin. αὖ, by a reverse of fortune; with πράξειν κακῶς.

l. 958. αὐτά, sc. τὸ καλῶς πράττειν, and τὸ κακῶς πράττειν.

l. 959. ἀγνωσίᾳ, sc. of the future : causal dative.

l. 961. προκόπτοντ' κ.τ.λ.: 'making no way ahead in evils': a common metaphor from pioneers clearing the way before an advancing army. κακῶν, partit. gen. after τὸ πρόσθεν, 'ahead in evils'; not 'ahead of evils': [cf. Plat. Rep. 550 C προϊόντες ἐς τὸ πρόσθεν τοῦ χρηματίζεσθαι; or, perhaps, partit. gen. after προκόπτοντ': see Prof. Jowett on Thuc. iv. 60. 2, vii. 56. 3.]

l. 962. τῆς ἐμῆς ἀπουσίας, partit. gen. after τι ('anything in' etc.): [cf. Thuc. i. 84. 1 ὃ μέμφονται μάλιστα ἡμῶν. Or gen. of cause ; τι being adverbial, and ἐμέ, understood, the object of μέμφει.]

l. 963. σχές, the Eng. 'hold!': so also ἔχε. The intransitive use may be explained grammatically by an ellipse of σεαυτήν or τὸ μέμφεσθαι. Cf. ἐπίσχες. τυγχάνω, ἦλθες : cf. sup. 21 ἀπόλλυται, κατεσκάφη.

ll. 964-5. ἐπεὶ δ' ἀφικόμην κ.τ.λ., 'but when I returned, even as I was lifting my foot from out the house'; i. e. to come to thee, Weil.

l. 966. ἐς ταὐτὸν συμπίτνει, 'falls in with me': one expression, ἐς ταὐτόν amplifying συμ-.: [Schol.; cf. Plat. Rep. 473 D. Others take ἐς ταὐτόν with αἴροντι, 'for this same purpose.']

ll. 970-2. αἰδώς μ' ἔχει, sc. τούτου, 'at him.' τυγχάνουσα, i. e. οὖσα: construe. ad sens., as if αἰδοῦμαι had preceded. προσβλέπειν, sc. τοῦτον. ὀρθαῖς κόραις, 'with straight eyes': the Eng. 'straight in the face': cf. Iph. A. 856 ὀρθοῖς ὄμμασιν. [So Kirch., Weil, omitting σ' after προσβλέπειν (Dind.), with the best MS. τυγχ., cf. Soph. El. 313 νῦν δ' ἀγροῖσι τυγχάνει ; (2) sc. τούτου, 'meeting him.' Nauck brackets τυγχάνουσ' . . δυναίμην : others, all three lines.]

l. 973. αὐτό, sc. τὸ μὴ δύνασθαι προσβλέπειν κ.τ.λ. σέθεν, objective genitive, 'ill-will toward thee.'

l. 974. ἄλλως, 'besides': contrast sup. 302.

l. 975. γυναῖκας κ.τ.λ., not after αἴτιον, but explanatory of νόμος: ὁ νόμος ὁ τοῦ γυναῖκας κ.τ.λ., 'the rule that' etc.

l. 976. τίς χρεία σ', sc. ἔχει. [The full phrase occurs Soph. Phil. 646 ὅτου σε χρεία .. ἔχει. Cf. Hom. τίπτε δέ σε χρεώ Od. i. 225, etc.; where the full Homeric phrase suggests rather an ellipse of ἵκει or γίγνεται.]

HECUBA.

l. 977. **τί χρῆμ'** κ.τ.λ., 'for what matter didst thou summon my steps from home?' τί χρῆμ': adverb. acc., like χάριν 874 sup. ἐπέμψω: N.B. middle: 'had me sent for' (causal); also, 'to come to thee':—almost μετεπέμψω, [as in Soph. O. C. 602. πόδα: for the periph., cf. Hipp. 661 σὺν πατρὸς μολὼν ποδί, Weil.]

l. 978. **πρὸς σὲ εἰπεῖν**: see sup. 217 πρὸς σὲ σημανῶν ἔπος.

l. 982. **φίλη μὲν** κ.τ.λ.: see sup. 7 and 858. But the friendship of the Greeks and its co-existence with the friendship of Hecuba, are unexplained.

ll. 986-8. **εἰπὲ παῖδ'.. εἰ ζῇ**: antiptosis; also called 'Attic construction': cf. N. T., 'I know thee who thou art.' παῖδ', acc. of respect. ἐξ: i.e. having received him from.

l. 987. **Πολύδωρον**: for the position of the word, see on sup. 771 Πολυμήστωρ.

l. 989. **τοὐκείνου μέρος**, 'as regardeth him'; adverbial acc.: see on 513 sup. τοὐπὶ σ'.

l. 990. **ὡς εὖ** κ.τ.λ.: irony: as inf. 1000, 1021. See on 430, sup. ζῇ κ.τ.λ.

l. 993. **ὡς**, 'to': used, in this prepositional sense, only with persons.

l. 996. **τῶν πλησίον**: neut. 'things near thee': a strangely elliptic phrase for τῶν τοῦ πλησίον, 'the things of thy neighbour': πλησίον, adverbial. [Or masc.? 'thy neighbours': in same sense: (v.l. τοῦ πλησίον: sc. τῶν τοῦ πλ., Herm.).]

l. 997. **ἥκιστ' ὀναίμην** κ.τ.λ., 'surely I will not; may I but enjoy what I have!': ἥκιστ', sc. ἐρασθήσομαι τῶν πλ. τοῦ παρόντος: causal gen., after ὀναίμην, lit. 'have profit because of': Jelf 491.

l. 998. **οἶσθ' ἅ**: see sup. 225 οἶσθ' οὖν ὃ ἔρασον.

l. 999. **σημανεῖς**: in sense, a polite imperative.

l. 1000. **ἔστ'**, 'there is': viz. κατώρυχες l. 1002: the 'Schema Pindaricum' junction of a singular verb and plural subject, not in the neuter), being softened down by the interposition of τί χρῆμ': Dind. ὦ φιληθεὶς κ.τ.λ.: sc. ὦ μισηθείς: for the irony, see on 990 sup. [ἔστ', ὦ φιλ.: Herm. emend. for MSS. ἔστω φιλ., i.e. φιληθήτω, the subject to which is λόγος, or, less probably, παῖς or χρόνος. Musgr. suggests τίς τῷ.]

l. 1004. **μάλιστα, διὰ σοῦ γ'**, 'aye, and through thee': γ' emphatic.

l. 1007. **τῇδε**, 'it were far wiser so': [Herm., Weil. Dind. destroys colon, 'herein thou speakest well' etc.]

l. 1008. **'Αθάνας**. Thinking, perhaps, of the temple of Athena at Athens; which possessed a large treasure, kept in the Parthenon. ἵνα, sc. εἰσίν: N. B. ἵνα a relative: so sc. τὸν τόπον ἵνα: see sup. on 112 οἶσθ' ὅτε, and 225 οἶσθ' ὅ.

l. 1010. γῆς: gen. after ὑπερ-. [Schol. finds in μέλαινα a reference to his coming blindness.]

l. 1011. τῶν ἐκεῖ, 'of the nature of the place': lit. 'things there': not in sense of περὶ τῶν, but part. gen. after τι. Cf. inf. 1017 τἄνδον.

l. 1013. κρύψασ' ἔχεις, 'hast thou them hidden': lit., 'thou hast them, having hidden them.' It is from such phrases that the auxiliary verb has sprung,—though, more commonly, the participle is passive and agrees with the object, as Lat. compertum habeo, O. Eng. I have him slain. [In ἔχει περάνας Soph. Aj. 22; ἀτιμάσας ἔχει Ant. 22, etc., ἔχω seems rather to bear the intrans. sense it has with adverbs, 'to be': implying continuance of result: Jelf 692.— ᾖ, Pors. (Dind.), for MSS. ἡ (Nauck, Weil).]

l. 1014. σκύλων ἐν ὄχλῳ, 'in a mass of spoils': ὄχλος, gen. a crowd of people. στέγαις: local dat.

l. 1015. αἴδ' κ.τ.λ., 'for here are,' etc., where the treasure would be unsafe. ναύλοχοι περιπτυχαί, the semi-circular fence which protected the ships, drawn up on land, from attack. [Schol., ναύσταθμα, the harbour; Paley, perhaps the tents of the men.]

l. 1017. τἄνδον κ.τ.λ., 'is all safe within, a male-less solitude?' lit. 'are things within to be trusted, and is there an absence of men?'

l. 1020. λῦσαι πόδα: prob. not 'loose the rope,' but 'stir their steps': metaphorical. See on 940 sup. ναῦς ἐκίνησεν πόδα. [So Weil. In the first rendering (which is more likely here than in 940), πόδα must be for πρυμνήσια; as λύειν πόδα means, strictly, 'to take down the sail': Od. 15. 496. Perhaps, in both passages, the two ideas are at the same time referred to.]

ll. 1021-2. Ironical: πράξας κ.τ.λ., viz. having paid the penalty; οὗπερ, viz. in Hades.

ll. 1024-8. ἀλίμενον κ.τ.λ., 'as one that falleth reeling into a harbourless deep, so shalt thou fall from thy dear heart (life), losing thy life.' ἄντλον: so in Pindar; generally hold of a ship. λέχριος: lit. slant-wise; perhaps owing to a lurch of the ship. ἀμέρσας βίον. ἀμέρσας seems here to be used in the sense of 'losing,' not, as elsewhere, of 'depriving.' See L. & S. [φίλας καρδίας: (2) 'cherished purpose,'!: cf. Soph. Ant. 1105 καρδίας ἐξίσταμαι. ἐκπεσεῖ, Herm. for MSS. ἐκπέσῃ (2nd pers. fut.; or 3rd pers. aor. subj., in the simile: Monro 283 a).]

ll. 1029-31. τὸ γὰρ ὑπέγγυον κ.τ.λ.: 'for where what is due to

HECUBA.

justice and to the gods coincide, deadly is the evil': i. e. when the gods and justice (human and divine vengeance) concur in enforcing a penalty, it is indeed heavy. [οὗ, Hemsterhuys for MSS. οὐ. If οὐ is read we must follow the Scholiast, who takes οὐ συμπίτνει = οὐκ ἀπόλλυται.]

l. 1032. ὁδοῦ, after ἐλπίς, 'hope in this journey'; not after ψεύσει.

l. 1033. θανάσιμον, proleptic, agreeing with σε: 'to thy death.'

l. 1034. ἀπολέμῳ χειρί, sc. of women: dat. instrum.

l. 1035. φέγγος: see on 367 ἐλεύθερον φέγγος: acc. of respect as ἀπὸ δὲ στεφάναν κέκαρσαι sup. 910.

l. 1037. δυστήνου σφαγῆς: not of the slaying of his children, but again of the putting out of his eyes: though his thoughts revert at the same time to the slain children. Weil.

l. 1038. καινά, 'strange,' 'terrible': cf. 689 sup.

l. 1039. οὐ μή. with aor. conjunc., usually implies a strong denial; with 2nd pers. of fut. indic., a strong prohibition. [The first has been explained by an ellipse of δέος ἐστί (sometimes inserted) between οὐ and μή; the second, as an interrog., 'will you not not' (οὐ being continued to a subsequent μηδέ), Elmsley. Both subj. and fut. indic., however, are found in both senses of denial and prohibition, and are best explained on the same principle, the subj. being a relic of the Homeric subj. with force of weaker fut. indic.: viz. either 1) as interrogs., in which οὐ μή = 'not not,' as sup. Elm., (Jelf, § 748. 2 b); or (2) as direct statements, in which οὐ μή = strong single negative. Goodw. M. & T. § 89. 2.) (N.B., on the last theory, such passages as Soph. Aj. 75 οὐ σῖγ' ἀνέξει, μηδὲ δειλίαν ἀρεῖ, are not cases of οὐ μή, but should be broken up into two distinct interrogs., the first, with οὐ, implying an affirm. answer (= exhortation), the second, with μή, a neg. answer (= prohibition); or ? an interrog. with οὐ, as before, and a direct prohib. with μή (not elliptic for ὅπως μή, but similar in force: M. & T. § 45. n. 7 b). Goodw. l. c.]

l. 1040. βάλλων, 'with blows.' μυχούς: perhaps the γυναικωνῖτις (women's apartments): but this need not be pressed.

l. 1041. ἰδοὺ κ.τ.λ., 'the blow of his heavy hand is launched forth': [or, 'hand used as a weapon,' Paley. Others take βέλος as a missile (which bursts through the walls, and falls on the stage before the chorus, Weil: but N.B. βαρείας, Paley); χειρός, as after ὁρμᾶται: the whole verse as spoken by Polymestor.]

l. 1042. ἐπεισπέσωμεν: delib. conjunc.: see on ἐσίδω 88 sup. ἀκμή, 'the full time,' 'the crisis.' (N.B. The murderesses must not be confused with the chorus: see note after 59 sup.)

NOTES. LINES 1030—1074.

l. 1044. μηδέν, adverbial. ἐκβάλλων, 'forcing out,' 'bursting open.' [(2) 'tearing up,' Paley; ἀνασπῶν, ἐς γῆν ῥίπτων, Schol.]
l. 1047. ἦ γὰρ καθεῖλες κ.τ.λ., 'what, hast thou overthrown the Thr., and hast thou the mastery over thy friend?': in prose, καθεῖλες Θρῆκα ξένον καὶ κρατεῖς αὐτοῦ. [Wakefield τέκνα, for Θρῆκα: Herm. ξένον: Weil, Θρηκίου κράτος ξένου.]
l. 1050. τυφλῷ κ.τ.λ., 'with blind and wandering feet.' [Cf. Soph. O. C. 182 ἀμαυρῷ κώλῳ: Milton, Sam. Ag. 'these dark steps.' τυφλὸν τυφλῷ: see on δυοῖν δύο 45 sup.]
l. 1052. ταῖς, sc. 'these': see sup. on 8 τὴν ἀρίστην πλάκα.
l. 1055. ῥέοντι: dissyllabic verbs in -εω (except δέω, bind) contract only -εε and -εει. θυμῷ δυσμαχωτάτῳ, together: dat. of manner with ῥέοντι. Θρῃκί, dative with ἀποστήσομαι. [ῥέοντι, most MSS.: cf. ? Dem. Cor. 272 πολλῷ ῥέοντι καθ' ὑμῶν. V. l. ζέοντι (Kirch., Nauck, Dind.).]
(Polymestor bursts out of the tent; from which, at the same time, an ἐκκύκλημα is rolled forward, disclosing to the spectators the dead bodies of his children: N.B. παῖδας τούσδ' 1118): see Introd., p. 13.)
l. 1057. κέλσω, 'where can I make the land?'; κέλλω, orig. trans., 'put ashore,' sc. τὴν ναῦν. Delib. conjunc.
ll. 1058-9. τετράποδος βάσιν κ.τ.λ. The construction may be continued from the preceding lines, i.e. πᾷ κέλσω βάσιν τετράπ.; if this view is taken, τιθέμενος ἐπὶ χεῖρα can be construed with Hermann, 'putting my hand down,' i.e. on the ground, or τιθέμενος αὐτὴν (sc. βάσιν) ἐπὶ χεῖρα = stepping on my hand. In the first case τιθέμενος ἐπί is = ἐπιτιθέμενος, in the second ἐπὶ χεῖρα is unusual for ἐπὶ χειρί. Or (2) the construction may be τιθέμενος βάσιν τετρ. θ. ἐπὶ χεῖρα, with which the question of the preceding line is, in thought, continued. 'Whither shall I go) stepping on my hand (like) a four-footed beast.' In his frenzy of rage and pain Polymestor crouches down like a wild beast. E. A. κατ' ἴχνος, 'in the tracks' (of the women who have blinded him).
ll. 1060-1. ποίαν .. ἐξαλλάξω; π., direct acc. after ἐξ.: 'what new way shall I take?'
l. 1064. ποῖ καί, emphatic: see on πῶς καί sup. 515. με, κατὰ σύνεσιν, after φυγᾷ πτώσσουσι, = φεύγουσι πτώσσουσαι.
l. 1065. μυχῶν, partit. gen. after ποῖ.
ll. 1067-8. Ἅλιε: as lord of light. τυφλὸν φέγγος, 'ridding me of this blind light': i.e. 'blindness': see 367 sup. Contrast inf. 1197, 1222, ἀπαλλάσσω τί τινος.
ll. 1071-4. πᾷ πόδ' ἐπᾴξας κ.τ.λ., 'whither can I dart my foot and be glutted with their flesh and bones, making me a banquet of

D 2   51

these wild beasts, winning their destruction, in requital for the outrage they have done me.' ἐπάξας: ἐπαίσσω, gen. intrans.; here trans.: see on περᾷ πόδα 53 sup. ἐμπλησθῶ, delib. conj. τιθέμενος: N.B. middle: 'for myself.' ἀντίποιν': in apposition, not to λώβαν only, but to the idea contained in the whole preceding sentence.
l. 1076. διαμοιρᾶσαι, 'for them to rend in pieces': infin., expressing possible result; often with ὥστε; but cf. 1107 inf. κρεῖσσον' ἢ φέρειν. N.B. the active: usual in such cases. Βάκχαις: the Bacchae were women maddened by the god of wine. [διαμ., and φέρειν 1107: Goodwin, M. & T. § 97, seems to regard these infins. as expressing purpose. On the question of their grammatical construction—as to whether they are datives or complementary accusatives— see Appendix, p. 64.]

ll. 1077-8. σφακτὰν κ.τ.λ., 'cruelly butchered, murdered, to feed the dogs, to be cast out on the mountain side': lit. a cruel butchered and murderous feast for the dogs, and a casting out upon the mountain; accs. in appos. to sentence. [MSS. Nauck, Kirch.-Herm., Dind. σφακτὰ κυσίν τε δαῖτ' ὀρείαν τ' ἐκβολάν.]

l. 1079. κάμψω, 'bend my course': metaphor from a ship doubling a headland. [2 Weil, Paley, Schol., sc. γόνυ, of bending the knee in rest: cf. 1150.]

l. 1080. ναῦς ὅπως κ.τ.λ., 'furling, like a ship, with sea-hawsers the flax-woven cloth.' πείσμασι, dat. instrum.: π., here = πύδες, 'the sheets': generally = πρυμνήσια, the stern-cables. λινόκροκον φᾶρος, i.e. my sails: metaph. στέλλων: almost στέλλουσ', but made masculine, by an afterthought, to retain the personality of Polymestor. [πείσμ.: for the opposite mistake, see ? on λῦσαι πόδα sup. 1020. (2) Schol., Paley, take λιν. φᾶρ. out of the metaphor, in sense of 'my mantle': making πείσμ. dat. of accompaniment with ναῦς, or understanding, with both, στέλλει κ.τ.λ.]

l. 1083. τέκνων ἐμῶν, after ὀλέθριον κοίταν: 'the place where my children lie dead:' (φύλαξ, 'to protect them'): [Weil. (2) after φύλ. ὀλέθριον κοίταν, 'deadly lair,' 'chamber of death.']

l. 1085. σοι, not dat. of agent, but dat. incommodi, 'upon thee.' εἴργασται, passive in sense (usually active). [Dind. Others εἴργ., active: sc. Ἑκάβη; or δαίμων 1087: but see next note.]

l. 1086. δεινά, predicate: N.B. position of article. Cf. the proverb: δράσαντι παθεῖν. [Line 1087 is almost a repetition of 722 sup. It is considered spurious by Herm., Nauck, and Kirch.]

l. 1089. Ἄρει κάτοχον, 'possessed by,' or, 'subject to, Mars,' viz. love of war.

l. 1094. ἢ οὐδείς, by synizesis, *you*: see 24.

l. 1100. αἰθέρ', acc. after ἀνα-, 'up through.' ἀμπτάμενος, contr. for ἀναπτ.; from ἀν-επτάμην, 2nd aor. of ἀν-ίπταμαι (collat. form of ἀνα-πέτομαι). Cf. inf. ἀμβήσει 1263; ἀμμένει 1281. [αἰθέρ', MSS.: omitted by Herm. and W. Dind. as superf.]
ll. 1101-3. Ὠρίων: a giant-hunter; changed, after death, into a star which rose soon after the summer-solstice. Σείριος, sc. the dog-star: lit. 'the scorching.' ὅσσων, gen. after ἀπο- in ἀφίησιν. [For Σείρ., cf. Verg. Aen. x. 274; on the whole sentiment, Med. 1276, Hipp. 732, etc.]
l. 1104. τὸν Ἅιδα πορθμόν, sc. the Styx: acc. of motion to. (Ἅιδ., see 483.) [Dind. MSS., τὸν ἐς Ἅιδα κ.τ.λ, Kirch., Nauck.]
l. 1107. συγγνωστά, 'it is pardonable': ironical. For plur., cf. συγγνωστά Med. 491, 703; ἄσημα Hipp. 269: Weil. φέρειν: for infin., see on sup. 1076 διαμοιρᾶσαι.
l. 1108. ἐξαπαλλάξαι: intrans.: 'to quit oneself of': the mid. would be more usual, but cf. on sup. 1061 ἐξαλλάσσω. ζόης: a lyrical form, required by the metre for MS. ζωῆς.
ll. 1109-10. οὐ γὰρ ἥσυχος κ.τ.λ.: 'for, with no quiet voice, Echo, the daughter of the mountain-rock, has cried aloud through the host, raising confusion.' λέλακ': or perhaps in present sense, 'cries': see on sup. 678 ζῶσιν λέλακας. ἥσυχος, in sense, ἡσύχως: cf. inf. 1226 σαφέστατοι.
l. 1112. ᾖσμεν: Attic contracted form of ᾔδειμεν: cf. ᾖσαν, for ᾔδεσαν, etc. On particip., see sup. 244 μεμνήμεθ' ἐλθόντες.
l. 1113. παρέσχεν, 'had caused,' 'would have caused.' The omission of ἄν in such cases seems to show how near the thing was to happening. [See Goodw. M. & T. 49. 2. n. 2. Cf. the use of the indic. for subjunc. in Latin, esp. in Tac. and the poets, e. g. Virg. Georg. ii. 131 et si non alium late jactaret odorem, laurus erat; and the Eng. 'were' and 'had been,' for 'would be' and 'would have been.' παρέσχ' ἄν has been suggested ('A' and 'B,' παρέσχεν ἄν); but this elision with ἄν is un-Attic: Weil.]
l. 1114. γάρ: accounting for the address, ὦ φίλτατ'. σέθεν: after ᾖσθ., genitive of the source of the perception.
l. 1118. τούσδ': see after 1055.
l. 1119. σοί, τέκνοισιν: dat. incom. ἆρα expresses slight surprise: Jelf 788. 4.
l. 1121. ἀπώλεσ', οὐκ ἀπώλεσ': cf. sup. 948 γάμος, οὐ γάμος.
l. 1123. τόλμαν, cog. acc.
l. 1124. τί λέξεις; 'what sayest thou?': see on 511 sup. ἐστί: viz. Hecuba.
l. 1125. ποῦ: the direct interrog. particle; often used for vivid-

53

ness, instead of the indirect: cf. reversion to tenses of direct orat. in obl. orat.

l. 1127. οὗτος: exclamatory nom, for voc. : cf. on 534 sup. πατήρ. τί πάσχεις; 'what ails thee?'

l. 1128. μέθες μ', lit. let me go so that I can etc., ὥστε ἐφεῖναι.

l. 1129. ἴσχ': from ἴσχω, form of ἔχω: here intrans. τὸ βάρβαρον, 'the barbaric passion': contrasted with Greek self-control,—μηδὲν ἄγαν. καρδίας: after ἐκβαλών.

l. 1132. λέγοιμ' ἄν, 'I will speak': see on 485 sup. ἂν ἐξεύροιμι. N.B. the equality in length of the two speeches, each of which contains 51 lines; and the law-court character of the scene generally, in keeping with the litigious spirit of the time. Aristophanes attacks this spirit, in the Wasps; and the νοῦς ἀγοραῖος (Ar. frag.) of Eur., in the Frogs. Cf. 1187 inf., on the sophists; and see Introd., p. 10. [Paley collects five or six such cases in Eur., where the two disputants are assigned an equal number of lines: e. g. in Med. 465-575, Medea and Jason each have 54.]

l. 1133. Ἑκάβης παῖς: Priam having had other wives. See note on l. 3 sup.

l. 1134. δίδωσι: hist. pres. τρέφειν: infin., expressing purpose: Goodw. M. &. T. 97. Distinguish διαμοιρᾶσαι sup. 1076.

l. 1135. ὕποπτος: active, 'suspecting': see sup. 5 and 11. Verbal adjectives in -τος are usually passive: but cf. μεμπτός Soph. Trach. 446.; πιστός Aesch. Prom. 917. δή: i. e. it seems; or, as the event showed: Paley. ἁλώσεως: objective gen.: see on καρδίας δηκτήρια sup. 235.

l. 1137. εὖ: i. e. I did well to do it: Weil. σοφῇ προμηθίᾳ: cf. 795 λαβὼν προμηθίαν.

l. 1139. ἀθροίσῃ, 'gather Troy together'; i.e. the débris of Troy, the Trojans. The subj. is a return to present narration (cp. sup. 27: [to gain vividness; or (2) to leave room for the expression of a remoter consequence in the optative, ἄρειαν, like Thuc. iii. 22. 5 παρανίσχον φρυκτοὺς ὅπως ἀσαφῆ τὰ σημεῖα ᾖ καὶ μὴ βοηθοῖεν (Arnold; discountenanced by Goodw. M. & T. 44. 2). Kirch. and Nauck read ἀθροῖσαι, ξυνοικίσαι: see on ἐλπίσαι, 820, sup.]

l. 1141. ἄρειαν. N.B. ἦρα (αἴρω) has ᾱ through all moods.

l. 1142. τρίβοιεν, 'waste': almost, 'wear.'

l. 1144. Τρώων: after γείτοσιν. ἐν ᾧπερ κ.τ.λ. (the evil), 'under which but now (νῦν) we were labouring.' [Τρώ., Weil; others, improbably = Τρώων ἕνεκα. Cf. Thuc. i. 11. 1 φαίνονται δέ (the Greeks at Troy) πρὸς γεωργίαν τῆς Χερσονήσου τραπόμενοι καὶ λῃστείαν τῆς τροφῆς ἀπορίᾳ.]

NOTES. LINES 1125—1168.

l. 1146. ὡς κ.τ.λ.: explanatory of λόγῳ τοιῷδε: 'by some pretence that she would take me' etc.

l. 1149. εἰδείη: optat.: perhaps, because the present εἰσάγει is historic (see on 11 sup. ἐκπέμπει ἵν' εἴη); but more probably, because εἰδ. expresses the aim of another person than the speaker, 'in order, she said, that' etc.: Jelf 807. β.

l. 1150. κάμψας γόνυ: common phrase for sitting or resting. [See sup. on 1079 κάμψω.]

l. 1151. χειρός: emend. the poet Milton for MSS. χεῖρες.

l. 1152. δή: sarcastic.

l. 1153. κερκίδ' Ἠδωνῆς χερός, 'the texture of the Edonian handiwork.' κερκίς: really the loom-comb, see sup. on 363. Ἠδωνῆς, i.e. Thracian; the Edonians being a people who lived in Thrace, near the Strymon. χερός: cf. Hom. Od. xv. 126 μνῆμ' Ἑλένης χειρῶν, sc. her art. [κερκ., use of ἱστός for tela; (2) τὸ Θρακικὸν ἀκόντιον, Schol. (cf. σπάθη; and see on 1156.) θάκους κ.τ.λ., Herm. emend. (Kirch., Nauck) for MSS. 'θάκουν, ἔχουσαι.. ἤνουν θ' (Dind.).]

l. 1154. ὑπ' αὐγὰς κ.τ.λ.: i.e. holding them up to the light: ὑπ. (bringing them) to under.

l. 1156. διπτύχου στολίσματος, 'two-fold equipment': i.e. his double cloak, in which a weapon might have been concealed: E. A.

l. 1159. γένοιντο: κατὰ σύνεσιν, as if παῖδες, not τέκνα, had preceded. A plural verb is often used with a neuter plural subject, when this refers to living persons, Pors. διαδοχαῖς κ.τ.λ., 'passing them in turn from hand to hand'; lit., exchanging them with succession of hands. On the absence of caesura, see 355 sup. [γέν.: cf. Thuc. i. 58 τὰ τέλη ὑπέσχοντο. V. l. γένοιτο (Dind.)]

l. 1160. κᾷτ': καὶ εἶτα: crasis. ἐκ, 'after': see on 55 ἐκ τυραννικῶν δόμων. πῶς δοκεῖς; parenthetic: 'what think you?': would you believe it? [Cf. Hipp. 446 τοῦτον λαβοῦσα, πῶς δοκεῖς; καθύβρισεν.]

l. 1162. αἱ δέ: as if αἱ μέν had preceded: cf. 28 ἄλλοτε.

l. 1164. χρῄζων: going, in construction, with the εἰ clauses.

l. 1165. ἐξανισταίην, 'if ever I tried to lift': the opt. expressing repeated; the imperf., attempted, action.

l. 1166. κατεῖχον, sc. με. κόμης, 'by the hair': partit. gen. like χερός, 523 sup.; though less directly after the verb, as in Hom. Od. iii. 439 βοῦν δ' ἀγέτην κεράων.

l. 1167. πλήθει, 'for the crowd,' 'because of the crowd': causal dat.: cf. inf. 1183 τοῖς κακοῖς. οὐδὲν ἤνυον: cf. sup. 937 οὐκ ἤνυσ'.

l. 1168. πῆμα πήματος πλέον, 'evil greater than evil'; i.e.

HECUBA.

demanding some greater name: acc. in appos. to sentence. [(2) Acc. or nom. of exclamation.]

l. 1170. πόρπας, 'brooch-pins.' So Oedipus puts out his eyes: Eur. Phoen. 62; Soph. O. T. 1268.

l. 1172. ἐκ δὲ πηδήσας: for the tmesis, cf. 928 ἀνὰ δὲ ἔμολε. It is especially common with δέ.

l. 1174. ὡς κυνηγέτης, viz. when searching the thickets. Yet 1173 θὴρ ὥς. (Weil limits θὴρ ὥς to ἐκ πηδ.)

l. 1175. σπεύδων χάριν τὴν σήν, 'urging thy interests': see on σπεύδων ἀγαθόν 122 sup.

l. 1178. εἴ τις κ.τ.λ., 'if any man of those of old time' etc. Eur. has been accused of misogynism by Aristoph., in the Thesm. and elsewhere. He has, in fact, written numerous invectives against women (see esp. the frags. of Eur.), and has introduced the blackest feminine characters into his plays, e. g. Phaedra, Stheneboea, Melanippe. But the invectives may be often accounted for by the plot; the darker characters are partly defensible as teaching virtue by strong pictures of vice and its fate; and are partly cancelled by some of the most human figures in ancient tragedy, such as Iphigenia and Polyxena herself. See Introd., p. 10.

l. 1180. συντεμών, 'all these things I will concisely say: Never' etc.: συντ. lit., 'cutting short'; Iph. Aul. 1249 ἐν συντεμοῦσα πάντα νικήσω λόγον. Cf. συνελών.

l. 1182. ὁ δ' ἀεὶ ξυντυχών, 'he who from time to time falls in with them': ἀεί, in this sense, more commonly with pres. part.

l. 1183. τοῖς κακοῖς, 'because of thy trouble': causal dat.: cf. 299 sup. τῷ θυμουμένῳ.

l. 1184. συνθείς, 'putting them together in one,' 'comprising them.'

ll. 1185-6. πολλαὶ γὰρ κ.τ.λ., 'for many of us are worthy of hatred, but the rest (the better women are equal in number with the bad.' εἰς ἀριθμόν: ? lit., come up to the number of. But the lines are spurious: G. Dind. [The usual interp., ἐπίφ. 'unjustly hated,' εἰς ἀρ. 'are numbered among,' is impossible: ἐπ. can hardly bear this meaning, and the 'bad' would be mentioned first. Paley suggests μὴ κακῶν; Reiske, τῶν καλῶν (=pulchrae, Herm.); Herm. (Weil) ἀντάριθμοι, from gloss ἰσάριθμοι. (ἰσάρ. itself might stand; but, in Trag. ἰσ- occurs only in three choric passages, Aesch. Pr. 549, Pers. 80, Cho. 319; and in the last two is emended to ἀντ-.)]

ll. 1187-94. Referring to the demagogues and sophistic rhetors. On the κρείττων and ἥττων λόγος, better and worse cause, of the sophists, cf. Clouds 112 sqq.; where, in the ἡττων λόγος, Eur. is said himself to have been personated. See on sup. 818, 1132; and Introd., p. 10.

ll. 1189-90. εἴτε .. εἴτ' αὖ, 'if on the one hand,—but if on the other hand': αὖ gives a preference to the alternative with which it goes. ἔδρασε, sc. τις, contained in ἀνθρώποισιν; though the third person of the verb is itself often used indefinitely. σαθρούς, 'unsound.'

l. 1191. δύνασθαι: the subject is not τἄδικα, but αὐτόν understood (τὸν λέγοντα, Weil).

l. 1192. οἱ τάδ' ἠκριβωκότες, 'that have mastered or, elaborated) these subtleties': sc. τὸ τἄδικα εὖ λέγειν.

l. 1193. διὰ τέλους, 'throughly,' like εἰς τέλος 817 sup.; or 'to the end' (Weil). [δύνανται, Nauck: Dind. δύναιντ' ἄν, from Vat. MS. δύναινται.]

l. 1194. ἀπώλοντο: for the gnomic aor., cf. sup. 598 διέφθειρ'.

l. 1195. καί μοι κ.τ.λ., 'so stands as preface what I would say to thee.' φροιμίοις, dat. of manner.

l. 1196. πρὸς τόνδε δ' εἶμι: the colloquial Eng., 'now will I come to him.' λόγοις ἀμείψομαι, 'make reply'; λ., dat. of manner. [2) Weil, λόγ. = τοῖς τοῦδε λόγοις: dat. incom.]

l. 1197. Ἀχαιῶν: after ἀπ-. Contrast ἀπαλλάσσω τι 1068 sup. ἀπαλλάσσων, present, expressing attempt, or purpose (cf. on 72 sup. ἀποπέμπομαι): almost = ἀπαλλάξων, to which Nauck emends.

l. 1199. ἄν .. ἄν: repetition emphatic: see sup. 359 ἴσως ἄν .. τύχοιμ' ἄν.

l. 1201. σπεύδων χάριν: see sup. 1175.

l. 1202. κηδεύσων: 'was it because you wished to ally yourself with someone by marriage?' τινά, i.e. some Greek prince; κηδ.: see on 511 sup. ὡς θανουμένους.

l. 1203. ἢ τίν' κ.τ.λ., 'or what other reason had you?'

l. 1205. τάδε, cog. acc.

l. 1206. βούλοιο: opt., expressing improbability. The sentence is protasis to a suppressed apodosis, λέγοις ἄν (ὅτι ὁ χρυσός κ.τ.λ. . Goodw. M. & T. § 50. 2; § 53. n. 2.

l. 1207. κέρδη τὰ σά, 'thy gain'; i.e. αἱ σαὶ πλεονεξίαι, thy avarice: Weil.

l. 1208. ἐπεί, 'for': cf. Soph. O. T. 390 ἐπεὶ φέρ' εἰπέ: Weil. πῶς: see on 1211 inf. ὅτ' ηὐτύχει: see sup. 16 sqq.

l. 1210. Ἕκτορος δόρυ, 'the warlike Hector.' See on 21 sup. Ἕκτορος ψυχή.

l. 1211. τί δ' οὐ τότ': recovering πῶς 1208: δέ, resumptive, 'I

HECUBA.

say': Weil. χάριν θέσθαι, 'to lay up for thyself gratitude with him.' τῷδ', dat. eth.

l. 1215. καπνῷ δ' ἐσήμην', sc. ὅν, Herm. 'and the city showed by its smoke it was under the enemy.' Cf. Aesch. Ag. 818 καπνῷ δ' ἁλοῦσα νῦν ἔτ' εὔσημος πόλις. [ἐσήμην', (2 sc. τοῦτο, τὸ ἡμᾶς μηκέτ' εἶναι ἐν φάει, Schol. ; (3 i. e. εὔσημον ἦν; not improbably, (4) gave the signal, i. e. for the death of Polydorus, Schaefer. Weil, δαμέν for ὕπο; Canter, καπνὸς ἔσ., 'defined').]

l. 1217. ὡς φανῇς, 'that thou mayst be seen'; 2nd aor. pass.: [Kirch., Nauck, Weil. V. l. φανεῖ (Dind.), 'how thou shalt' etc.]

l. 1219. οὐ, not μή, is generally used with infin. of obl. orat., to retain negative of direct orat.: Goodw. G. G. 283. σόν, predicate. τοῦδε: Polydorus. Polymestor did not refer to this.

l. 1220. πενομένοις: [Paley thinks that Hecuba is speaking of the time before Troy was taken; but the drift of the passage is against this: the word perhaps involves a rhetorical exaggeration.]

l. 1222. ἀπαλλάξαι ‚τὸν χρυσὸν) χερός: χερ. after ἀπ.: cf. 1197 sup. Ἀχαιῶν ἀπαλλάσσων. See on 1068 sup.

l. 1223. τολμᾷς, 'canst find the heart.' καρτερεῖς, 'persistest.'

ll. 1224-5. καὶ μήν: introducing a new idea; as, sup. 216, a new person. τρέφων .. τὸν ἐμόν: sc. τρέφων μὲν σώσας τε τὸν ἐμὸν παῖδα ὥς σ' ἐχρῆν τρέφειν καὶ σῶσαι αὐτόν. Participle hypothetic, like 756 τιμωρουμένη.

ll. 1226-7. ἐν τοῖς κακοῖς κ.τ.λ., 'for it is in times of trouble the good are plainest friends: prosperity hath of itself friends in every case'; cf. Ov. Trist. i. 8. 5 donec eris felix, multos numerabis amicos; nullus ad amissas ibit amicus opes; Ennius, ap. Cic. de Am. 17. 64 amicus certus in re incerta cernitur ‚Weil). ἀγαθοί, οἱ ἀγαθοί: crasis. σαφέστατοι: in sense almost σαφέστατα: cf. sup. 1109 ἥσυχος. αὐτά: per se.

l. 1228. χρημάτων: priv. gen., after a verb implying want. ὁ δέ: Polydorus.

l. 1229. ὑπῆρχε: 'there would he have been, a great treasure, ready at hand for thee.'

l. 1230. ἐκεῖνον: prob. not Agamemnon, as some think, but Polydorus. N.B. in poetry, the article is often omitted after ἐκεῖνος, οὗτος, etc.

l. 1234. εὐσεβῆ κ.τ.λ.: predicates. οἷς ἐχρῆν: sc. ἐκείνοις οἷς ἐχρῆν πιστὸν εἶναι. But see on 864 sup. θνητῶν ὅστις.

l. 1236. τοῖς κακοῖς: masculine.

l. 1237. τοιοῦτον: sc. κακόν: for which it is apologetically substituted. δεσπότας : generalising plural : cf. inf. 1253 τοῖς κακίοσιν. [See on 237 sup.]

l. 1239. ἀφορμάς, 'basis for good words.'

l. 1240. ἀχθεινά : prob. not like the plural. συγγνώσθ' 1107 sup., but pred. of κακά: κρίνειν being epexegetic, an acc. of respect, Goodw. M. & T. 93. 2. [See on 1076 sup.]

l. 1242. πρᾶγμ' κ.τ.λ. : sc. τὸ ἐμὲ πρᾶγμ' κ.τ.λ., nom. to φέρει : Goodw. M. & T. 91.

l. 1243. ἐμὴν χάριν : 'for my sake': see on sup. 874.

l. 1244. οὔτ' οὖν : 'nor yet indeed.' Ἀχαιῶν : sc. χάριν.

l. 1245. ἔχης. The mood may be explained grammatically as depending on δοκεῖς; but see on 27 sup. μεθῆχ' ἵν' ἔχῃ.

l. 1247. τάχ' : 'perhaps.' ῥᾴδιον, 'a light thing.'

l. 1249. μὴ ἀδικεῖν : to be pronounced μỵἀδικεῖν, by synizesis. φύγω : delib. conj.

l. 1251. ἐτόλμας, τλῆθι : 'endured' (sc. had the heart); 'endure' (sc. suffer). The words are probably intended to resemble one another.

l. 1252. γυναικὸς ἡσσώμενος : 'worsted of a woman': gen. of cause or agent, rather than comparative gen.: cf. Soph. Aj. 807 φωτὸς ἠπατημένη : Eur. El. 123 σᾶς ἀλόχου σφαγείς, Weil.

l. 1253. τοῖς κακίοσιν : 'to those that are inferior to me': cf. δούλης. For generalising plur., cf. 1237 sup. δεσπότας.

l. 1254. ΕΚΑΒΗ. [So Herm., after MS. A. Pors., with the other MSS., gives the verse to Ag.]

l. 1256. τί δαί 'μέ; sc. πάσχειν δοκεῖς : δαί, colloq. form of δή, used by Eur. ; only after interrog. παιδός : 'for my child': gen. of cause. [MSS., τί δαί με and τί δέ με : for which Pors. (Weil, Dind.), τί δ' ἡμᾶς (taken by some with παιδ. κ.τ.λ.); Nauck, τί δ'; ἢ 'μὲ κ.τ.λ.; Kirch., τί δὴ 'μέ.]

l. 1259. ἀλλ' οὐ τάχ', sc. χαιρήσεις : τάχ', 'perchance,' as in 1247 sup.

l. 1260. ὄρους : acc. of motion to, without prep. : confined, in Attic, to poetry. [See on 146 sup. ἀλλ' ἴθι ναούς.]

l. 1261. μὲν οὖν : 'nay rather, shall bury thee out of sight, having fallen from the mast-head': μὲν οὖν corrects a previous statement, by adding to it : like Lat. immo. Cf. Aesch. Eum. 38 δείσασα γὰρ γραῦς οὐδέν, ἀντίπαις μὲν οὖν.

l. 1262. πρὸς τοῦ κ.τ.λ., 'at whose hands meeting with a leap perforce.'

l. 1263. πρὸς ἱστόν, 'thou shalt climb up by the mast': πρός, lit. with reference to, expressing the manner, as in the adverbial

HECUBA.

πρὸς βίαν etc. ναός: Dor. gen., for νεώς. ἀμ-, sc. ἀνα-: cf. 1100 ἀμπτάμενος.

l. 1265. δέργματα, not 'eyes' (Paley), but 'glances.'

l. 1267. ὁ Θρῃξὶ μάντις: 'seer to the Thracians': dat. of respect, almost possessive: cf. sup. 816 τύραννον ἀνθρώποις: Phoen. 17 ὦ Θήβαισιν εὐίπποις ἄναξ: N. T. 'sister's son to Barnabas.' [Herodotus (vii. 111) speaks of an oracle of Dionysus among the Thracian Satrae; probably the one consulted by Octavius, father of Augustus. (Suet. Aug. 94). On the prophetic power of Bacchus, see Bacch. 298, Rhes. 972: Weil.]

l. 1268. ἔχρησεν. χράω is used of an oracle, answering; χράομαι, of a man, consulting it. ὧν: sc. τούτων ἅ: 'Attic Attraction,' attraction of rel. to anteced.; almost confined to cases where the rel. should be acc., the antec. gen. or dat.

l. 1269. γάρ, 'else had thou not': no, for if he had, thou wouldst not have, etc. Weil.

l. 1270. θανοῦσα δ', κ.τ.λ., 'shall I be changed after death? or in life, and, as a dog, fulfil my length of days on earth?' θανοῦσα: sc. κύων γενήσομαι. ἐνθάδ': opposed to ἐκεῖ, 'in Hades': see on 418 sup. ἐκπλήσω βίον: sc. κύων οὖσα: going only with ζῶσα, which it expands. [ἐνθάδ': (2) = οὕτως, sc. as a dog, Schol.; (3) sc. ἐκεῖ, in the sea, going with θαν. ἢ ζῶσ', Herm. βίον, MSS.: Musgr. emend. πότμον (Dind.); Brunck, μόρον; Weil, ἐνθάδ' ἐκστήσω βίον, i. e. μεταβαλῶ βίον εἰς τάδε.]

l. 1271. τύμβῳ κ.τ.λ.: a confusion between τύμβῳ ὄνομα δοθήσεται, and τύμβος ὄνομα κεκλήσεται: Paley.

l. 1272. μορφῆς: obj. gen. ἐπῳδόν, 'named after:' ἐπώνυμον. ἢ τί: parenth.: cf. πῶς δοκεῖς; 1160.

l. 1273. κυνὸς σῆμα. The legend of Hecuba's metamorphosis into a dog was probably invented to explain the name of Cynossema, a promontory in the Thracian Chersonese, where Hecuba's tomb is still shown; the name itself being probably astronomical in origin. [Paley; cf. ? sup. 1265 πυρσ' ἔχουσα δέργματα. According to Ovid (Met. xiii. 565), Hecuba was turned into a dog, on being stoned by the Thracians for the murder of Polymestor; according to Cicero (Tusc. Disp. iii. 26) the change was a picturesque fiction, invented to represent her 'animi acerbitatem et rabiem': cf. Juv. x. 271 torva canino latravit rictu.]

l. 1276. ἀπέπτυσ', 'I spurn thy predictions and bestow them on thyself to keep': ἀπ., almost 'abominor.' Aor., momentary: see on sup. 583 ἐπέζεσε.

l. 1278. μήπω, 'not yet,' i. e. may it be long before:=μήποτε, understated: as in Soph. El. 403 μήπω νοῦ τοσόνδ' εἴην κενή, Weil. **Τυνδαρὶς παῖς**: Clytaemnestra, wife of Agam. N.B. the patronymic: almost adjectival; amplified by παῖς. [See on 191 sup. v. l. Πηλείδᾳ γέννᾳ.]

l. 1279. **τοῦτον**, sc. κτενεῖ. [γε, Pors., Herm., Weil, from 'C': W. Dind., Nauck, with other MSS., σε; but σε τοῦτον is a doubtful altern. for σε τόνδε (in spite of οὗτος σύ), and would almost necessitate giving the previous verse to Agam.: (Paley, Weil.]

l. 1281. **κτεῖν', ὡς κ.τ.λ.**: i.e. you may kill me, but you will not save yourself thereby: ὡς, 'since,' 'for.' **ἀμμένει**: =ἀναμ.: see on 1100 sup. ἀμπτάμενος.

ll. 1282–3. **οὐχ ἕλξετ'; οὐκ ἐφέξετε**: The interrog. fut. with οὐ is equiv. to a strong command: cf. Soph. Aj. 75 οὐ σῖγ' ἀνέξει: [See on οὐ μή 1039 sup.]

l. 1284. **ἐγκλῄετ'**: sc. στόμα. **εἴρηται**, 'I have spoken'; i.e. said what I wanted to say (Weil): formula perorandi. See on 236 sup. εἰρῆσθαι. **ὅσον τάχος**, 'with all speed': elliptic adverbial phrase for ὅσον τάχος ἐστί, 'as there is speed.' So ὡς τάχος, ὡς τάχιστα, ὅσον τάχιστα.

l. 1285. **νήσων ἐρήμων**, after που. [On the artistic point of Agam. banishing Polym., like a common soldier, see Introd., p. 10. For the punishment, cf. Aegisthus and the minstrel: Od. iii. 270.]

l. 1286. **οὕτω καὶ λίαν**: together, 'thus so overbold of speech': [Weil. Others separate: (*a*) καὶ λίαν, vel maxime: οὕτω, 'in this plight'; (*b*) Paley, ἐπεὶ καί.]

l. 1287. **Ἑκάβη, σὺ δ'**: for position of δέ, see on sup. 372 μῆτερ, σὺ δ'. **διπτύχους**, sc. δύο: cf. sup. 126 δισπῶν.

l. 1288. **δεσποτῶν δ' κ.τ.λ.** [A stage contrivance to make the chorus leave the orchestra in procession: Paley.]

l. 1290. **πρὸς οἶκον**: with πομπίμους, which = πέμψοντας,—'to convey us.' See sup. 35 sqq. and 113. **τάσδε**: pred.

l. 1291. **εὖ δὲ τὰν δόμοις κ.τ.λ.**: 'Sophoclean irony' (see on sup. 430): the infidelity of Clytaemnestra is known to the spectators.

l. 1294. **τῶν δεσποσύνων μόχθων**, 'the toils of slavery': Weil. **δεσποσύνων**, attrib. adj.: see on 101 sup. δεσποσύνους σκηνάς.

APPENDICES.

List of chief variations from the MSS. (and Dindorf's Oxford Text).

l. 80. ἄγκυρ' ἀμῶν, Nauck :—most MSS. ἄγκυρά τ' ἐμῶν; (1 MS. Dind. ἄγκυρ' ἔτ' ἐμῶν).
l. 164. ποῖ δ' ἧσω πόδα ; τίς, Reiske and Musgr. ;—MSS. Dind. ποῖ δ' ἧσω; ποῦ τις.
l. 165. δαίμων νῷν, Kirch., Nauck :—MSS. δαιμόνων, (Dind., δαίμων).
l. 191. Πηλείᾳ γέννᾳ, Weil :—MSS. Πηλείδᾳ γέννᾳ, Kirch., Nauck ; Πηλείδα γέννᾳ, Brunck, Dind. ; etc.
l. 211. (καὶ σὲ μέν, μᾶτερ δύστανε, Nauck with best MSS. :—v. l. Dind., σὲ μέν, ὦ μᾶτερ δύστανε βίου.)
l. 231. κἄγωγ' ἄρ', Dind. :—MSS., κἀγὼ γάρ.
l. 293. λέγῃς, Kirch., Dind., following Muretus :—MSS. Nauck, λέγῃ.
l. 312. (ὄλωλε, Kirch., Nauck, with most MSS. :—Dind., with Parisian MS., ἄπεστι.)
l. 332. πέφυκ' ἀεί, Kirch., Nauck, Dind. :—MSS. πεφυκέναι.
l. 373. μήτε, Pors. :—MSS., (Dind.) μηδέ.
l. 392. πῶμ', Dind. et al. :—MSS. πόμ'.
l. 394. (εἷς, MS. 'Λ,' followed by Kirch., Nauck :—cet. MSS., Dind.,σῆς.)
l. 425. (ἀθλίας, MSS., Kirch., Nauck :—Dind., ἀθλία.)
l. 454. γύας, Herm., Dind. :—MSS., Kirch., Nauck, πεδία.
l. 467. (θεᾶς ναίουσ', Nauck :—Kirch., Dind., 'Αθαναίας.)
l. 469. (ἆρα, Kirch., Nauck :—Dind. ἅρματι.)
l. 470. (δαιδαλέαισι, Kirch., Nauck :—Dind., δαιδαλταῖσι.)
ll. 478-9. (δορίκτητος 'Αργείων, Kirch., Nauck, Weil :—Dind. δορίληπτος πρὸς 'Αργείων.)
l. 528. (αἵρει, Kirch., from Marcianus :—cet. MSS., Dind.. ἔρρει.
l. 574. δὲ πληροῦσιν, Kirch., Dind. :—δ' ἐπληροῦσαν, Nauck.
l. 580. λέγω, Dind. :—most MSS., Kirch., Nauck, λέγων.
l. 595. ἄνθρωποι, Herm., Kirch., Nauck, Dind. :—MSS., ἀνθρώποις.
l. 720. (ᾠκτίσω, Kirch., Nauck :—Dind., ᾤκτισας.)

APPENDICES.

l. 742. (ἄλγος ἄν, some MSS., Kirch., Nauck :—Brunck, Dind., ἄ. αὖ.)
l. 818. ἵν' ἦν, Elmsley, (Dind. et al.) :—MS. ἵν' ᾖ.
l. 821. (οἱ μὲν γὰρ ὄντες, Kirch., Nauck : -v. l. Dind., οἱ μὲν τοσοῦτοι.)
l. 831. (βροτοῖς, Kirch., Nauck :—v. l., Dind., πάνυ.)
l. 972. (προσβλέπειν, MS. 'A.', Kirch., Weil :—cet. MSS., Nauck, Dind., προσβλέπειν σ'.)
l. 1000. ἔστ', ὦ, Herm. em., Dind. :—MSS. ἔστω.
l. 1026. ἐκπεσεῖ, Herm. em., Dind. :—MSS. ἐκπέσῃ.
l. 1055. (ῥέοντι, MSS. :—Barnes em., Dind., Nauck, Kirch., ζέοντι.)
l. 1077. (σφακτὰν κ.τ.λ., MSS., Kirch., Nauck :—Herm. em., Dind., σφακτὰ κυσίν τε δαῖτ' ὀρείαν τ' ἐκβολάν.)
l. 1104. τὸν "Αιδα, Dind. :—MSS., Kirch., Nauck, τὸν ἐς "Αιδα.
l. 1112. ᾖσμεν, Dind. et al. :—MSS. ἴσμεν.
ll. 1153, 4. θάκους .. ἤνουν, Herm. em., Kirch., Nauck :—MSS. (Dind.) 'θάκουν .. ἤνουν θ'.
l. 1159. 'γένοιντο, Kirch., Nauck :—v. l., Dind., γένοιτο.)
l. 1217. (φανῇς, Kirch., Nauck, Weil :—v. l., Dind., φανεῖ.)
l. 1256. (τί δαὶ 'μέ; some MSS. :—Pors. em., Dind., τί δ' ἡμᾶς.)

(*Note.*—In ll. 59-215, and ll. 1056-1085, the lines have been numbered according to Dindorf's Oxford Text; which differs slightly, in this respect, from the text of Nauck.)

On the infinitive. The infinitive is, philologically, the dative case of a feminine noun of the first declension (N.B. the older form in -αι, τιθέναι etc.); and appears, in many cases, to be also used as a dative, grammatically: (see Monro, H. G., § 231). But there is some doubt whether, in its later grammatical development, this dative-origin is not sometimes lost sight of and the infinitive should not rather be regarded, grammatically, as a nominative or an accusative (Goodwin, M. & T. § 91): e.g. θανεῖν, l. 214, as a nominative; λῦσαι, l. 539, as a direct accusative; πεσεῖν, l. 5, as a cognate accusative; διαμοιρᾶσαι, l. 1076, and φέρειν, l. 1107, as complementary accusatives.

INDICES TO NOTES.

I. GREEK.

ἀεί, and particip., 1182.
αἰσχύνομαι, and infin., 552, 968.
ἀκούω, 'be called,' 576.
ἀλάστωρ, 'tormentor, 686.
ἀλίμενον, of the high seas, 1025.
ἀλλά, then, 391.
ἀλλὰ γάρ, 724.
ἀλλὰ μήν, 401.
ἄλλοτε, omitted, 28.
ἄλλως, ' besides,' 974; 'idly,' 302.
ἀμ-, = ἀνα-, 1100, 1281.
ἀμπτάμενος, from ἀνίπταμαι, 1100.
ἀμφιθείς, 'cover,' 432.
ἄν, doubled, 359, 742, 1199.
,, omitted, 1113.
,, (with opt., and after ὡς, see opt. and ὡς).
ἀνάγκη, 'slavery,' 362, 639; 'situations forced,' 847.
ἀναδέτοις, active, 923.
ἀνέστηκεν, ' be dispeopled,' 494.
ἀντισηκώσας, 57.
ἄντλον, ' sea,' 1025.
ἀπαλλάσσω, τι, 1068; τί τινος, 1197, 1222.
ἀπέπτυσ', ' I spurn,' 1276.
ἀπόβλεπτος, 355.
ἀποπέμπομαι, abominor, 72.
ἀποσταθείς, 807.
ἆρα, 1119.
ἀτέρμονας αὐγάς, 926.

βέλος, 'blow,' 1041.

γε, emphat.: by strengthening, 246, 346, 745, 1004; by limiting, 766, 854.
γύας, 454.

δαί, 1256.
δαιδάλεος, 470.
δέ, postponed, 372, 1286.
,, resumptive, 1211.
δειμαίνω τί, 186.
δέμας, periphr., 724.
δή, 'it seems,' 1135; sarcastic, 1152.
δή ποτε, 484.
διά, and gen.: manner, 673, 851, 1193.
διάδοχος, active, and gen., 588.
διαύλοις κυμάτων, 28.
διαφέρω, 'make a difference,' 595.
διπτύχους, = δύο, 1287.
δισσῶν, = δυοῖν, 126.
δοκοῦντες, οἱ, 295.
δορί, of sway, 5.
δορίκτητος, and gen., 479.
δόρυ, periphr., 1210.
δύνᾳ, = δύνασαι, 253.
δύρομαι, and ὀδύρομαι, 740.

εἰ, and opt., = wish, 836.
,, = to see if, 680.
εἰ καί, 843.
εἰμί, verb, 284, 683.
,, copula, with adverb, 532, 732.
,, with particip. (vid. sub partic. as adj.).

E   65

INDICES TO NOTES.

εἴργασται, = passive, 1085.
εἴργω, = 'constrain,' 867.
εἰρῆσθαι, form. peror., 236, 1284.
εἰς, and acc., after verb of speaking, 303.
„ „ = adverb, 817.
εἰς ἀριθμόν, 'up to the number,' 1186.
ἐκ, = 'after,' 55, 915, 1160.
„ = 'by,' 407.
„ pregnant, 986.
ἐκεῖ, in Hades, 418.
ἐκεῖθεν, preg., = ἐκεῖ, 731.
ἐν, and dat., = 'at,' ἐπί, 624.
„ of time within which, 44.
ἐνθάδε, 'on earth,' 1270.
ἐπάξας, trans., 1071.
ἐπέζεσε, sudden aor., 583.
ἐπεί, 'for,' 1208.
ἐπερειδομένας, 114.
ἐπεύχομαι, 'pray after,' 542.
ἐπί, with acc. : reference, 514 : 'go for,' 522, 635.
„ with dat., 'in terms of,' 648, 727, 822; 'near,' 733.
ἐπίσχες, trans., 895.
ἐπῳδός, and gen., 1272.
ἐξαιτέομαι, = exoro, 49.
ἐξαλλάξω, intrans., 1060.
ἐξαπαλλάξαι, intrans., 1108.
ἐξέπτοξας, trans., 180.
ἐξιστορῆσαι, τινά τι, 236.
ἔστιν ᾗ, 857.
εὐφημέω, 664.
ἔχω, with διά, and gen., 851.
„ with particip., 1013.
-εω, dissyl. verbs in, 1055.

ζόης, - ζωῆς, 1108.
ζῆλον, and interrog. pron., 352.

ἠκριβωκότες, 1192.
ᾔσμεν, = ᾔδειμεν, 1112.
ἥσυχον πλοῦν, 901.
-ην, augm. : ηὐτύχει, 18 ; ἐπηύξατο, 542 ; ηὑρέθη, 770.

θεοδμήτῳ, 'built for a god,' 23.
θεράπναν. = θεράπαιναν, 482.
θῆλυς, two terms., 659.

ἱκετεύω, and gen., 752.
ἱκέτις, and gen., 147.
ἵνα, with indic. ; purpose, 818.
„ ' where,' 711.

καὶ γάρ, 898.
καὶ εἰ, 318.
καὶ μήν, 216, 1224.
καὶ πῶς, 883.
κάμπτω, 1079, 1150.
κάρα, periphr., 676.
κατὰ σύνεσιν, (vid. sub schema).
καταπαύσας ἄπο, 916.
κατάρχομαι, and acc., 685.
καταστάζω, intrans., 241 ; trans., 760.
κέλσω, intrans., 1057.
κερκίς, 363, 1153.
κινεῖν πόδα, 940.
κύπις, ' quibbler,' 134.
κρύπτω, τινά τι, 570.

λέλακα, as pres., 678, 1110.
λέξει, pass., 906.
λύειν πόδα, ' depart,' 1020.

μελανοπτερύγων, of dreams, 71.
μέμφομαί τι, and gen., 962.
μὲν οὖν, ' then,' 729 ; corrective, 1261.
μετακλαίομαι, ' regret,' 213.
μεταξύ, ' before,' 437.
μή, hypoth. with εἰ, 235.
„ with hypoth. adv., 378.
„ with infin., 867.
„ with indefinite relative, 282.
„ with partic. = imperat., 874.
„ postponed, 12.
μηδέ, and indic., of wish, 395.
μηδέν, τό, 622.
„ after indefinite relative, 628.
μήπω, = μήποτε, 1278.
μὴ σύ γε, 408.

66

μήτε, omitted, 373.
μῶν, num, 754.

νήνεμον, with ὄχλον, 733.
νόμος, 800, 847.
νόμων γραφαί, 866.
νύμφην ἄνυμφον, 612.
νῦν, argumentative, 900.

ὅ, 'therefore,' 13.
ὅδε, = preceding, 273.
οἷός τε, 15.
οἶσθα, and relative: ὅτε, 112; ἡνίκ', 239; ἵνα, 1008; οἶσθ' οὖν ὃ δρᾶσον, 225.
ὅλωλα, of captivity, 914.
ὀνίνημι, and gen., 997.
ὁποῖα, ὅπως, double compar., 398.
ὁράω, 'look for,' 901, 921.
ὀρρωδεῖν, and infin., 768.
ὅσον οὐ, 143.
ὅσον τάχος, 1284.
ὅστις, and indic. = quippe qui 55.
,, and opt. with ἄν, consecutive, 297.
,, indef. = plur., 360.
οὐ, with infin., 1219.
,, redundant, 956.
οὐ μή, and aor. subj., 1039.
οὖν, resumptive, 1244.
οὗτος, exclamatory, 1127, 1280.
ὀφλεῖν ἀμαθίαν, 327.

πάθω, like δράσω, 614.
πάρα, = πάρεστι, 34.
παρα- : παραιρέω, 591; παρακαλέω, 587; παρηγορέω, 288.
παράσχες, (2 -σχε, 842.)
πατήρ, as voc., 534.
πείσματα = πόδες, 1080.
περᾷ, trans., 53.
πέπλος, 933 ; of Athene, 467.
περιπίπτω, fall in with, 498.
πλαθεῖσα, from πλάθω, 890.
πλησίον, τῶν, neut., 996.
ποῖ, = πως, 419.
ποῖ καί, 1064.

πύλεος, = πύλεως, 866.
πομπίμους πρός, 1290.
ποῦ, = ὅπου, 1125.
,, like πῶς, 828.
προκόπτω, 961.
προλείπω, intrans., 438.
πρός, postponed, 146.
,, and acc., = adverb ; πρὸς βίαν, 406.
,, ,, ,, πρὸς ταῦτα, 861.
,, ,, ,, = 'at,' 190, 221.
,, ,, ,, after verb of speaking, 217, 422, 978.
προστιθεῖσ', addicens, 368.
προτίθεσθαι, 'lay out,' 613.
πρότονοι, = haul-yards, 114.
πρωτόγονος, 'then first born,' 458.
πως, and adj., 133.
πῶς καί, 515.
πῶς δοκεῖς, parenth., 1160.

σῖγα, σῖγα, 532.
σκύτος, gender, 1.
στεροπά Διός, = light of day, 68.
στεφάναν πύργων, 910.
συγκεκλημένη, 'huddled,' 487.
συμπίτνω : = συμβαίνω, 846 ; 'meet, 1028, + ἐς ταὐτόν, 966.
συνέπαισε, intrans., 118.
σχῆμα, καθ' ὅλον etc., (vid. sub schema).
σχῆματ', periphr., 619.
σωζομένου, 'in safety,' 73.

τάχα, perhaps, 1247, 1257.
τε, misplaced, 80, 426, 462, 848, 854.
,, indef., (οἷός τε), 15.
τίθημι, periphr., 111, 656, 754, 869.
τιμωρέω, and acc, 756, 882.
,, and dat., 749.
τις, = many, 649.
τοῦ, postponed, 370.
τριταῖος, 'of third day,' 32.
τυγχάνω, and acc., 51
τῷ, = τίνι, 448.

INDICES TO NOTES.

ὑπέγγυον, and dat., 1028.
ὑπεξάγεις πόδα, and acc., 812.
ὑπό, and gen., 'from under,' 53, 605.
„ and acc., pregnant, 149, 1154.
ὑπο-, 'secretly,' 6, 207, 812.
ὕποπτος, active, with gen., 1135.
ὕστερον πρότερον, (vid. sub schema).

φέγγος, 'eyes,' 1035; (sight, life, 368; τυφλὸν φ., blindness, 1067).
φέρειν, 'steal,' 804.
φθονεῖν, and gen., 238.
φονέα, 882.
φόνου, 'blood,' 241.
φυλλοβολία, 574.
φύρω, 496.

χαίρω, 'fare-well,' 427.
χαλάω, intrans., 403.
χαλιναςτήρια,= πρυμνήσια, 539.

χαρακτήρ, 379.
χάρις, pleasure, 320; thanks, 830, 832.
χηλή, of a wolf, 90.
χθόνιοι, 77.
χράω, of an oracle, 1268.
χρεία σ', sc. ἔχει, 976.
χρῆν,=infin., 260; = imperf., 629.
χρυσοφόρου, of a maiden, 153.

ψυχή, periphr., 21, 87.

ᾤκισται, midd.. 2.
ὡς, exclamatory, 56.
„ = ἴσθι ὡς, 400.
„ = 'since,' 346, 506.
„ prepos.='to,' 993.
ὡς ἄν, and subj., 330.
ὥς,=οὕτως, 441, 888.
ὥστε, and infin., 246; (after φανείη, 854.)
ὤφειλον, and infin., of wishes, 395.

68

II. ENGLISH.

abstract for concrete, 241.
accusative, absolute, 121, 506.
,, adverbial, 514, 874, 892, 977, 989.
,, in apposition to sentence, 461, 529, 1074, 1077.
,, cognate, 163, 644, 912, 1058, etc.
,, double, 236, 265, 285, 570.
,, of duration, 436.
,, of motion to, 450, 1104, 1260.
,, of respect, 114, 664, etc.
active for middle, (vid. sub verb).
Achilles, tomb of, 37.
adjective, active, with gen. (vid. sub obj. gen.); with πρός, 1290.
,, adverbial, 1109, 1226.
,, attributive, 101, 130, 1294.
,, proleptic, 367, 533, 691, 782, etc.
,, with genitive, = superlative, 193, 717.
,, repeated, 45, 203, 205.
Aegyptus, 886.
Alexander, 630.
anachronism, 291, 510.
antiptosis, 986.
aorist, gnomic, 598, 847, 1194.
,, momentary, 583, 881, 1276.
,, = pluperfect, (583.)
aposiopesis, 843.
Artemis, 936.
article, generic, 328.
,, omitted, 599, 1230.
,, as relative, 473, 637.

attraction of dat. to acc., 541, 605.
,, of gen. to nom., 906.
,, of antec. into rel. clause, 771, 989.
,, of verb (vid. sub ind., opt., partic.).

Bacchae, 1076.

caesura, absence of, 355, 549, 1159.
Cassandra, 88.
Cisseus, 3.
comparative, double, 377.
conjunctive: (vid. sub subj. and opt.)
crasis, 725, 1160, 1226, 1249.
cretic pause, 729.

Daedalus, 838.
dative, of agent, 309, 863.
,, causal, 958, 1167.
,, commodi, 160, 380, 460, 749.
,, ethical, 53, 197, 409, 674, 889, 1055, etc.
,, of giver, 535.
,, incommodi, 140, 1085, 1119.
,, of instrument, 251.
,, local, 82, 121, 300, 457.
,, of manner, 1055, 1195, 1196.
,, of motion to, 207.
,, possessive, 816, 1267.
,, of respect, 271.
,, of resemblance, 61.
Delos, 458.
Dioscuri, 943.

epic forms, 323, 441, 767, 888, 915.
Eris, 644.

future, midd. = pass., 906.

69

INDICES TO NOTES.

future, neg. interrog., = command,
  1282, 1283.
" part., = purpose, 511, 579,
  634, 731, 1202.
" sudden, for pres., 511, 713,
  (863, 1124.

genitive, of agent, 1252.
" causal after adj., 661;
  interj., 183; verb, 238,
  752, 760, 997, etc.
" descriptive, 199.
" objective: after adj., 235,
  536, 588, 1135, 1272;
  subs., 147, 352, 973, etc.;
  obj. and subj., 715.
" material, 241, 1228.
" of origin, 380, 584.
" partitive, after adverb,
  961; ὅστις, 864; verb
  of bringing, 610, of
  touching, 64, 242, 523,
  1166.
" possessive, 66, 268, 478,
  844, 1267.
" of price, 360.
" privative, after adj., 151,
  etc.; verb, 622.
  of relation, 152.

Hecuba, 3, 1273.

imperfect, of attempt. 1165 (cf.
  sub pres.).
indicative, fut. for opt. fut., 353,
  360.
" with ἵνα, purpose, 818.
" of wish, ὤφειλ., 395.
infinitive, as subst.: subj., 214; obj.,
  541; cog. acc., 5; acc.
  of resp., 1240.
" epex., 41, 410.
" purpose, 338, 1134.
" result, 1076, 1107.
" imperative, 305.
intransitive, as transitive: (vid. sub
  verb.)

irony, simple, 990, 1000, 1021,
  1107.
" Sophoclean, 430, 1291.

Lemnos, 887.
locative, (vid. sub dat.).

middle, self: on self, 107; from
  self, 72; for self, 308, 1072,—
  causal, 754, 977.

Neoptolemus, 24.
nominative, for acc. (vid. sub
  schema κατ. συν.).
" exclamatory, 1127.
" for voc., 534.

optative, and ἄν, = fut., 485, 789,
  1132.
" by attraction, 839.
" deliberative, 854.
" expressing improbability,
  1149, 1206.
" indefinite, 819, 1165.
Orion, 1101.
oxymoron, 612.

participle, as adj., 122, 358, (579),
  668.
" attracted to subj. of
  main verb, 244, 397; to
  acc. infin., 541.
" fut, (sub fut.)
" hypothetic, 756, 1224.
" omitted, 423, 734, 1215.
" with verbs of emotion,
  244, 397.
" with ἔχω (vid. sub ἔχω).
perfect, as present, 880.
Pergamus, 931.
periphrasis, (vid. sub substantive,
  and verb.)
pleonasm, 104, 489.
plural, generalising, for sing., 403,
  1237, 1253.
" masc., = sing. fem., 237, 511.
" in appos. to sing., 265

INDICES TO NOTES.

plural, adj. pred., for sing., 1107.
Polydorus, 3.
Polyxena. 40.
present, historic, 25, 645, 963, etc.
,, of attempt, 72, 340, 1197.
,, = 'it is who,' etc., 266, 696.
,, with οὔποτε, 86.
primary, for historic, (vid. sub indic. and subj.).
Pyrrhus, 24.
repetition, (vid. sub adj.).
relative, (vid. sub article; and οἶσθα).

schema, Atticon, 986.
,, Pindaricon, 1000.
,, κατὰ σύνεσιν : agreement of particip., 39, 430, 971 ; of verb, 1159.
,, καθ' ὅλον καὶ μέρος : acc., 432; dat. 202 ; gen., 62, 147, 275, 344.
,, ὕστερον πρότερον, 762.
sequence of tenses (vid. sub subj. and opt.).
spoils, system of distrib., 102.
subjunctive, deliberative, 88, 422, 1042, etc.

subjunctive, after historic tenses, 27, 712, 1139, 1245.
substantive, adjectival, 137, 406, 921.
,, contained in another word, 23, 416, 430, 479, etc.
,, periphrastic, 22, 87, 676, 1210, etc.
superlative, double, 620.
synizesis, 24, 523, 551, 852, 1094.

Theseidae, 129.
tmesis, 911, 928, 1172, etc.
transitive, as intrans. : (vid. sub verb.)

verb, intrans., as trans., 53, 180.
,, omitted, 520, 626, 748.
,, periphrastic, (τίθημι), 111, 636.
,, plural, with n. pl. subj., 1159.
,, singular, with f. pl. subj., 1000.
,, trans., as intrans., 118, (164), 403, 963, 1057, 1071 ; (active, as midd., 1060, 1108).

THE END.

Clarendon Press Series.

Latin School-books.

GRAMMARS, LEXICONS, etc.

Allen. *Rudimenta Latina.* Comprising Accidence, and Exercises of a very Elementary Character, for the use of Beginners. By J. BARROW ALLEN, M.A. . . . . [Extra fcap. 8vo. 2s.

—— *An Elementary Latin Grammar.* By the same Author. *Fifty-seventh Thousand.* . . . . . . [Extra fcap. 8vo. 2s. 6d.

—— *A First Latin Exercise Book.* By the same Author. *Fourth Edition.* . . . . [Extra fcap. 8vo. 2s. 6d.

—— *A Second Latin Exercise Book.* By the same Author.
[Extra fcap. 8vo. 3s. 6d.

[*A Key to First and Second Latin Exercise Books : for Teachers only, price* 5s.]

Gibson. *An Introduction to Latin Syntax.* By W. S. GIBSON, M.A.
[Extra fcap. 8vo. 2s.

Jerram. *Reddenda Minora.* By C. S. JERRAM, M.A.
[Extra fcap. 8vo. 1s. 6d.

—— *Anglice Reddenda.* By the same Author. *Fourth Edition.*
[Extra fcap. 8vo. 2s. 6d.

—— *Anglice Reddenda.* SECOND SERIES. By the same Author.
[Extra fcap. 8vo. 3s.

Lee-Warner. *Hints and Helps for Latin Elegiacs.* By H. LEE-WARNER, M.A. . . . . [Extra fcap. 8vo. 3s. 6d.
[*A Key is provided: for Teachers only, price* 4s. 6d.]

Lewis and Short. *A Latin Dictionary, founded on Andrews' edition of Freund's Latin Dictionary.* By CHARLTON T. LEWIS, Ph.D., and CHARLES SHORT, LL.D. . . . . [4to. 25s.

Lewis. *A Latin Dictionary for Schools.* By CHARLTON T. LEWIS, Ph.D. . . . . [Small 4to. 18s.

Nunns. *First Latin Reader.* By T. J. NUNNS, M.A. *Third Edition.*
[Extra fcap. 8vo. 2s.

Ramsay. *Exercises in Latin Prose Composition.* With Introduction, Notes, and Passages of graduated difficulty for Translation into Latin. By G. G. RAMSAY, M.A., Professor of Humanity, Glasgow. *Second Edition.*
[Extra fcap. 8vo. 4s. 6d.

[A]

Sargent. *Easy Passages for Translation into Latin.* By J. Y. SARGENT, M.A. *Seventh Edition.* . . . . . . [Extra fcap. 8vo. 2s. 6d.
[*A Key to this Edition is provided : for Teachers only, price* 5s.]

—— *A Latin Prose Primer.* By the same Author.
[Extra fcap. 8vo. 2s. 6d.

King and Cookson. The Principles of Sound and Inflexion, as illustrated in the Greek and Latin Languages. By J. E. KING, M.A., and CHRISTOPHER COOKSON, M.A. [8vo. 18s.

Papillon. *A Manual of Comparative Philology.* By T. L. PAPILLON, M.A. *Third Edition.* [Crown 8vo. 6s.

LATIN CLASSICS FOR SCHOOLS.

Caesar. *The Commentaries* (for Schools). With Notes and Maps. BY CHARLES E. MOBERLY, M.A.

The Gallic War. Second Edition. . [Extra fcap. 8vo. 4s. 6d.
The Gallic War. Books I, II. . . . [Extra fcap. 8vo. 2s.
The Gallic War. Books III-V. . . . . [*In the Press.*
The Civil War. Second Edition. . [Extra fcap. 8vo. 3s. 6d.
The Civil War. Book I. . . . . [Extra fcap. 8vo. 2s.

Catulli Veronensis *Carmina Selecta,* secundum recognitionem ROBINSON ELLIS, A.M. . . . . . . [Extra fcap. 8vo. 3s. 6d.

Cicero. *Selection of Interesting and Descriptive Passages.* With Notes. By HENRY WALFORD, M.A. In three Parts. *Third Edition.*
[Extra fcap. 8vo. 4s. 6d.
Part I. *Anecdotes from Grecian and Roman History.* . [*limp*, 1s. 6d.
Part II. *Omens and Dreams; Beauties of Nature.* . . [„ 1s. 6d.
Part III. *Rome's Rule of her Provinces.* . . . . [„ 1s. 6d.

—— *De Senectute.* With Introduction and Notes. By LEONARD HUXLEY, B.A. *In one or two Parts.* . . . . [Extra fcap. 8vo. 2s.

—— *Pro Cluentio.* With Introduction and Notes. By W. RAMSAY, M.A. Edited by G. G. RAMSAY, M.A. *Second Edition.* [Extra fcap. 8vo. 3s. 6d.

—— *Select Orations* (for Schools). *In Verrem Actio Prima. De Imperio Gn. Pompeii. Pro Archia. Philippica IX.* With Introduction and Notes. By J. R. KING, M.A. *Second Edition.* [Extra fcap. 8vo. 2s. 6d.

—— *In Q. Caecilium Divinatio* and *In C. Verrem Actio Prima.* With Introduction and Notes. By J. R. KING, M.A. [Extra fcap. 8vo., 1s. 6d.

—— *Speeches against Catilina.* With Introduction and Notes. By E. A. UPCOTT M.A. *In one or two Parts.* . . [Extra fcap. 8vo. 2s. 6d.

—— *Philippic Orations.* With Notes, etc., by J. R. KING, M.A. *Second Edition.* . . . . [8vo. 10s. 6d.

LATIN SCHOOL-BOOKS.

Cicero. *Selected Letters* (for Schools). With Notes. By C. E. PRICHARD, M.A., and E. R. BERNARD, M.A. *Second Edition.*
[Extra fcap. 8vo. 3s.

—— *Select Letters.* With English Introductions, Notes, and Appendices. By ALBERT WATSON, M.A. *Third Edition.* . . [8vo. 18s.

—— *Select Letters.* Text. By the same Editor. *Second Edition.*
[Extra fcap. 8vo. 4s.

Cornelius Nepos. With Notes. By OSCAR BROWNING, M.A. *Third Edition.* Revised by W. R. INGE, M.A. . . [Extra fcap. 8vo. 3s.

Horace. With a Commentary. Volume I. *The Odes, Carmen, Seculare,* and *Epodes.* By EDWARD C. WICKHAM, M.A., Head Master of Wellington College. *New Edition. In one or two Parts.* [Extra fcap. 8vo. 6s.

—— *Selected Odes.* With Notes for the use of a Fifth Form. By E. C. WICKHAM, M.A. *In one or two Parts.* . . . [Extra fcap. 8vo. 2s.

Juvenal. *XIII Satires.* Edited, with Introduction, Notes, etc., by C. H. PEARSON, M.A., and H. A. STRONG, M.A. . . [Crown 8vo. 6s.
Or separately, Text and Introduction, 3s. ; *Notes,* 3s. 6d.

Livy. *Selections* (for Schools). With Notes and Maps. By H. LEE-WARNER, M.A. . . . . [Extra fcap. 8vo.

Part I. *The Caudine Disaster.* . . . . . [limp, 1s. 6d.
Part II. *Hannibal's Campaign in Italy.* . . . [„ 1s. 6d.
Part III. *The Macedonian War.* . . . . . [„ 1s. 6d.

—— *Book I.* With Introduction, Historical Examination, and Notes. By J. R. SEELEY, M.A. *Second Edition.* . . . . . . [8vo. 6s.

—— *Books V—VII.* With Introduction and Notes. By A. R. CLUER, B.A. *Second Edition.* Revised by P. E. MATHESON, M.A. *In one or two Parts.* . . . . [Extra fcap. 8vo. 5s.

—— *Book V.* By the same Editors. . . . [*In the Press.*

—— *Books XXI—XXIII.* With Introduction, Notes and Maps. By M. T. TATHAM, M.A. *Second Edition. In one or two Parts.*
[Extra fcap. 8vo. 5s.

—— *Book XXI.* By the same Editor. . . . [*In the Press.*

—— *Book XXII.* With Introduction, Notes and Maps. By the same Editor. . . . . . . [Extra fcap. 8vo. 2s. 6d.

Ovid. *Selections* (for the use of Schools). With Introductions and Notes, and an Appendix on the Roman Calendar. By W. RAMSAY, M.A. Edited by G. G. RAMSAY, M.A. *Third Edition.* . [Extra fcap. 8vo. 5s. 6d.

—— *Tristia,* Book I. The Text revised, with an Introduction and Notes. By S. G. OWEN, B.A. . . . [Extra fcap. 8vo. 3s. 6d.

Persius. *The Satires.* With Translation and Commentary by J. CONINGTON, M.A., edited by H. NETTLESHIP, M.A. *Second Edition.*
[8vo. 7s. 6d.

CLARENDON PRESS SERIES.

Plautus. *Captivi.* With Introduction and Notes. By W. M. LINDSAY, M.A. *In one or two Parts.* . . . . . [Extra fcap. 8vo. 2s. 6d.

—— *Trinummus.* With Notes and Introductions. (Intended for the Higher Forms of Public Schools.) By C. E. FREEMAN, M.A., and A. SLOMAN, M.A. . . . . [Extra fcap. 8vo. 3s.

Pliny. *Selected Letters* (for Schools). With Notes. By C. E. PRICHARD, M.A., and E. R. BERNARD, M.A. *New Edition. In one or two Parts.* . . . . [Extra fcap. 8vo. 3s.

Sallust. *Bellum Catilinarium* and *Jugurthinum*. With Introduction and Notes, by W. W. CAPES, M.A. . . [Extra fcap. 8vo. 4s. 6d.

Tacitus. *The Annals.* Books I—IV. Edited, with Introduction and Notes for the use of Schools and Junior Students, by H. FURNEAUX, M A. [Extra fcap. 8vo. 5s.

—— *The Annals.* Book I. By the same Editor. [Extra fcap. 8vo. *limp*, 2s.

Terence. *Adelphi.* With Notes and Introductions. By A. SLOMAN, M.A. . . . . [Extra fcap. 8vo. 3s.

—— *Andria.* With Notes and Introductions. By C. E. FREEMAN, M.A., and A. SLOMAN, M.A. . . . . . [Extra fcap. 8vo. 3s.

—— *Phormio.* With Notes and Introductions. By A. SLOMAN, M.A. . . . . [Extra fcap. 8vo. 3s.

Tibullus and **Propertius.** *Selections.* Edited, with Introduction and Notes, by G. G. RAMSAY, M.A. *In one or two Parts.* [Extra fcap. 8vo. 6s.

Virgil. With Introduction and Notes, by T. L. PAPILLON, M.A. In Two Volumes. . . . (Crown 8vo. 10s. 6d.; Text separately, 4s. 6d.

—— *Bucolics.* With Introduction and Notes, by C. S. JERRAM, M.A. *In one or two Parts.* [Extra fcap. 8vo. 2s. 6d.

—— *Georgics.* By the same Editor. . . . [*In the Press.*

—— *Aeneid I.* With Introduction and Notes, by the same Editor. [Extra fcap. 8vo. *limp*, 1s. 6d.

—— *Aeneid IX.* Edited with Introduction and Notes, by A. E. HAIGH, M.A. . . . [Extra fcap. 8vo. *limp*, 1s. 6d. *In two Parts*, 2s.

London: HENRY FROWDE,
OXFORD UNIVERSITY PRESS WAREHOUSE, AMEN CORNER.

Edinburgh: 6 QUEEN STREET.

Oxford: CLARENDON PRESS DEPOSITORY,
116 HIGH STREET.

A Reading Room has been opened at the Clarendon Press Warehouse, Amen Corner, for the use of members of the University of Oxford. Schoolmasters and others, not being members, can also use it on obtaining permission.

www.ingramcontent.com/pod-product-compliance
Lightning Source LLC
Chambersburg PA
CBHW030316170426
43202CB00009B/1028